P9-DNB-747

DATE DUE

Black Rage Confronts the Law

CRITICAL AMERICA
General Editors: Richard Delgado and Jean Stefancic

Paul Harris

BLACK RAGE
CONFRONTS THE LAW

NEW YORK UNIVERSITY PRESS | NEW YORK AND LONDON

345.04
H 3156

New York University Press
New York and London

Copyright © 1997 by New York University

Library of Congress Cataloging-in-Publication Data
Harris, Paul, 1943 Feb. 17–
Black rage confronts the law / Paul Harris.
p.   cm. — (Critical America)
Includes bibliographical references and index.
ISBN 0-8147-3527-4 (cl : acid-free paper)
1. Defense (Criminal procedure)—United States.   2. Afro-
Americans—Psychology.   3. Racism—United States.   4. United
States—Race relations.   5. Afro-Americans—Social conditions.
6. Extenuating circumstances—United States.   I. Title.
II. Series.
KF9244.5.H37   1997
345.73′04—dc21   97-2379
                               CIP

New York University Press books are printed on
acid-free paper, and their binding materials are
chosen for strength and durability.

Manufactured in the United States of America

10 9 8 7 6 5 4 3 2 1

To the members of the San Francisco Community Law Collective. For sixteen years we built community power, demystified the law, dignified our clients, and won more than our share of cases.

26.95

9-18-97

Contents

Acknowledgments

To my wife, Barbara Newman, for her love, encouragement, good humor, ideas, and editing.

To my children—Josh, Carmen, and Corey—for keeping me young and strong in spirit.

To Bernadette Aguilar for keeping her cool in the chaos of typing and retyping the manuscript.

To my parents, Sydney Harris and Rose Fine; my stepfather, Jerry Atinsky; and my brother, Jerry Harris—for living in a manner consistent with their beliefs in racial and economic justice.

To my uncle, Fred Fine, for surviving McCarthyism and four years underground with his profound intellect and humanity intact.

To Stan Zaks for making our vision of a radical, multiracial community law collective a reality.

To Jeff Wilkinson and the Harp-Tones for "Sunday Kind of Love."

To Bob Feinglass, Karen Jo Koonan, Ricky Jacobs, Peter Haberfeld, Ellen Zucker, Michael Griffith, Seiko Fuapopo, and Richard Ingram for helping me weather the storms of illness and disability.

To Dennis Roberts, Peter Gabel, and Chris Kanios, who created opportunities for me to work and contribute while disabled.

To my special clients, Huey Newton, Stephanie Kline, Stephen Bingham, Ronald Stevenson, and Leonard McNeil, for the courage they showed by fighting back while facing prison.

To my editors, Niko Pfund, Richard Delgado, Despina Papazoglou Gimbel, and Jean Stefancic, for their help and enthusiasm.

To Otilia Parra, Patrick Romero Guillory, Susan Gzesh, Jonathan Mosby, Catherine Carroll, Hazel Weiser, John Brittain, Haywood Burns, Charles Berrard, Dale Minami, George Colbert, Shirley Keller, Steve Saltzman, Newton Lam, Fred Setterberg, Joe Matthews, Pamela Harrington and Abby Ginzberg, for research, commentary, and encouragement.

And to Nelson Mandela and Che Guevara; Frodo and Sam.

Black Rage Confronts the Law

To be black and conscious in
America is to be in a constant
state of rage.
—James Baldwin

Introduction

Felicia Morgan was beaten at home by her parents and in the streets by
strangers. She was raped at fourteen and robbed at gunpoint at fifteen.
Her fear and anger began to devour her. At seventeen, Felicia took a gun
and, with her eyes closed, put one bullet in the head of Brenda Adams.
She was tried for robbery and murder in 1992 in a Milwaukee courtroom.
Had her abusive childhood led to the homicide? Had growing up in a
community devastated by poverty and racism shaped her criminal behavior? *Black Rage Confronts the Law* explores these questions as it shows the
connection between a society infected by white supremacy and the crimes
its citizens commit.

Black Rage Confronts the Law is about race, crime, and the legal system.
It tells the story of men, women, and teenagers who have robbed banks
and committed homicides. It is about trials in which defense lawyers have
argued that their clients' crimes were in part a product of societal racism.
It is the first attempt to document and critique the *black rage defense* in
American legal history.

Black rage and the black rage defense are not synonymous. Black rage,
in its positive and negative aspects, is examined insightfully by psychiatrists Price Cobbs and William Grier in their widely discussed 1968 book
Black Rage. The frustration and anger of African Americans and their
consequences for this country are also articulated in James Baldwin's *The*

Fire Next Time. Black rage is eloquently expressed in the works of Alice Walker, Gloria Naylor, and Walter Mosley. It is found in the poems of Gwendolyn Bennett, in the music of KRS-One, in the essays of bell hooks, in the speeches of Malcolm X, in the "Ten-Point Program" of the Black Panther Party, and in the very history of African Americans.

The black rage defense is a *legal strategy* used in criminal cases. It is not a simplistic environmental defense. The overwhelming majority of African Americans who never commit crimes and who lead productive lives against overwhelming odds prove that poverty and racial oppression do not necessarily cause an individual to resort to theft, drugs, and violence. But it cannot be denied that there is a causal connection between environment and crime. A black rage defense explores that connection in the context of an individual defendant on trial.

There has always been a strain in American jurisprudence which argued that the social and economic system must bear part of the responsibility for crime. Even the dominant legal philosophy, which perpetuates the myth that each person is free to act as he or she wishes, acknowledges that environmental conditions may lead to criminal behavior. Criminal law is based on the doctrine that the individual must be held responsible for his or her acts. But it has also reluctantly recognized that in cases where environmental factors do contribute to the crime, lawyers must be free to argue factors such as poverty and racism in defense of the charges or in mitigation of the penalties.

In a country divided by color and class, racial oppression and poverty have always been causal agents of theft and violence. However, lawyers have had difficulty translating these consequences of racism into the language of the criminal courtroom. The law does not allow the simple fact of racial discrimination as a defense to murder. Long-term unemployment is not accepted as a defense to bank robbery. French novelist Anatole France's famous ironic quote about the law is an accurate explanation of the inequality of the American legal system: "The law, in its majestic equality, forbids the rich as well as the poor to sleep under bridges, to beg in the streets, and to steal bread." Although legal doctrine has maintained a claim of class neutrality and a façade of colorblindness, in some cases lawyers have been able to break through the criminal law's resistance to allowing social reality into the courtroom. In 1846 William Henry Seward, one of the foremost lawyers and politicians of the time, defended twenty-one-year-old-William Freeman by arguing that the consequences of slavery and the continued oppression of black people had driven his client mad and caused him to commit murder. Seward thrust the awful conditions suffered by black people into the crucible of the trial. Unfortunately, this ground-breaking defense has basically been lost to the modern generation.

In 1925 Clarence Darrow, the most famous criminal lawyer in American history, again confronted the criminal law with the reality of discrimination and hatred against blacks. He defended Dr. Ossian Sweet, his wife Gladys, his brother Henry, and seven other blacks who were tried for murder when one of them shot into a mob of white people attempting to force the Sweets out of their home in a previously all-white neighborhood in Detroit.

The Freeman and Sweet cases were not described at the time as black rage defenses. But they were stunning examples of lawyers articulating how white supremacy had led to murder charges against blacks. They also were examples of confronting white juries, white judges, and a white legal system with the rage, pride, and strength of black people.

Between the 1930s and the 1970s the best-known black rage case was a fictional one. Richard Wright, in *Native Son,* created the classic case of a lawyer arguing that the system of white supremacy had produced his client's crimes. Although *Native Son* was published in 1940, Wright depicted the anguish and bottled-up fury experienced by many of today's black youth. In the opening scene Bigger Thomas, a young black man, kills a huge rat that has attacked him in his family's ghetto apartment. As his sister comforts their mother, Bigger tries to shut the crying out of his mind.

> He hated his family because he knew that they were suffering and that he was powerless to help them. He knew that the moment he allowed himself to feel to its fulness how they lived, the shame and misery of their lives, he would be swept out of himself with fear and despair. So he held toward them an attitude of iron reserve; he lived with them, but behind a wall, a curtain. And toward himself he was even more exacting. He knew that the moment he allowed what his life meant to enter fully into his consciousness, he would either kill himself or someone else. So he denied himself and acted tough.

Bigger begins to work for a wealthy white family whose daughter Mary attempts to befriend him. One night, after heavy drinking, he helps her into her room and puts the semiconscious young woman in her bed. He then lies down next to her and kisses her. Suddenly, Mary's blind mother knocks on the door. Terrified that he will be found in her bed, Bigger puts a pillow over Mary's mouth to keep her quiet. She suffocates, and in a frenzy of fear Bigger tries to dispose of the body in the furnace. Later in the novel he murders his girlfriend because he is afraid that she will talk and give him away.

Bigger is charged with murdering Mary and raping her (which he did not do). His lawyer knows that in the prejudiced public atmosphere there is no chance for a manslaughter verdict, so he has Bigger plead guilty. He then argues to the judge to give Bigger life imprisonment instead of the death penalty.

Wright was a leftist, and in *Native Son* he created a Communist defense attorney who delivers a passionate indictment of racism. In the attorney's plea for life imprisonment he attempts to answer the question of "why a man killed." The answer he proposes is found in the nexus between racial oppression and Bigger's life. This link between society and the individual is at the crux of the black rage defense.

Thirty-one years after *Native Son* was written, black rage and black pride became the defining characteristics of two seminal criminal cases. The murder trial of a Chrysler autoworker in Detroit and the bank robbery trial of an unemployed draftsman in San Francisco were the incarnation of what became known as the black rage defense.

What is the black rage defense? It is a legal strategy that centers on the racial oppression experienced by the defendant. It is an attempt to explain to the judge and jury how the defendant's environment contributed to his or her crime. It shows how concrete instances of racial discrimination impacted on the mental state of the defendant.

It is essential to understand that the black rage defense is not an independent, freestanding defense. That is, one cannot argue that a defendant should be acquitted of murdering his boss because the boss fired him out of racial prejudice. The innovation inherent in the black rage defense is that it merges racial oppression with more conventional criminal defenses.

The law has always recognized state-of-mind defenses. For example, if a person is insane at the time of the criminal act, he can raise his mental condition as a defense. So if, in the above example, the white boss's racist behavior caused the black worker to lose the ability to control himself, a defense of diminished capacity would be allowed. Such a defense would reduce first-degree murder to second-degree murder or manslaughter. Another example is a young African American surrounded by three skinheads wearing Nazi symbols and calling him "nigger." If he pulls a gun and shoots one of them, he can raise a self-defense claim. As part of the defense he would be allowed to argue that given his experience with racists it was "reasonable" for him to assume that he was in danger of serious bodily injury, and therefore it was legally justifiable to shoot before he was actually attacked.

State-of-mind defenses allow us to bring the racial reality of America into the court by presenting "social context" or "social framework" evidence. I have also described it to judges as "social reality" or "racial reality" evidence. The phrase "black rage defense" describes a lawyer's gestalt, a theory of the case, an all-emcompassing strategy that uses racial reality evidence to establish self-defense, diminished capacity, insanity, mistake of fact, duress, or other state-of-mind defenses allowed by the criminal law.

In a larger sense, the black rage defense educates the judge and jury about society's role in contributing to the criminal act. It is part of a growing body of recognized criminal defenses that have forced the courts to consider the effects of environmental hardship. The Vietnam Vet Syndrome and post-traumatic stress disorder used to defend veterans scarred by the war in Vietnam and African American teenagers scarred by the war in urban America illustrates state-of-mind defenses rooted in social reality. The battered woman defense parallels the black rage defense, in introducing evidence of gender oppression in defense of women charged with crimes of violence against their abusive husbands and boyfriends. The cultural defense, another rapidly growing legal strategy, uses evidence of a defendant's culture (e.g., Laotian and Vietnamese refugees, Chinese immigrants, or Native Americans) to explain his or her state-of-mind in defense or mitigation of criminal charges.

One major misconception surrounding the black rage defense is that it is a race hatred defense. This notion grew out of cases such as that of

Colin Ferguson. Ferguson is the Jamaican immigrant living in New York who killed six people and wounded nineteen others on a Long Island commuter train in 1993. Initially his lawyers said they were going to use a black rage defense as part of an insanity claim. Ferguson later fired them and represented himself, denying that he had done the shootings. In the massive publicity surrounding the case many pundits portrayed the black rage defense as an attempt to justify violence against white people solely on the basis of previous racial oppression. Commentators also criticized the defense as an abdication of individual responsibility. These criticisms are enshrined in Alan Dershowitz's book *The Abuse Excuse,* which attacks all environmentally based defenses.

In fact, no black rage defense has ever argued that African Americans are entitled to attack whites solely because of a history of oppression. However, the improper use of the defense by well-meaning lawyers can leave an impression that racial violence against individual whites is a legitimate response to racial discrimination. A mistaken strategy can also lead to a "poor-me" characterization of the defendant. A review of actual cases reveals that judges and juries will reject a defense based on race hatred or victimization.

These inaccurate stereotypes of black rage cases can be symbolized by the picture of an angry black male with a gun in his hand standing over a dead white man. In fact, the cases include all types of crimes, and the black rage defense is often used in positive situations such as self-defense. Nor is it limited to men — African American women also feel agony, grief, misery and anger. The richness of African American literature reminds us of their rage. Just a few years after the success of *Native Son,* Ann Petry's novel *The Street* was published. Petry's heroine, Lutie Johnson, uses a candlestick to crush the skull of a black man who has abused her. Her violence is described as a reaction to a "lifetime of pent-up resentment."

> First she was venting her rage against the dirty, crowded street. She saw the rows of dilapidated old houses; the small dark rooms; the long steep flights of stairs; the narrow dingy hallways; the little lost girls in Mrs. Hedges' apartment; the smashed homes where the women did drudgery because their men had deserted them.
>
> Then the limp figure on the sofa became . . . the insult in the moist-eyed glances of white men on the subway; became the unconcealed hostility in

the eyes of white women; became the gaunt Super pulling her down, down into the basement.

Finally, and the blows were heavier, faster, now she was striking at the white world which thrust black people into a walled enclosure from which there was no escape. . . .

She saw the face and head of the man on the sofa through waves of anger in which he represented all these things and she was destroying them.

Although almost all recorded black rage defenses involve male defendants, chapter 10 in this book, on post-traumatic stress disorder, highlights the juvenile case of seventeen-year-old Felicia Morgan, who in 1991 robbed and killed a teenage girl in Milwaukee. Chapter 9 critiques the two high-profile trials of Inez Garcia, who shot and killed a man who aided his friend in raping her. Garcia is not African American, but the strategy of the black rage defense can and should be used by other races.

The concept that environmental hardship leads to criminal acts regardless of a person's race can also be found in African American literature. Black rage is the rage of the oppressed. Willard Motley, in his 1947 bestselling novel *Knock on Any Door*, shows how poverty and police abuse cause an Italian American to turn to crime. Like Bigger Thomas, Nick Romano grew up in Chicago. Although their worlds are separated because of segregation, much of their lives are similar. Motley created a defense lawyer who asks the jury to answer the question, "Who is Nick Romano."

All of his life has been a dirty, murky, rainy, foggy night. . . . We might say Nick is guilty—he is guilty of having been reared in desperate poverty in the slums of a big city. . . . At home, a father who does not understand and who, with a stick or club chases you into the street. Walk with Nick along West Madison at night when the beat cop comes swaggering down the street. . . . Stay two nights in jail for no other reason than that you were walking on the street. Be slapped!—punched!—kicked!—if you so much as answer—*the law*—back.

Nick Romano, twenty-one years old, is executed, just as Bigger Thomas is executed. Motley ends the novel by warning the reader that if one were to walk down Maxwell Street and "knock on any door," they would find another boy just like Nick Romano, filled with rage.

The criminal courtroom has always been a place where the law focuses on the individual. The defense lawyers in Wright's and Motley's novels try unsuccessfully to force the legal process to focus on the relationship between society and the alleged criminal. The black rage defense has succeeded in the same endeavor. Although this book concentrates on African Americans, it also discusses cases in which the environmental defense has been extended to a Native American who killed a policeman, and to a poor white ex-convict who robbed six banks.

There has been growing criticism of the political separation of the races in the United States. Social critic Todd Gitlin, in his book *The Twilight of Common Dreams,* writes that we have developed an "obsession with difference" and have fallen into "identity politics" in which cultural and political debates pit race against race, gender against gender, and lifestyle against lifestyle. Although the black rage defense, by its very name, emphasizes race, it is actually an attempt to bring all Americans closer together. Its premise is that although there are essential differences in the ways people grow up, there are profound underlying similarities in their responses to deprivation, violence, and injustice. Closing our eyes to the impact on social behavior of factors such as racism and poverty takes us down the path to ever more prisons and executions. We will be locked into these and other fruitless responses to crime unless we cross racial and class barriers in order to understand the social forces that contribute to crime. The black rage defense plays one small part in the very large and important movement to break down those barriers.

The sword comes into the world
because of justice delayed and
justice denied.

—The Talmud, Pirkei; Avot 5:11

Chapter 1

The Black Rage Defense, 1846:
The Trial of William Freeman

The first recorded black rage defense took place in 1846. The parties involved included the son of an ex-slave and the wealthiest family in Cayuga County, New York. The prosecutor was the son of a U.S. president, and the defense lawyer was a former governor of New York. The trial was described as "one of the most interesting and extraordinary criminal trials that ever occurred in our country." [1] It is a story of oppression and blood. It is a story of race and America.

William Freeman was born in a little settlement called New Guinea, a half mile from the town of Auburn, New York, in the year 1824. His father, James, a former slave, had been able to purchase his freedom in 1815. His mother, Sally, was part Native American, part African American, and was said to have some French blood. Therefore, William, or Bill as he was called, was considered a "quadroon of Tartar and African descent with a visage strongly marked with the distinctive features of the North American Indian."

Sally's tribe was virtually wiped out in the area near Berkshire, Massachusetts. She was a house servant and was sent to work in Auburn in 1817.

There she and James were married, and William was born. Just three years after Bill was born, his father fell off the dock where he was working in Albany and died from the injuries. As was the custom with black children, Bill was sent to work as a servant boy for a white family when he was only seven years old. When he was nine he was transferred to the family of Ethan Warden, but he was fired because "of an uncontrollable disposition for play with other colored boys, which rendered his services valueless."

Bill was then sent to work in the home of a judge. But he often left the estate to play in the countryside. He was so good at figuring out how to get away that this skill was blamed on his Indian heritage.

In the winter he worked doing household chores for a family named Lynch. When he was truant in his duties, Mrs. Lynch would whip him. Finally, unable to bear these whippings, the little boy escaped from the house and in his night clothes, in the freezing New York winter, fled home to his mother.

As Bill grew up he worked many places in and around Auburn, sometimes in private homes, sometimes as a waiter in local hotels. He was an intelligent, friendly, honest teenager who occasionally drank, as did his mother. When he was sixteen, however, an event took place that changed his life forever.

A woman named Martha Godfrey, in a town five miles from Auburn, had one of her horses stolen. Bill, who had been in the area, was arrested. After an examination by the magistrate, however, he was released. Weeks later the horse was found in a nearby county. It had been sold by a black man named Jack Furman. Furman knew that Bill had been a suspect and blamed the theft on him. Bill was again arrested. After a month in jail, frightened and desperate, he managed to break the lock of his cell, and he and another prisoner escaped. His cellmate was captured almost immediately, but Bill reached the woods and for two weeks was able to avoid the search parties. Finally, he was caught in a nearby town and returned to jail. Two months later he went on trial for larceny and breaking jail.

There were only three witnesses for the prosecution. Mrs. Godfrey testified to the loss and recovery of her horse. Mr. Doty, a neighbor, testified that he saw a Negro on the horse the night it was stolen. Jack Furman said that he went to the stable with Bill and saw him steal it. Bill testified that he was innocent and that he had only broken out of jail because he had heard Furman was going to lie about him in order to avoid prosecution.

The jury convicted Bill, and he was sentenced to five years at one of two large penitentiaries in New York, the State Prison at Auburn. Charges against Furman were dismissed. Evidence was later discovered that placed Bill at a different location on the night the horse was stolen. Furman, in the meantime, was arrested for another horse theft and was tried and sentenced to prison. But it was too late for Bill; he had been shipped off to what would become a nightmare of tragic proportions.

When sixteen-year-old Bill arrived at the prison he began to weep. Every person has a little place in his or her soul where hope is kept alive. Even though Bill had lived under an unjust system, some small part of him believed in justice. He was aware that new evidence had been found proving he was nowhere near the stable of the stolen horse, so Bill waited to be set free, but no relief came. The eyes of justice were indeed, in the words of the poet Langston Hughes, "two festering sores."[2] How long can a man—or a sixteen-year-old boy—be in a prison cell wondering why he has been locked away for a crime he did not commit, without terrible changes taking place in his psyche?

Bill had been sentenced to hard labor. The prison had many shops where convicts worked under the supervision of private contractors. For two years Bill worked, mainly filing iron for plating. As time went on Bill became less intimidated and more angry. He resolved to struggle for the justice he felt he deserved. He told his bosses he should not have to work because he had done nothing to deserve being locked up in prison. The response he received was threats of punishment. So Bill worked less and less, which created hostility among his bosses, who viewed him as ignorant and incorrigible.

The keeper of the shop where Bill worked most of the time was a man named James Tyler. Tyler did not like Bill's attitude and felt he was not doing enough work. He repeatedly threatened Bill with punishment. One day Tyler told Bill he didn't want to hear any more excuses about being imprisoned. He said he was done trying to talk to him and was going to flog him. He ordered Bill to take off his clothes, and then turned around to get a cat-o'-nine-tails. Tyler later claimed that at this point Bill attacked him, and that during the fight Bill got hold of a knife. This was never confirmed by any other witnesses. But one thing was clear: Tyler hit Bill on the left side of his head with a large board that broke into pieces from the force of the blow. Tyler denied that the blow could have hurt Bill. Years later, however, a medical examination confirmed that the force of the board on Bill's left ear had broken the ear drum and permanently damaged his left temporal bone.

Bill was now deaf in his left ear. His spirit seemed broken. He worked carrying yarn to and from the dye shop. He became sullen, morose, and easily provoked. He had two fights with other convicts over minor disputes, and both times Bill was flogged. The second time, the whipping was so bad that he could put his fingers into the hole that had been cut between his ribs.

His mental condition deteriorated. Prison rules did not allow conversation between inmates, and prisoners were supposed to talk to their bosses and guards only when it was necessary in performing their duties. With such disciplinary rules, no one recognized Bill's worsening condition. They stereotyped him as a stupid, childlike Negro with a bad attitude. His brother-in-law, John Depuy, came to the prison five times to visit Bill. He was shocked at Bill's state. He came home to tell Bill's mother that her son had become deranged. The mother was so pained by what had happened to her son that she was unable to bring herself to go to the prison and face Bill.

After five years of prison, the day of Bill's release arrived. The prison chaplain offered him a Bible, but Bill couldn't read. Then the clerk told him to sign a voucher to receive two dollars. Bill looked at the voucher and said, "I have been in prison five years unjustly, and ain't going to settle so." The prison officers and the chaplain laughed.

John Depuy took him from the cold, foreboding halls of Auburn State Prison. Bill hardly recognized his brother-in-law. As they traveled home, Bill said he had accidently broken a dinner knife while eating and the guards had threatened to give him five more years in prison. He was afraid and asked John if they could do that to him. Over and over he said he needed to find the people who had caused him to be imprisoned and to make them pay him for the injustice he had suffered.

For months he lived with John. The people who had known him, both black and white, were stunned by the changes in him. He rarely talked, and when he did he often made little sense. People had described him as "a lad of good understanding and of kind and gentle disposition." Now he seemed stupid, angry, and prone to break out in loud laughter for no reason.

One day, Bill walked the five miles to Mrs. Godfrey's house and told her that he was innocent of stealing her horse and that he wanted her to pay him a settlement. She felt sorry for him and gave him some cakes. He left quietly.

Bill then went to a lawyer and asked for a warrant for the man whose testimony had put him in prison, saying that he wanted to get damages. The lawyer's clerk told him to go to the justice of the peace's office. A few days later he went to see a lawyer named Lyman Paine, who was a justice of the peace. Bill said he wanted "a warrant for the man who put me to State Prison." Paine told him that the only warrant he could make out would be for perjury, and that he would need detailed facts to issue such a warrant. But Bill could not understand and just kept repeating himself. Finally, Bill threw a quarter on the table and said, "Sir, I demand a warrant." He soon left the office but returned in the afternoon and gave Paine the names of Mr. Doty and Mrs. Godfrey. Paine would not issue a warrant and sent him away again. Refused a warrant, but unwilling to give up, Bill went to another justice two days later. Again he was denied a warrant and was informed that there was no legal remedy for his problem.

During the same period of time, Bill went to the John Van Nest farm, on Owasco Lake, four miles from Auburn. The Van Nests were a very wealthy and well-respected family. They had no previous relationship with Bill and had never seen him before. He asked for a job, was politely refused, and left the farm.

After being refused a warrant and visiting the Van Nest farm, Bill became more and more agitated. He bought two knives and, while showing them to John Depuy, started to threaten him. After John calmed him down, Bill said that he had found the folks that had put him in prison— "they were Mr. Van Nest"—and that he was going to kill them.

On the night of March 12, 1846, twenty-two-year-old William Freeman left the settlement at New Guinea with his knives, drank a pint of liquor, and walked to the Van Nest farm. He walked back and forth outside the yard, until after a long wait he saw Mrs. Van Nest open the back door and step outside. He ran toward her and began stabbing her. Her husband, John Van Nest, heard her screams and opened the door. Bill jumped on him and quickly killed him. He then ran upstairs and into a room where George, their two-year-old son, was sleeping, stabbing the boy so hard the knife pierced the bed. One of the men in the house, Cornelius Van Arsdale, confronted Bill and was also stabbed, but he managed to hit Bill with a candlestick and knock him down the stairs. As Bill left the house he ran into Mrs. Wyckoff, the mother-in-law, who attacked him with a carving knife and severed the tendons in his wrist. In the struggle, he stabbed her in the stomach. She too would die, two days later. Bill ran to the stable, took an old horse, and fled.

After some miles the horse gave out and fell. Bill killed the horse and stole another from a nearby barn. By the next day he was forty miles away in another village. When he tried to sell the horse, people became suspicious and called the authorities. A Mr. Alonzo Taylor found Bill in Gregg's Tavern and arrested him. He accused Bill of the murder. When Bill denied, Taylor said, "You black rascal, you do know about it," and raised his cane to hit him. He was stopped from striking Bill, but he then allowed two men to take Bill into another room "to get something out of him." The two men beat Bill. He was then taken back to the Van Nest farm, where he was identified by Van Arsdale. He was continually interrogated and gave many different responses, from denials to statements that he wanted to get paid for being in prison, to sentences that just made no sense. One sentence, however, did make sense. Bill said: "You know there is no law for me."

As word of the murders spread, people from all over the countryside gathered at the Van Nest farm. When Bill was brought there to be identified the crowd screamed for his death. They called out that he should be put on a rack, or burned at the stake. Some people had brought ropes and called for a lynching. However, the officers "by a diversion artfully contrived" escaped from the mob and managed to get Bill safely into the county jail. The mood in Auburn and Cayuga County was ugly. People were outraged when anyone even raised the idea that Bill might have been insane. The funeral services acted as a platform for Reverend A. B. Winfield, who used the sad occasion to stir up hatred against the "assassin" and to lobby for the death penalty. Winfield's speech is one that could be given today by proponents of capital punishment, as it criticized lawyers, judges, and the appeals process.

Winfield warned against "adroit counsel" who would use confusion and sympathy to pervert the law. He raised the specter of judges infected with sympathy who would thereby charge the jury in favor of the criminal. And he warned that the appeals process might put off the trial so long that witnesses would die. He railed against "false sympathy," which would lead the murderer to be acquitted. He concluded by appealing to the assembly "to maintain the laws of their country inviolate" and put the murderer to death.

Given the atmosphere of the day, and the fact that the jurors would be drawn from the same county in which Winfield spoke, the reverend's tirade served to inflame people even more against Bill and a possible insanity defense. His sermon was published and thousands of copies were given away free throughout the state of New York. The public was characterized by one of Bill's attorneys as having "a demon thirst for blood, and unchristian thirst for revenge." The *Albany Argus* observed: "It was with the utmost difficulty that the people of Auburn could be prevented from executing summary justice upon the fiend in human shape."[3]

Bill, meanwhile, sat in his stone cell, chained at all times, as people from the community came and peered through the bars of the cell and doctors, law officers, and even the district attorney were allowed to question him.

As William Freeman lay chained in his cell, William Seward, the former governor of New York and one of America's most prestigious lawyers, was talking with friends and associates from Auburn. A few of them pleaded with him to take up Bill's defense. What kind of man was William Henry Seward, and why would he defend such an unpopular case? Seward was born in the farm country of New York State in 1801. His parents were of English, Welsh, and Irish extraction, leaving Seward with an affinity for Irish independence from Great Britain. His father, a Jeffersonian Republican, was a doctor, merchant, land speculator, and county judge. His mother was a compassionate woman, well respected in the community. Over the years his father amassed a fortune, and Henry (as he was then called) and his four siblings grew up in comfortable surroundings. In accordance with his father's wishes, Henry went to college and then took up the study of law. He studied in school for one year and apprenticed in a law office for another year. At the age of twenty-two Henry passed his bar examination. He went to Auburn and began to practice law in the same firm as Judge Elijah Miller, a fortuitous move both professionally and socially. He met the judge's daughter, Frances, and two years later they were married. Frances was an intelligent, strong, empathetic woman with a liberal Quaker background.

In 1830, Seward was elected to the state senate on the freedom and social equality program of the Anti-Mason party. He developed a reputation as a man who could forge idealism with political pragmatism. In 1838 he was elected governor of New York on the Whig party platform. An effective and respected politician, Seward advocated for penal reform, education for women, and schools for immigrants. When his term ended he returned to private law practice in Auburn, and no one doubted that at the propitious time he would again hold public office.

When William Freeman was captured and taken to jail, Frances Seward stood looking out the window of her house and watched the mob parading along South Street yelling for Bill's death. She was quite shaken by the hate and thirst for vengeance she witnessed. She was also shaken by the murders. She had known the Van Nest family, and indeed, her husband had done legal work for them. She wrote to Henry in Albany, describing what she had seen and expressing concern for the prisoner.

Seward had developed an interest in the insane. His expertise was so great that social reformer Dorothea Dix visited him in Auburn in 1843 to get advice on how to improve conditions for the mentally ill. Months before Bill killed the Van Nest family, Seward represented another man accused of murder. The trial of that man, a black convict named Henry Wyatt, had taken place in Auburn. Seward defended Wyatt, who had killed another convict, on the grounds of insanity and obtained a hung jury. Retrial was set for June. Seward was encouraged to take Bill's case and thereby increase his knowledge and skill in the defense of the criminally insane. He hoped that, through his defense of the case, the law of insanity would be developed to a more scientific and, in Seward's mind, more humanistic level.

Seward was also drawn to Bill's case due to his sympathy for the black race and his hatred of slavery and racism. Although he believed that whites were a "superior race" to blacks, he also believed and fought for the right of all men to vote. In 1846 he had declared that he would "give the ballot to every man, learned or unlearned, bound or free."[4]

Along with his genuine humanitarianism, Seward also took Freeman's case for pragmatic political reasons. Seward was a member of the Whig party. Its opposition, the Democratic party, was controlled by the proslavery forces of the South. The Democratic party had shown signs of growing strength in the North. At the same time, the antislavery Liberty party was gaining adherents in the North. Seward was afraid that the Liberty party would take votes away from the Whig party, resulting in a Democratic party victory in New York and in the nation. Seward and other influential Whigs pushed their compatriots to adopt positions against slavery and for Negro suffrage. He hoped his defenses of Wyatt and Freeman would gain publicity for the Whig program and expose the horrors of the existing racist system.

When Seward returned to his home and law office in Auburn and people heard that he was preparing to take Bill's case, he began to receive hate mail and some of his friends urged him to reconsider. His father-in-law told him to "abandon the nigger." But Frances encouraged her husband to defend Bill. He agreed with her, and ultimately Frances became active in the defense, doing research on mental illness. Seward's strong feelings are evident in a letter he wrote to his best friend, Thurlow Weed.

> There is a busy war around me, to drive me from defending and securing a fair trial for the negro Freeman. People now rejoice that they did not lynch him; but they have all things prepared for . . . a mock trial. . . . He is deaf, deserted, ignorant, and his conduct is unexplainable on any principle of sanity. It is natural that he should turn to me to defend him. If he does, I shall do so.

Seward met with Freeman, who agreed that Seward and two other lawyers would defend him. There were almost no black lawyers in the entire United States. Two years earlier, in 1844, Macon B. Allen, the first African American attorney in America, was first allowed to practice law in Maine.

The preliminary hearing began in Auburn on June 1, 1846, after a motion to change venue to a location where the public was not as enraged and potentially prejudiced was denied. Judge Bowen Whiting presided over the trial, and State Attorney General John Van Buren, son of former president Martin Van Buren, was sent from Albany to prosecute the case.

Under the law as it now exists, a judge determines whether a defendant is sane enough to stand trial. The rule is that a person has to be able to understand the nature of the proceeding and to help his lawyer prepare a defense by providing facts, witnesses, and potential evidence. If a defendant cannot do these things because of a mental illness, he is considered incompetent to stand trial. Such a person is kept in custody until he regains, if ever, enough sanity to go through a trial. The requirements of the law were generally the same in 1846, except that a jury decided the issue of competency to stand trial.

In Freeman's case, the jury decided by a vote of eleven to one that he was "sufficiently sane" to go through a trial. There was a strong feeling among those sympathetic to Bill that the jury was prejudiced against him and that the judge was making every ruling against him. Seward also was upset and wrote to his friend Weed, "I am crushed between the nether millstones of judicial tyranny and popular anger. But there will be a consoling reflection by and by that I was not guilty of hanging the poor wretches whom the State Prison tormentors drive to madness."

After the preliminary hearing, Seward was forced to retry the case of the convict. Wyatt was convicted and sentenced to be hanged. Seward then had only a few weeks to prepare Freeman's trial, which began on July 10, after a motion for a continuance was denied.

The jury consisted of twelve white men; at that time, women were not allowed to serve as jurors. Among the twelve were three abolitionists. The prosecutor asked them the following question: "Suppose it should be proved that the prisoner is a poor demented negro, would you think society ought to be punished and not the negro?" Juror Norman Peters replied, "I should hold him responsible the same as any other man." The prosecutor was satisfied with the answers the men gave and left them on the jury.

The state presented its case, calling seventy-two witnesses. As in most insanity cases, the prosecution attempted to elicit evidence that showed a rational planning and execution of the crime, from which the jury could infer that the defendant knew what he was doing was wrong and that he was in control of his actions. The testimony showed that a week before the murders Bill bought two knives, that he hid the knives, and that he wanted to get the persons who caused him to be sent to prison. The evidence showed that he waited outside the Van Nest farm before trying to enter, and that after the murders he attempted an escape and lied when captured. In addition to the lay witnesses, eight physicians testified to their opinions that Bill was not insane. Dr. Bigelow, a leading witness for the state, summed up their medical case when he testified: "I believe him to be a dull, stupid, moody, morose, depraved, degraded negro, but not insane."

Bill sat at the counsel table and watched the proceedings, which would likely have been even more traumatic for him had he been able to comprehend what was taking place. He sat quietly, his small body (five-foot-seven, 115 pounds) slumped over. He laughed for no reason. He continually smiled, seemingly unaware of the hate directed at him in the crowded courtroom.[5]

After the prosecution finished, Seward began his defense. He called thirty-six witnesses, among them nine doctors who testified that William Freeman was insane at the time he committed the murders. The essence of the psychiatric defense was that he suffered from a delusion that the Van Nest family had caused him to be put in prison for stealing a horse. Obviously, claimed Seward, this was a delusion because the Van Nest family had nothing to do with the horse-stealing case. This delusion was so strong that it overwhelmed Freeman's rational thought; the criminal act he committed was "an immediate, unqualified offspring of the delusion."

There was a great deal of testimony regarding mental disease, but the heart of Seward's defense was to explain how social conditions caused the insanity. He would not have called his strategy a black rage defense. The very words "black rage" would have conjured up a strong, black man acting in rebellion against his oppression. Seward, limited by his own racial prejudices, felt more comfortable describing Bill as a "child" and a "wretch." The implications of a black man so enraged at his condition that he would strike out against white people were not only terrifying, but threatened the entire social construct of blacks as a docile, weak, subservient race. So Seward did not talk about black rage; he probably did not even consider it. He did understand, however, that blacks lived under an unfair, oppressive system. He recognized that such a system had driven Freeman mad and was willing to put the system of racism on trial.

Seward's two-day-long closing argument gives flavor and political context to the case. He showed no hesitation in putting forward the theme of racial injustice, arguing that if a white man or white woman had exhibited the signs of mental disease that Freeman exhibited, his or her case would have been dismissed.

Seward argued that prejudice infected the standards by which his client was judged. The symptoms of Freeman's mental disorder were being misinterpreted simply as the normal behavior of an inferior race. He pleaded with the jury to look deeper than this stereotype and to treat Freeman as a man.

> An inferior standard of intelligence has been set up here as the standard of the Negro race, and a false one as the standard of the Asiatic race. This Prisoner traces a divided lineage. On the paternal side his ancestry is lost among the tiger hunters on the Gold Coast of Africa, while his mother constitutes a portion of the small remnant of the Narragansett tribe. Hence it is held that the Prisoner's intellect is to be compared with the depreciating standard of the African, and his passions with the violent and ferocious character erroneously imputed to the Aborigines. Indications of manifest derangement, or at least of imbecility, approaching to Idiocy, are, therefore set aside, on the ground that they harmonize with the legitimate but degraded characteristics of the races from which he is descended. You, gentlemen, have, or ought to have, lifted up your souls above the bondage of prejudices so narrow and so mean as these.

At this point, Seward pursued a strategy quite common in the nineteenth century: he brought religion into his argument. He reminded the jurors that all men, including black men, were created by God. He attempted to reach through their prejudice and feelings of superiority, to their shared Christian beliefs that all men are brothers.

> The color of the Prisoner's skin, and the form of his features, are not impressed upon the spiritual, immortal mind which works beneath. In spite of human pride, he is still your brother, and mine, in form and color accepted and approved by his Father, and yours and mine, and bears equally with us the proudest inheritance of our race—the image of our Maker. Hold him then to be MAN. Exact of him all the responsibilities which should be exacted under like circumstances if he belonged to the Anglo-Saxon race, and make for him all the allowances which, under like circumstances, you would expect for yourselves.

Seward sought to demonstrate that Bill went insane by describing his life. Although he mentioned hereditary insanity as a predisposing cause, pointing out that Bill's aunt died in a lunatic asylum and that his uncle was considered a lunatic, he focused primarily on the social conditions under which blacks suffered.

> If neglect of education produces crimes, it equally produces Insanity. Here was a bright, cheerful, happy child, destined to become a member of the social state, entitled by the principles of our Government to equal advantages for perfecting himself in intelligence, and even in political rights, with each of the three millions of our citizens, and blessed by our religion with equal hopes. . . . [But] there was no school for him . . . there has been no school here for children of his caste. A school for colored children was never established here, and all the common schools were closed against them.

Seward explained that when he tried to send colored children who worked for him to school with his own children, they were sent back to him with a message that black children could not go to the school.

He described how Bill was "subjected, in his tender years, to severe and undeserved oppression," recounting how Bill was whipped by the family he worked for, beaten at another house because he forgot to return an umbrella, falsely convicted of stealing a horse, and at only sixteen years old sent to a state prison instead of a house of refuge. Seward railed against the prison, saying that "mere imprisonment is often a cause of insanity." In Bill's experience prison was a terrible nightmare, filled with beatings. The result was a descent into madness. Seward described it thus: "Such a life, so filled with neglect, injustice and severity, with anxiety, pain, disappointment, solicitude and grief, would have its fitting conclusion in a madhouse."

An understanding of racial oppression was at the heart of Seward's masterful closing arguments as he attempted to illustrate the consequences of Bill's treatment at the hands of a prejudiced legal and penal system. One of the most powerful expressions of this injustice was articulated in John Depuy's testimony, repeated by Seward in his closing argument: "They have made William Freeman what he is, a brute beast; they don't make anything else of any of our people but brute beasts."

In the cross-examination of the black witnessess, Hiram Depuy's common-law wife, Deborah, was attacked for not being legally married, and Bill's mother, Sally Freeman, was characterized by the prosecution as a drunk. Seward's defense of these witnesses is interesting because it provides us with a window into the philosophical views of a racist nineteenth-century America and exposes the paternalism and notions of superiority of William Seward himself, one of the country's leading white liberals.

> Deborah De Puy is also assailed as unworthy of credit. She calls herself the wife of Hiram De Puy, with whom she has lived ostensibly in the relations of seven years, in, I believe, unquestioned fidelity to him and her children. But it appears that she has not been married with the proper legal solemnities. If she were a white woman, I should regard her testimony with caution, but the securities of marriage are denied to the African race over more than half this country. It is within our own memory that the master's cupidity could divorce husband and wife within this State, and sell their children into perpetual bondage. Since the Act of Emancipation here, what has been done by the white man to lift up the race from the debasement into which he has plunged it? Let us impart to Negroes the knowledge and spirit of Christianity, and share with them the privileges, dignity and hopes of citizens and Christians, before we expect of them purity and self respect.
>
> But, gentlemen, even in a slave State, the testimony of this witness would receive credit in such a cause, for Negroes may be witnesses there for and against persons of their own caste. It is only when the life, liberty or property of the white man is invaded, that the Negro is disqualified. Let us not be too severe. There was once upon the earth a Divine Teacher who shall come again to judge the work in righteousness. They brought to him a woman taken in adultery, and said to him that the law of Moses directed that such should be stoned to death, and he answered: "Let him that is without sin cast the first stone."

Seward's defense of Sally Freeman shows his heartfelt compassion and his shame for what the white man did to Africans and Indians. Yet even here, the disease of superiority seeps through his oratory.

> The testimony of Sally Freeman, the mother of the Prisoner, is questioned. She utters the voice of nature. She is the guardian whom God assigned to study, to watch, to learn, to know what the Prisoner was, and is, and to cherish the memory of it forever. She could not forget it if she would. There is not a blemish on the person of any one of us, born with us or

coming from disease or accident, nor have we committed a right or wrong action, that has not been treasured up in the memory of a mother. Juror! roll up the sleeve from your manly arm, and you will find a scar there of which you know nothing. Your mother will give you the detail of every day's progress of the preventive disease. Sally Freeman has the mingled blood of the African and Indian races. She is nevertheless a woman, and a mother, and nature bears witness in every climate and every country, to the singleness and uniformity of those characters. I have known and proved them in the hovel of the slave, and in the wigwam of the Chippewa. But Sally Freeman has been intemperate. The white man enslaved her ancestors of the one race, exiled and destroyed those of the other, and debased them all by corrupting their natural and healthful appetites. She comes honestly by her only vice. Yet when she comes here to testify for a life that is dearer to her than her own, to say she knows her own son, the white man says she is a drunkard! May Heaven forgive the white man for adding this last, this cruel injury to the wrongs of such a mother! Fortunately, gentlemen, her character and conduct are before you. NO woman has ever appeared with more decency, modesty, and propriety than she has exhibited here. No witness has dared to say or think that Sally Freeman is not a woman of truth. Dr. Clary, a witness for the prosection, who knows her well, says, that with all her infirmities of temper and of habit, Sally "was always a truthful woman."

Seward finished his two-day-long closing argument with a rhetorical flourish and poetic language rarely found in today's courtrooms.

The Prisoner, though in the greenness of youth, is withered, decayed, senseless, almost lifeless. He has no father here. The descendant of slaves, that father died a victim to the vices of a superior race. There is no mother here, for her child is stained and polluted with the blood of mothers and of a sleeping infant; and "he looks and laughs so that she cannot bear to look upon him." There is no brother, or sister, or friend here. Popular rage against the accused has driven them hence, and scattered his kindred and people. . . .

I must say to you that we live in a Christian and not in a Savage State, and that the affliction which has fallen upon these mourners and us, were sent to teach them and us mercy and not retaliation; that although we may send this Maniac to the scaffold, it will not recall to life the manly form of Van Nest, nor reanimate the exhausted frame of the aged matron, nor restore to life, and grace, and beauty, the murdered mother, nor call back the infant boy from the arms of his Savior. Such a verdict can do no good to the living, and carry no joy to the dead. If your judgment shall be swayed at all by sympathies so wrong, although so natural, you will find the saddest hour of your life to be that in which you will look down upon the grave of your victim, and "mourn with compunctious sorrow" that you should have done so great injustice to the "poor handful of earth that will lie mouldering before you."

John Van Buren did not have the oratorical skills of William Seward, but his presentation was a model of logic and persuasiveness. Van Buren, like most prosecutors faced with a political trial, tried to deny the politics of the case, defining it solely as "a criminal case." When confronted with racial issues the typical prosecutor will reject the idea that racial oppression can lead to a crime, stressing instead the criminal nature of the defendant and commending the law for its equal treatment of different races and classes. Van Buren's argument is an early example of this traditional response of the state's representatives. He praised the "impartial administration of justice" and told the jury that the trial had taken place in an atmosphere of "calm and dispassionate examination." His opening words describe Bill as a member of an inferior race, a criminal personality who is fortunate to have the benefit of a great lawyer and distinguished witnesses.

> It is a gratifying feature in our institutions, that an ignorant and degraded criminal like the prisoner, who has spent a large portion of his life in prison; vicious and intemperate of his habits; of a race socially and politically debased; having confessedly slaughtered a husband, wife, son and mother-in-law, composing one of the first families of the State; and arrested with but one cent in his pocket, can enlist in his defense the most eminent counsel in the country, bring upon the witness' stand Professors of the highest distinction in their departments of science, members and trustees of churches, and even pious divines. It is particularly gratifying to those whose official duty requires them to participate in this prosecution, because it assures them that there is no danger that the slightest injustice can be done to the prisoner from an inability to secure friends and testimony, at any distance or at any cost.

Van Buren's argument contains within it the contradiction of a system of justice built on democratic rules in a society that reeked of racial and class inequality. He correctly praised the system for securing the finest defense for a man with no financial or social resources. But he avoided the reality that even with such a fine defense William Freeman could not find justice in front of an all-white jury sitting in the same county in which the murders had taken place. Van Buren was also correct when he suggested that the law, on its face, applies to all races equally. But in reality the application of the law was warped by racism. That is why Bill was convicted of horse stealing and sent him to state prison at the age of sixteen, even though he was innocent.

With regard to the medical testimony, Van Buren made the same argument prosecutors are making today—doctors don't decide the case, jurors do. He accurately stated the law: "had the prisoner, when he killed John G. Van Nest, sufficient capacity to judge whether it was right or wrong so to do? And if he had, did any disease divest him of control over his actions?" He then spent six hours going over all the evidence in support of his argument that Bill planned the murders in a rational, legally sane manner, and had control over his behavior when he committed them.

> I hope I have satisfied you that this Prisoner is clearly responsible for his acts. He is not an idiot. This is not pretended. He has not dementia. His attention, coherence, memory of events, ancient and recent, keen and steady glance, healthy appearance—all triumphantly repel the idea of dementia. He had no disease when these murders were committed, nor has he now. He has never had an insane delusion.

Van Buren was afraid that testimony linking racial oppression to mental illness might have found a sympathetic ear among some of the jurors, so he tried to scare them by implying that civilized society will be destroyed if these theories are accepted.

> Doctrines have been advanced by counsel and witnesses in the course of this trial, dangerous to the peace of society and fatal to good government. The laws and institutions under which we live have been assailed. The maxims of law which have emanated from the wisest and most humane jurist that ever lived—maxims of which the security of liberty, property, and life have reposed for ages; which the successive wisdom of centuries has confirmed, and under which the safety of Prisoners, as well as of society, has been protected—are now openly derided and defied.

In many ways Van Buren's closing argument foreshadows the arguments of twentieth-century prosecutors. He raised theories that find support today when he suggested that acquittal would cause other criminals to excuse their behavior by pleading insanity. He informed the jury that Freeman attended Henry Wyatt's first insanity trial, which ended in a hung jury, suggesting that Bill got the idea from the defense that he could commit a murder and get away with it by pleading insanity like Wyatt.

> Now, is there not reason to fear that this depraved criminal may have caught from the theories broached on Wyatt's trial, and from the result, an impression that he could commit this crime with impunity? Far be it from me to suggest that the distinguished Counsel or witnesses on that occasion ever imagined or contemplated such a frightful consequence. But is it beyond the range of possibilities?

It is hard to take such an argument seriously, particularly when we recall that a verdict of not guilty by reason of insanity would cause Bill to be locked up for the rest of his life in the state lunatic asylum.

Van Buren attempted to frighten the jury by raising the image of cunning individuals committing crimes all over the state and using the defense of insanity as a justification for their acts.

> Is it not the imperative duty of those charged in any way with the faithful execution of the laws, to remember that the audience who throng a Criminal Court Room, are not exclusively composed of the upright, the intelligent or the humane, and when theories are advanced in such a presence, which strike at the root of Law and Order, and furnish a perfect license for Crime, by rendering its detection impossible, to sift them thoroughly, and if as unsound as they are dangerous, to condemn them publicly and boldly? It needed not the fearful conjectures as to the origin of this crime, to induce courts, juries and public prosecutors, by very just means, to extinguish sparks which threaten such wide-spread conflagration.

Van Buren's arguments were not foolish attempts to manipulate the jurors' prejudices. His closing argument is a fascinating historical document precisely because it represents the same values prevalent in the law today, 150 years and one Civil War later. Van Buren viewed Seward's attempt to tie together the concepts of racial oppression, mental illness, and criminal responsibility as an attack "at the root of Law and Order." The fears and responses of government to this argument in our day have been strikingly similar. The law of insanity has been changed in every federal jurisdiction so that it is now the same conservative rule that it was in 1846. Three states have abolished the insanity defense altogether. Numerous states are passing laws restricting insanity defenses. And commentators are suggesting, like Van Buren, that insanity defenses based on the oppressive nature of social conditions are "a perfect license for Crime."

In Van Buren's argument we find the myth of an impartial system of equal justice that is still the prevalent ideological underpinning of American law. We also find the deeply ingrained fear of allowing social reality into the courtroom. A defense which contends that there is a link between social conditions such as racial oppression and antisocial acts is interpreted as a threat to law and order and to America's institutions.

Identifying with the forces of law and order, Van Buren closed by appealing to the patriotism and fears of the jurors.

> The danger to the peace of this community only affects me, as a lover of good order. If crimes of this magnitude are to go unpunished, and thus to invite imitation, it is your hearth-stones, not mine, that may be drenched in blood. But I do confess to a feeling of pride at the administration of justice in our State. Elsewhere, the murderer may go at large as a Somnambulist, an Insane Man, or a Justifiable Homicide. But in New York, thus far, the steady good sense and integrity of our Juries, and the enlightened wisdom of our Judges, have saved our Jurisprudence from ridicule, and firmly upheld Law and Order. Thus may it ever be; and I feel entire confidence, not withstanding the extraordinary appeals that have been made to you in this case, that your verdict will be in keeping with the high character our tribunals have thus acquired, and will prove that the Jurors of Cayuga fully equal their fellow citizens of other counties, in intelligence to perceive, and independence to declare the guilt of a criminal.

The jury deliberated for only one hour and found William Freeman guilty.

By the day of the sentencing Bill's mental condition had worsened. He either did not understand or did not care that he was going to be hanged. When the Judge asked him if he understood he was going to be sentenced to die, he simply responded, "I don't know."

One reason the legal system in the United States and England has been so successful in protecting existing institutions and power relations is that the participants actually believe the fictitious stories embedded in the legal culture. Judges in particular accept the myth of equal justice for all people. The Honorable Bowen Whiting was no exception. He was preparing to send William Freeman to his death. To make that act palatable and legitimate, both to himself and to the public, in what was considered the most important criminal trial in America in the first half of the nineteenth century, Judge Whiting needed to choose the right myths to express in the sentencing. He needed to talk of equal justice and to praise the law as the protector of all citizens, and he did so.

> Let it not be said that the administration of justice is partial or prejudiced by reason of his color, his social degradation, or his monstrous crimes. Slow and tedious as these proceedings have been, the Court are certain that in the minds of all reflecting men, a confidence will arise in the power of the laws to protect the rights of our fellow citizens, and that the result will reflect honor upon the institutions and law of the country.

There is one particularly revealing section in the judge's sentencing speech. He says that the most important lesson to be drawn from the case is the recognition of "a duty upon society to see to the moral cultivation of the colored youth, now being educated for good or evil in the midst of us." Judge Whiting was warning the public that if they did not educate young blacks to respect law and white institutions, then the same kind of violence expressed by Freeman would be visited upon the entire society. In a warped way, the judge recognized the black rage that filled the African American community.

Having set out the facts of the case as he interpreted them, having praised the fairness and justice of the law, and having warned the public about colored youth, Judge Whiting then pronounced sentence:

> The Judgment of the law is, that the prisoner at the bar, William Freeman, be taken from this place to the place from whence he came, there to remain until Friday, the eighteenth day of September next, and that on that day, between the hours of one and four in the afternoon, he be taken from thence to the place of execution appointed by law, and there BE HUNG BY THE NECK UNTIL HE SHALL BE DEAD.

Bill's hanging was delayed after William Seward obtained a stay of execution in order to appeal. During that time Frances Seward went to visit

Bill. She described her visit in a letter to her sister: "I was affected to tears by his helpless condition—I pray God that he may be insensible to the inhumanity of his relentless keepers—He stood upon the cold stone floor with bare feet, a cot bedstead with nothing but the sacking underneath, and a small filthy blanket to cover him."[6]

Four months after the trial, oral argument on the appeal was heard by the three judges constituting the New York Supreme Court. In the Bill of Exceptions filed by the defense attorneys, twenty-seven errors of law were alleged. The court, well aware that this case was being watched by the public and the country's entire legal community, wrote a thoughtful and well-reasoned opinion.[7] The decision, written by Judge Beardsley, found four errors of law, reversed the conviction, and ordered a new trial.

The first error the court found was made at the preliminary hearing. The judge incorrectly instructed the jury that if the prisoner knew the difference between right and wrong he was sane. The correct rule of law was that the defendant had to know the difference between right and wrong *at the time he committed the crime.* The difference is important, as a person can generally know what is right and wrong but can act under an insane delusion, as Bill did.

The second error also took place at the preliminary hearing. The jury found that Bill was *"sufficiently* sane, in mind and memory, to distinguish between right and wrong." The court considered this verdict to be argumentative and evasive, like saying someone is a little bit pregnant.

The third error of law was at the trial. One of the jurors, a man named Taylor, had a general and fairly strong opinion that Bill was guilty. Today, if lawyers object to a juror, the trial judge rules on the objection. In Bill's trial the procedure was to have two neutral lawyers called "triors" rule on objections to jurors. The judge, however, was to give the triors the law that controlled their decision. In Bill's case, the judge incorrectly told the triors that a juror could not be found prejudiced on the grounds that he had already formed a hypothetical opinion of guilt. The appeal court stated that the judge should have allowed the triors to weigh the strength of the juror's opinion of guilt and then determine whether he could be impartial.

The final legal mistake the trial judge made in his haste to ensure Bill's conviction was to restrict the testimony of the defense doctors. The judge had ruled that they could not testify to the results of the examinations they performed after the preliminary hearing. The judge reasoned that the verdict at the preliminary hearing had already found Bill sane. But that was not correct. The preliminary verdict was only to determine if Bill was competent to stand trial; it did not determine the issue at trial, which was whether or not he was sane when he committed the murders. Therefore, if the doctors felt their examinations after the preliminary hearing were relevant to their expert opinions as to Bill's sanity at the time of the crime, their testimony should have been allowed. Based on all of the above errors, the conviction was reversed.

Meanwhile, Bill lay in manacles on the stone floor of his cell, his mind shattered, his spirit listless. The circuit judge visited the cell and verbally examined Bill, concluding that the prisoner was mentally unfit to be tried again. Approximately eighteen months after he was arrested, still chained in that same stone-walled cell, twenty-three-year-old William Freeman died of complications from a cold, his lungs failing him.

William Henry Seward went on to a distinguished career as secretary of state for Abraham Lincoln, becoming known as the man who persuaded the government to purchase Alaska. William Freeman's case was considered so important that the U.S. Congress passed an Act in 1848 entering the report of the proceedings into the Clerk's Office of the District Court of the United States for the Northern District of New York.

Seward had brought the reality of racism into the courtroom. For the next 110 years African Americans struggled to win their constitutional right to equal protection of the law. But during those years Seward's theme that white supremacy causes black violence was rarely debated in criminal courtrooms. The anger of African Americans was as yet too threatening to acknowledge. Society had to be shaken by the civil rights sit-ins and black power movement of the sixties before white Americans would open their eyes to the rage of black America.

By the end of the sixties the country had been forced to confront its racist institutions. The stage was set for black rage to enter the courtroom without the burden of nineteenth-century paternalism and without the fear of a jury's blind rejection. In the midst of these changes two cases evolved that would lay the groundwork for what is now know as the black rage defense.

My skin is like my shadow,
I can't seem to shake it.
— M. C. Identity, San Francisco
Street Music

Chapter 2

The Black Rage Defense, 1971

In the years since William Freeman died in a jail cell, many lawyers have argued that there is a causal relationship between suffering from racism and engaging in a criminal act. Some of those attempts, such as Clarence Darrow's defense of Henry Sweet for shooting into a white mob and Charles Garry's defense of Black Panther leader Huey Newton for shooting a policeman, have been preserved in our legal literature. But most of those attempts have been lost to history. Lawyers less famous than Darrow or Garry have stood next to their clients and urged judges or juries to recognize racial oppression as an accomplice in crime. But before 1970, in these unsung trials, it is doubtful that the lawyers used the words "black rage." Lawyers and the language they use are bound by their historical circumstances; the time was not yet right for the acceptance of a concept as threatening as black rage. But times change.

In the early 1960s the civil rights movement was struggling for the right of blacks to sit in the front of a bus, to go to the school of their choice, to eat at a lunch counter, to gain employment according to their skills, and to vote in elections. People such as Ella Baker, Bob Moses, and Fannie Lou Hamer organized in the South against America's version of apartheid.

In 1962, the National Lawyers Guild opened a law office in Jackson, Mississippi, specifically to provide legal support for the hundreds of black people who were trying to register to vote and to destroy segregation. In June 1963 Medgar Evers, president of the Mississippi chapter of the National Association for the Advancement of Colored People (NAACP), was assassinated. Three months later in Birmingham, Alabama, four girls, ages eleven to fourteen, were killed when their church was bombed. Still, people refused to give up and organizing intensified. Martin Luther King, Jr., viewed as the national spokesman for the civil rights movement, called for integration, equality, and nonviolence. These were the dominant words in the public dialogue.

The courage and contributions of the civil rights workers would leave a lasting mark on the country. But in some ways the movement was failing. The right to sit in the front of the bus did not change the fact that the transportation system in Watts was hopelessly inadequate. The right to go to school with whites did not change the fact that in the North the proportion of black children going to segregated schools had increased since 1954. The right to eat anywhere one chose did not change the fact that food costs money and that, between 1949 and 1959, the income of black men relative to white men had declined in every section of the county. The right to vote did not change the fact that Californians voted nearly two to one to repeal fair housing laws. The right to be employed according to one's abilities did not change the reality that in the major ghettos one out of three black men was either jobless or earning too little to live on.

Having black skin not only meant suffering economic and social discrimination, it meant a lack of positive identity, a vague but corrosive sense of shame, a hostility that vented itself on others in the community, and a volatile, building frustration that often destroyed the self as well as others. Roy Wilkins and the NAACP and Whitney Young and the National Urban League did not speak to the problem of pride; they spoke of integration. The philosophy of integration encouraged the black person to get rid of his ghetto accent, to speak like white people, dress like them, and accept their values and aspirations. Hopefully the white society would then accept the black person, and the end result would be a world of equality and brotherhood. But the means to that goal did not work. In fact, the means never were accepted by the majority of black people. Blackness and poverty, not integration, were the issues for the man and woman in the ghetto.

By 1964, a new voice was commanding attention. Malcolm X's message of black pride and self-determination rapidly gained adherents, particularly among northern urban blacks. In February 1965 Malcolm was assassinated while giving a speech at the Audubon Ballroom in New York City. But his message found new ears and minds, and thousands began to advocate his ideas.

Meanwhile, the civil rights movement grew stronger. In 1964 the Mississippi Summer Project sent hundreds of students into the belly of the beast to register voters. By the end of the project, James Chaney, Andrew Goodman, and Michael Schwerner had been murdered, one thousand people had been arrested, eighty people had been beaten, three people had been wounded by shotguns, thirty-five churches had been torched, and thirty-one homes and stores had been burned to the ground. But the project was successful, and the Mississippi Freedom Democratic Party sent delegates to the National Democratic Convention and forever changed the racist face of southern politics.

That same summer, the Harlem section of New York erupted in violence after a thirteen-year-old boy named James Powell was killed by a policeman. This was the first of five years of black uprisings, usually referred to as riots by the media and the government. Race riots were not new in America. After a white police sergeant was killed in 1917 in East St. Louis, mobs of whites marched on the ghetto, and thirty-nine blacks and nine whites were killed. That same year, in Chicago, a seven-day riot left twenty-three blacks and fifteen whites dead. In 1920 in Elaine, Arkansas, eighteen blacks and five whites were killed in racial fighting. In 1921 in Tulsa, Oklahoma, twenty-one blacks and ten whites died. In Detroit, on June 20, 1943, a fight started between a couple of black youths and a white man. Soon white sailors joined in and within hours a major race riot was in progress. White mobs, estimated at over a thousand people, attempted to march into the black ghetto but were turned back. When the violence ended two days later, twenty-four blacks and nine whites had been killed. In the same month in Los Angeles, large groups of white soldiers and sailors attacked Mexican Americans and blacks in what was described by the media as the "zoot-suit riots." Fifty people were seriously injured and some four hundred Mexican Americans were jailed. All these riots were marked by intensive fighting between people of different races. The Harlem uprising of 1964 was different, however, because it did not involve fighting between black people and white mobs. Rather, it was distinguished by blacks attacking the most visible signs of their oppression — police and merchants. It was a difference that would become clearer in the next few years.

In 1965, one year after the Harlem uprising, the ghetto of Watts, California, exploded to the cry of "burn, baby burn." Millions of dollars worth of property was destroyed. Thirty-three blacks were killed as police, the National Guard, and the Army surrounded and marched into Watts. Only two whites died in the violence.

In 1966 there was a large civil rights march in Mississippi. At the march, one of the nation's young civil rights leaders, Stokely Carmichael, coined the slogan "black power." The television news showed images of young black people shouting "black power" as they marched through Mississippi for twenty-one days.

In the spring of 1967 black uprisings occurred around the country, including five days of violence in Cleveland and four in Boston. In July, Newark, New Jersey, broke loose with a fury that caused the governor to describe it as an "open rebellion" and "criminal insurrection." One month after Newark, a storm of fire and violence hit Detroit. In many sections of the city, poor whites and poor blacks looted side by side; more than seven thousand people were arrested. During that summer there were over a hundred days of uprisings. The National Advisory Commission on Civil Disorders summed up five years of violence: "While the civil disorders of 1967 were racial in character, they were not *inter*racial. The 1967 disorders, as well as earlier disorders of the recent period, involved action within Negro neighborhoods against symbols of white American society — authority and property — rather than against white persons" (emphasis in original).

In 1968 Martin Luther King, Jr., was assassinated in Memphis, Tennessee, where he had gone to support sanitation workers in their quest for better working conditions and higher wages. Integration into white society, melting into white America, would never again be the overwhelming focus of black politics.

In 1970 a book was published that had a transformative impact on millions of people of all races. Its title was *Soledad Brother: The Prison Letters of George Jackson*. This was a book about the raw, ugly, brutal experience of prison. It was also about the strength, rage, and courage of one young black man. When he was eighteen years old, George Jackson had pled guilty to robbing a gas station of seventy dollars. He was sentenced to one year to life under California's indeterminate sentencing law. He spent over seven years in solitary confinement. He became a symbol of resistance for prisoners throughout the country. In his letters we find words that could just as easily have expressed the anguish of William Freeman in Auburn State Prison:

> If I leave here alive, I'll leave nothing behind. They'll never count me among the broken men, but I can't say that I'm normal either. I've been hungry too long, I've gotten angry too often. I've been lied to and insulted too many times. They've pushed me over the line from which there can be no retreat. I know that they will not be satisfied until they've pushed me out of this existence altogether. I've been the victim of so many racist attacks that I could never relax again. . . . I can still smile now, after ten years of blocking knife thrusts, and the pick handles of faceless sadistic pigs, of anticipating and reacting for ten years, seven of them in solitary. I can still smile sometimes, but by the time this thing is over I may not be a nice person.

Seething anger in the prisons, on the streets. The anger has always been there, since the first young African man and woman were ripped from their families, kidnapped, and forced to cut cotton without pay. Resentment, bitterness, hostility, vehemence, and madness had been there for hundreds of years. Now, white America was for the first time forced to listen to this anger in its purest form—BLACK RAGE.

In the midst of these changes, on July 15, 1970, a workday like any other, black autoworker James Johnson walked into the dirty, hazardous Eldon Avenue Gear and Axle Plant in Detroit, Michigan. He walked strangely, hindered by the M-1 carbine he had hidden in the pant leg of his overalls. He stepped over the oil slicks on the plant floor, the deafening noise from the machinery hammering in his head. Stalking the black foreman who had illegally suspended him earlier that day, he raised the M-1 and fired.

As the foreman fell and then struggled to get up Johnson stood over him firing again and again. Johnson then began to look for Jim Rhoades, the general foreman who had called him "boy" and had told the gate guard to take away the badge that allowed Johnson to come into the plant. Unable to find Rhoades he entered a room and began firing. When the M-1 ran out of bullets two white men, a foreman and a job setter, lay dead. As Johnson walked out of the plant two union stewards approached him. He gave one of them his empty rifle. A few minutes later, he quietly gave up to the police.

Six months later, Steven Robinson, a twenty-nine-year-old black man, walked into a bank in the Fillmore district of San Francisco and pulled an unloaded .22 caliber derringer out of his overalls. He lined up the four women tellers against the wall and emptied each cash drawer into a striped laundry bag. As he went from drawer to drawer, two police officers, Jordan and Johnson, responding to the bank's silent alarm, arrived on the scene. Officer Jordan slowly moved into the bank, aimed his service revolver at Robinson, and ordered him to drop his gun. After Robinson dropped his gun, the police began to handcuff him. The six-foot Robinson suddenly turned and grabbed the officer. The three men punched and kicked each other until finally one of the policemen got his baton against Robinson's neck and choked the bank robber briefly into unconsciousness.

As they walked out the front door, a large crowd of black people from the neighborhood gathered around. Robinson, his hands cuffed behind his back, his nose streaming blood, stopped suddenly and held his head high. The two officers who were holding his arms came to an abrupt halt. Looking at the crowd, Steven Robinson shouted in a loud voice, "Why are black people without jobs or homes when there is so much money in America's banks?" Many of the people in the crowd shouted their agreement and a few even began to applaud. The police hurriedly shoved Robinson into the squad car.

James Johnson and Steven Robinson went to trial, respectively, in the spring and summer of 1971. In both trials the political reality of what it means to be black in America became an essential part of the defense. These trials marked the modern development of the black rage defense.

"Black rage" is the term commentators and the media have used to describe a defense strategy that attempts to bring a very particular social reality into the courtroom. But while the term evokes violent, aggressive images, the black rage defense encompasses a broader view of African American life than just rage and violence. It includes pride in one's heritage. It explains hopelessness and sheds light on the darkness of fear and abuse. Most of all, it says to the American legal system: You cannot convict me without hearing who I am and what shaped me. I was not born with an M-1 carbine in my hands. My childhood dreams did not include robbing a bank.

The black rage defense raises fundamental issues regarding crime, race, and justice. It forces us to grapple with questions the criminal justice system does not want to hear. Why does a person commit a crime? What is society's responsibility for shaping the person who commits a crime? These and many other questions that lie festering in the juncture between race and the law will be addressed in the following pages. But first we need to get a grasp on the black rage defense. Therefore, let us look in depth at the Steven Robinson case. (The James Johnson case is discussed in chapter 4.)

San Francisco is a city divided up into distinct neighborhoods. After World War II, the city had two primarily black neighborhoods. One was Hunter's Point, a remote district that was home to the Naval shipyards. The other, near the heart of the city, was called the Fillmore. Running through its heart was Fillmore Street. At one time Fillmore Street had been a thriving business and cultural section. But then urban redevelopment came along and much of the Fillmore ended up being divided into real estate parcels as many black people were moved out. April 4, 1968, the day Martin Luther King, Jr., was assassinated, marked the death knell for the Fillmore. There was an uprising of black people who as in other cities, burned what was nearest to them. They burned down building after building along Fillmore Street, and for years afterwards the economics of the free market resulted in nothing new being built.

In 1969, among the rubble and vacant lots, a small community school was started. It was called the Malcolm X School, and the teachers taught the children black history and black culture along with a standard curriculum. They tried to instill in the children respect for each other and pride in themselves. Steven Robinson was music director at the school. He loved teaching even though there was no money to pay him.

The school was housed in the back of a church on Fillmore Street, but the church was slated to be torn down and the school needed financial help. Many of the children came to school without breakfast, and the staff could not always provide hot lunches. Steven watched the children trying to learn, reaching out for a better life. He cherished running the music program, integrating traditional African music into the curriculum and making jazz accessible to young minds.

Since the Malcolm X School could not put Steven on salary, he looked elsewhere for employment. Having been trained as a draftsman, he went to many job interviews at architectural firms. But there seemed to be no place for a black draftsman. After a number of failed attempts he sought out the help of the Bay Area Urban League. The League's veterans' affairs coordinator thought highly of Steven and was able to obtain a position for him. The work situation turned out to be difficult. He was not accepted by the white employees, and when the firm's business slowed down he was let go. He got another draftsman's job, but again he was laid off. In early 1970 he was without work and unable to find a job. He continued his volunteer position at the Malcolm X School, but he became more and more frustrated as he watched the young, gifted black teachers confronting the overwhelming problems of poverty and dislocation.

Fortunately, Steven had met a wonderful woman named Elaine. He took her and her eight-year-old daughter into his heart and the couple was soon married. They lived in a small apartment and struggled to survive. After he became unemployed their situation worsened. Elaine could not find work, and in the fall of 1970 both she and their daughter Kamisha developed a persistent, deep cough. Steven took them to the Blackman's Free Clinic, where they were examined and given antibiotics. But neither of them got better. Steven worried that they might have tuberculosis like his uncle, and he took them back to the clinic. This time the doctor recommended they see a specialist. But they had no money for a specialist. Elaine asked Steven if she could apply for welfare. His response was angry and bitter. "No wife of mine will ever take the white man's handout," he shouted. "I can take care of my family; I'm the man of the house." They had discussed and argued about accepting welfare before; each time Steven's pride was wounded and he would retreat into a shell of silence. This time the frustration of days of knocking on doors for jobs that were not to be seemed to rush out of him in a torrent of words. Elaine understood that his failure to provide for them went to the core of his being. There would be no more discussions.

Christmas passed. The New Year brought only more frustration. Steven allowed Elaine to go to Sacred Heart Parish on Fillmore, where Eugene Judge, president of the Sacred Heart Conference, had won the respect of the community for his work. Judge gave Elaine a food package and offered to help obtain a new stove for them. A week later Steven fixed a car for a neighbor. He was paid twenty dollars and given a .22 caliber derringer for the other ten dollars he was owed.

Kamisha's cough had not gotten better, and now there was a new worry—Elaine was pregnant. Instead of joy and excitement Steven felt only anxiety and anger: anger at himself for failing to protect his family, and at society for limiting his dreams.

Elaine was worried about her husband. He wasn't acting like himself. They argued. He yelled at Kamisha. He was distant and strange. On the evening of January 21, 1971, Steven left the apartment, simply saying he was going to a friend's house. He hung out with his friend listening to music until after midnight. Then he started home, but confused, he found himself two miles away, near Golden Gate Park. He fingered the unloaded derringer in his pocket. He thought of robbing a bank. Yes, that way he could take Kamisha and Elaine to a specialist and could buy a new stove. He wandered for a long time, along the streets of the Western Addition and along the confused pathways of his mind. He soon found himself in front of a burned-out, boarded-up building near the bus stop at Eddy and Fillmore streets. That ugly building had been standing like that for two and a half years. The vacant, garbage-filled lots were all around him. Why didn't white investors build something here? he wondered. Black people needed jobs, needed homes. How many years would the Fillmore stand as a monument to the black rage of 1968 and to the white neglect of always? Steven's thoughts, usually precise and organized like his drawings, were jumbled and hazy. But his emotions were powerfully clear—rage boiled inside him.

He spent the rest of the night at his friend's apartment thinking about his father, his own life in Chicago, his failures in San Francisco. He fell asleep in the early morning. Upon waking, he got dressed, grabbed a pillowcase and began walking down Fillmore Street. He saw the Malcolm X School but could not bring himself to go in. He stopped and talked to the hardcore unemployed young black men who hung out in the tiny park on the corner of Ellis and Fillmore. He passed the old winos and saw the contours of his own future in the faces of all those jobless men. He saw the pawnshop and decided to pawn the derringer to buy some food for Elaine and Kamisha. He stood in line, but the pawnshop was crowded and it seemed to be taking forever. He left, walked another block, and stood in front of the First Western Bank. He saw that the bank was empty. Then, as if propelled, he was inside the bank.

The next morning Steven sat in a jail cell on the seventh floor of the courthouse known to Bay Area radicals as "The Hall of Injustice." At the same time Dee Reid sat at her kitchen table scanning the *San Francisco Chronicle* for an article about the bank robbery. She had been in the crowd when Steven had been taken out of the bank. She had seen him pull up suddenly, stopping the two policemen in their tracks. She felt that he had carried himself with dignity and had spoken with pride. As a community activist she wanted him to have good legal representation. She found the short news clip and wrote down Steven Robinson's name. She recalled a small radical law firm called the San Francisco Community Law Collective and one of its lawyers, Paul Harris. She looked up his number and called.

I was sitting in our storefront office, across from Mission High School. Bernadette Aguilar and Ricky Jacobs were hard at work, Bernadette interviewing a woman in Spanish about her car accident, Ricky editing and typing a brief in a draft resistance case. The other attorney, Stan Zaks, was talking to Francisco, one of the members of Los Siete (a leftist group named after seven Latinos who had been charged with killing a policeman). Francisco had been harassed by police for passing out the organization's newspaper, *Basta Ya* (Enough Already!). I took Dee Reid's call and agreed to go to the jail and interview this bank robber.

The loud, harsh clanking of the steel doors, the stink of food and sweat—I was entering San Francisco County Jail, where federal prisoners were held in custody. Steven and I met in one of the tiny, airless rooms set aside for lawyer–client conferences. Steven was both mistrustful and happy. He didn't know me or Dee Reid, but he sure needed a lawyer and didn't want a public defender. We went over the facts briefly. I agreed to take the case, hoping I could get the federal magistrate to appoint me so I could get paid. I told him I'd meet him at the bail hearing and would get some references from people at Sacred Heart and the Urban League. He said that the teachers at the Malcolm X School would not talk to a white lawyer they didn't know without him first paving the way.

As I left the jail I had no idea how I would fight the case. He had been caught red-handed. So I focused on the bail hearing and two days later persuaded the magistrate to release Steven on his own recognizance.

Over the next two months I got to know Steven and Elaine. As I learned of Steven's life, a plan began to form in my mind. I did not call it a black rage defense, but I did believe I could fit together three elements: Steven's personal life history, what it means to be black in America, and the law of temporary insanity. I grew more and more excited. I read *Black Rage* by black psychiatrists William Grier and Price Cobbs. I reread *Wretched of the Earth* by Algerian psychiatrist Frantz Fanon. These books have a common theme: Oppressed people fill with rage, which they turn upon themselves, causing mental illness and crime.

I knew that rhetoric alone would not persuade a jury. Yet the truth of these books, written by men who had examined and treated hundreds of people, could not be denied. There was a link between social existence and acts of criminality. There was a nexus between racism and crime. Steven Robinson had broken the law, but he was not a criminal. He was not classically insane, either, but his mental state at the time of the crime could fit within the then prevailing definition of temporary legal insanity. I felt I had a defense. Steven didn't agree.

"How many jury trials have you had?" Steven asked me on April Fools' Day.

"None," I replied, "but I spent a year as a law clerk for Federal Judge Alfonso Zirpoli, and I watched lots of trials and discussed and dissected them with the judge."

"How old are you, Paul?"

"I'm twenty-eight, but I won my practice trial in law school at Berkeley, and I've won both judge trials I had in federal court."

"Do you know anyone who has done the kind of defense you are suggesting?" Steven asked.

"No, but Clarence Darrow brought the reality of racism into court when defending Henry Sweet, who shot into a mob outside his house. And Charles Garry did the same when defending Black Panther Huey Newton for shooting a cop. Of course, those were self-defense cases. This is different."

"It's too different—it won't work," said Steven.

And then he left. He really left. In twenty-eight years of practice, Steven Robinson is the only client I've ever represented who jumped bail.

Six weeks later Steven was arrested in Savannah, Georgia. He and a friend had been stopped for a traffic violation. When the police found a gun in the car, they ran a warrant check and found out that Steven was a federal fugitive. He was returned to San Francisco County Jail, where I once again sat with him in the small, airless interviewing room. Steven was depressed and could not be consoled. He had no hope; he just wanted to plead guilty and do his five years in prison. A black rage defense was the furthest thing from his mind.

A few days later I walked through the long Kafkaesque hallways of the federal building on my way to court. I could not help but recognize that in this hallowed building of the law, all eight judges were white, all the U.S. attorneys were white, all the federal public defenders were white, all the probation officers, bailiffs, law clerks, and secretaries were white. Everyone was white except the defendant.

We stood in court facing U.S. District Court Judge Stanley A. Weigel.[1] Judge Weigel was a liberal in matters of civil liberties and civil rights, but he was strict with criminals and even stricter with lawyers. He was an intelligent and thorough jurist. His Yale law clerks read every motion and brief and prepared detailed memos for him. A lawyer had to be completely prepared when appearing before him. He also had a reputation for running a dictatorial courtroom. He would fine a lawyer for the violation of any one of over a hundred technical, local court rules. At times, he would lash out at attorneys, humiliating them in open court. One lawyer I knew often threw up before working a trial at which Judge Weigel presided. But you could rely on him to give a defendant a fair trial.

The judge began to take Steven's guilty plea: "You know you have a right to remain silent and not incriminate yourself," he said. "Do you waive that right?"

"Yes, I do," answered Steven.

"You have a right to call witnesses in your behalf. Do you waive that right?"

"Yes, I do.

"You have a right to confront and, through your lawyer, cross-examine all witnesses. Do you waive that right?"

"Yes, I do."

"You have a right to a jury trial, a jury of your peers. Do you understand that right?"

"If I had a jury of my peers, I would be found not guilty," replied Steven.

There was a pause as the judge stared at the defendant. "What do you mean?" he asked.

"If I had twelve people who were really my peers they would understand my action," Steven answered.

The Judge leaned forward, his eyes piercing into mine. "This is not a guilty plea. Counsel, I thought you told the court this was a guilty plea?"

I had been taken completely off guard by Steven's statements. I quickly asked for some time to confer with my client. The judge motioned to the U.S. marshals. "Take the defendant and his lawyer, and put them in the holding cell until they straighten things out."

For half an hour Steven and I sat in the cell behind the courtroom as once again I explained my idea of a political, psychiatric defense. Once again he refused, feeling it was hopeless. He said he would plead guilty and answer all the judge's questions the way the judge expected. We returned to court and went through the litany of rights one waives when one pleads guilty. But when the judge got to the part about a jury of peers, there was only silence. Then Steven spoke out clearly and strongly. "If I had a jury made up of people from Ellis and Fillmore Streets I would be found not guilty!"

Judge Weigel was seconds from exploding. "This is not a guilty plea. I refuse to accept the plea. You are going to trial!"

At the time, none of us expected that a new defense would be the consequence of Steven's pride and stubborn refusal to accept the legitimacy of a white legal system.

The next month was a busy one. My second child, Jamie Carmen, was born, and two weeks later I had my first jury trial, four counts of post office embezzlement. The assistant U.S. attorney and the postal inspector were sure of conviction, but the jury brought in a verdict of not guilty on the first two counts and was divided on the remaining two counts. When Steven heard the news, he seemed to relax; maybe his young lawyer did know what he was doing.

Our law collective had a summer program in which five law students, including one from back East, worked in the office. We couldn't pay them, but we offered involvement in every aspect of the cases. Two of the students, Willie Phillips and George Colbert, attended Hastings Law School in San Francisco. There were more than three hundred students in their graduating class, yet they were two of only six African Americans. They wanted to work on Steven's case, so we sat down and started to divide tasks. Since Steven was in custody we needed to have as much contact with him as possible. I obtained a judicial order allowing Willie to visit him in jail. George began to do the investigation, including trying to get an interview with the bank manager. We brainstormed. Was it possible to explain the life of Steven Robinson to what would probably be an all-white jury? Was it possible to make this robbery a political case in the broadest sense—that is, bring political reality into the vast, intimidating federal courtroom? Our instincts told us yes. We began to mold our idealism into legal strategy.

Lucy Harris, my wife, had some background in psychology. She went through the *Diagnostic and Statistical Manual of Mental Disorders* (second edition), the official publication of the American Psychiatric Association, and found a mental condition called transient situational disturbance.[2] It seemed accurately to describe Steven's actions: a temporary "cracking up" caused by situational stress. The psychiatrist who had been referred to us by Price Cobbs, coauthor of *Black Rage,* agreed to examine Steven. His conclusion was that Steven's robbery of the bank was a result of a transient situational disturbance. The pieces were falling into place.

I sat with Steven and tried to get him to remember everything he could about that fateful morning of January 22. He could vividly remember the faces of the unemployed men hanging out in the tiny park. He remembered going into the bank and stuffing the cash into the pillowcase. He remembered the crushing baton across his throat, squeezing out the air. He recalled walking out of the bank, seeing the crowd, tasting the blood dripping from his nose into his mouth. He remembered saying something about lots of money in the bank and poor children in the neighborhood. He could not remember much else. And he could not explain why he robbed the bank. By now it was eight o'clock at night and I had to get home to my family. As the deputy led him back to his cell, Steven asked me to call his wife and daughter.

That night, I laid down with my two-year-old son Josh and told him a story about our family dragon until he fell asleep. I tucked in my new daughter, said good night to my wife, and opened the investigation file George had given me. Why had Steven robbed the bank? Had he intended to get money for a doctor for Kamisha? Had he intended to get money for the children at the Malcolm X School? I was asking the wrong questions. Steven had not made a rational decision to commit the crime. He had no conscious intent; he was driven into the bank. The question to be asked was: How had life shaped Steven to compel him toward this criminal action? How had his unique individual experience interacted with the racism of our society to produce this explosion? I had to understand his experience if I hoped to help a jury, one composed *not* of his peers, to understand his actions.

I began reading George's thorough interview with the bank manager, Mr. Hanston. Steven had pulled his unloaded gun on an employee of the bank, twisted his arm behind his back, and forced him behind the tellers' windows. He told Hanston that if he moved he would blow a hole in the employee's back. At the same time, as the police arrived in the bank, an FBI agent telephoned. Hanston told the agent that the police were wrestling with the robber, and the agent said, "Why don't they just shoot him?" Yet for all this violence, the bank manager felt that Steven didn't want to hurt anyone, and that he seemed to be "a very proud man."

Suddenly something jumped out at me. Hanston said he thought the robber "must be crazy to stay here so long and to take this much time going through each drawer, he was going to be caught for sure." I reread this quote from George's report, and I began to think it was strange that Steven had robbed the same bank he used to cash his occasional checks. Wouldn't they recognize him? And how did he think he was going to get away? He had no car, and the bank was right in the middle of an area frequently patrolled by the police. Maybe the robbery was a cry for help.

Unable to get a job, unable to care for his family, too proud to accept welfare—was this Steven's unconscious way of reaching out? Certainly, that was something a jury could understand. But first I had to spend more time with Steven. I had to discover the motivating forces in his life.

The first day of trial is always nerve-racking. There is an initial jockeying for position between the prosecutor and the defense lawyer, and between the judge and the defense. This power struggle continues throughout the trial. The judge controls the courtroom, but the lawyer must carve out space in which to put forth his arguments. If he fails to achieve this, the dynamics of the courtroom will crush the defendant.

You walk into court with your stomach churning and adrenalin surging through your body. You have to control the wild forces, focus your energy and not give in to the fear that your mistakes will send your client to prison. The two most traumatic moments in a trial are at the beginning and at the end. At the end you and the defendant stand as the verdict is read and his fate decided. At the beginning, after voir dire (the questioning of the jury), the twelve actual jurors are accepted. At this precise instant, you realize you are stuck. The trial has begun. Everything you have prepared for has become real.

Steven and I looked at the twelve jurors. Eleven whites, one Latino, one under thirty, no one from the Fillmore. The one potential black juror had been dismissed by the prosecutor, John Milano. Milano was one of the two top criminal trial lawyers in the United States Attorney's office. He was experienced, skilled, and had a killer instinct. Judge Weigel surveyed his courtroom and invited opening statements.

Our strategy was to communicate the black experience to the judge and jurors. First, we needed to reduce the overwhelming whiteness of the courtroom, the white judge, jurors, lawyers, FBI agent, U.S. marshals, bailiff, calendar clerk, law clerk, and court reporter. I obtained permission for the two black law students to sit at counsel table, since they were working on the case. And we also had the students from the Malcolm X School attend the daily court sessions. The students and their teachers filled half of the courtroom's large seating capacity. As part of our strategy I ended my opening statement with these words: "Whether you find Steven Robinson guilty or not guilty, we hope that at the end of this trial you will have begun to understand the intensity and the profound nature of the black experience in America and Steven Robinson's reaction to that experience."

After opening statements there were five segments to the trial. First, the witnesses from the bank and the police officers testified. This testimony was straightforward and not surprising, since we had admitted to the robbery in our opening statement. Our issue was not whether he had robbed the bank, but why he had done it.

Second, the two psychiatrists testified, one for the government and one for the defense. The psychiatrist called by the prosecution testified that Steven may have been in a "neurotic state of depression" but was not insane at the time of the crime. There were two flaws in his testimony. First, his definition of legal insanity was limited to psychoses. This was not the actual law, which was much broader. In 1971, the federal test of insanity was "a mental disease or defect which caused the person to not know the difference between right or wrong, or lack the substantial capacity to conform his conduct to law." A "mental disease" was not restricted to a psychotic condition.

The psychiatrist also admitted, under cross-examination, that he had never read *Black Rage*. This emphasized his second mistake—his denial that it was necessary to take racial environmental factors into consideration when diagnosing Steven Robinson.

The psychiatrist called by the defense wasn't much better. It seemed that he had not read all the reports and documents with which we had provided him. Though he had been articulate and confident in his office, we felt his presentation on the witness stand was weak (an observation confirmed by the jurors with whom we spoke after the trial).

Fortunately, our strategy did not rely on psychiatric testimony. This is a mistake many lawyers make: hoping the expertise of the psychiatrist will persuade the jurors. In fact, "expert witnesses" on each side usually cancel each other out. Also, the psychiatric testimony often paints the defendant as so crazy that the jury cannot identify with the defendant and does not want to find him or her not guilty.

Expert witnesses, by virtue of their expertise, are allowed to state their opinions instead of sticking to observable facts. For example, a psychiatrist can give his opinion as to whether a person is suffering from a mental illness, or an orthopedist can give her opinion as to the cause of a fractured leg. In our case, however, we relied more on "lay witnesses," that is, people who had observed facts relevant to the issues in the case. These lay witnesses were the third segment of the case. We called the veterans' affairs coordinator from the Bay Area Urban League, who testified about his attempts to get Steven a job. Although we did not attempt to prove the pervasive job discrimination in the Bay Area, the impact of his testimony underlined the existing racism. We then called Elaine, who testified to the family's illnesses, how her husband wouldn't let her apply for welfare, and how strange he had acted during the week before the robbery. The last witness was Mr. Judge from Sacred Heart Parish, who testified to providing a food order for the family and to Steven's obvious need to be the main supporter of his wife and child. These witnesses took no more than half a day of testimony. Jurors get bored sitting in those chairs all day long. We did not want to lecture them about racism; we did not want to create a classroom atmosphere. White people know there is discrimination. We didn't feel we had to hit them over the head with what they already knew in their hearts. The idea was to get them to look into their hearts.

The fourth and most important segment of the trial took place when Steven took the stand. Cases are often won or lost by the defendant's own testimony. Too many times a lawyer takes the credit for winning a case, but blames the client if he loses.

There are two different theories on how to relate to a client. The prevailing theory was put forth succinctly by my trial practice teacher in law school at Berkeley: Never explain the case to the client, because one of two things will result. The client will understand you and wonder why he is paying you so much for something so simple. Or he won't understand you and therefore will waste your valuable time asking questions. Our law collective rejected this elitism. We were committed to demystifying the law and dignifying the client. This required the full participation of the person we represented. Yes, it took more time. But it was rewarding to see clients in crisis able to overcome their fears and anxieties, to help clients educate themselves about how the legal system actually worked, and to engage with them as partners in a joint effort to achieve some measure of justice. It was also more effective than having a client who felt isolated, alienated, and completely at the mercy of forces beyond his or her comprehension and control. An empowered client can offer a different point of view from the lawyer's, who is often limited by his professionalism. And although 90 percent of the clients' suggestions are inappropriate or useless, the other 10 percent are often gems that help win the case.

In Steven's case, once he was encouraged to participate in his own defense he began to play an active role. He agreed with or deferred to our judgment in almost all decisions. But he had two points he felt very strongly about. First, he refused to *blame* racism for his crime. Second, he would not say he was "insane" at the time of the robbery. He would not use that word. Fortunately, we agreed with him.

Our strategy was to argue that racism is a major factor in the equation that causes a person to strike out. A different strategy is to *blame* racism for one's predicament. The former has the potential to open people's eyes to the powerful impact of environment. But the latter points the finger at others for one's failings and results in closing people's eyes to social reality. We chose the course that retained Steven's dignity and pride, and rejected the course that led to pity and victimization.

Steven took the stand as our last witness. In a typical bank robbery trial, the issue is whether or not the defendant in fact robbed the bank. He may have the defense of alibi. For example, "I was in the park with friends at the time of the crime." So, the dispute is whether he was in the bank or in the park. The defendant's mental state is not an issue, nor are the factors that shaped his behavior. Therefore, no testimony is allowed as to the defendant's social background. In a psychiatric case, however, the issue for the jury is whether or not the person who admits robbing the bank was suffering from a mental state that is considered insanity under the law. A person who was "insane" at the time he committed a crime is not considered morally responsible, because he did not have knowledge of the consequences of his behavior or was not in rational control of his behavior. In such a trial the entire life of the defendant becomes relevant because it has formed his mental state. Therefore, the psychiatrist and Steven were allowed to testify to Steven's life experience.

Steven was born on the south side of Chicago in September 1941. His parents were divorced at an early age, and he lived with his mother and grandmother. He lived a life fairly typical of a black child in the ghetto on the south side of Chicago. His mother worked at various unskilled jobs, earning less than a dollar per hour. His grandmother cleaned white people's homes as a domestic. For the first ten years of his life, Steven rarely saw his father. His uncle, however, took him to zoos, museums, and the ballgames. When Steven was ten years old, his uncle, the most important male in his life, whom he loved dearly, died of tuberculosis.

At fourteen Steven moved in with his father. As he grew older, people commented on how much he looked like his dad, and Steven identified with his father. His father, for all his harshness and discipline, cared deeply about Steven and loved him. But their poverty continued. They lived in hotels, always moving from one to another. They often had to live in slums infested with roaches and rats. Steven's father, like so many black men, just could not provide economically for his family. Steven swore to himself that he would never fail his family like his father had.

After high school, Steven joined the Air Force, where he was an air policeman. He was honorably discharged and returned to Chicago, where he worked seriously on his music. He became involved with a community organization of musicians who played high-quality live jazz for free throughout the ghetto. Soon thereafter he moved to San Francisco and met Elaine and Kamisha, who were to become his wife and daughter.

Steven specifically testified to his wife's and child's illnesses and how his failure to afford a specialist affected him. He testified to walking the streets the night before the robbery and how he felt the next morning. He was not overly emotional. The only time he showed the depth of his feelings was when he said that the last month before the robbery was like experiencing water torture: "The drops of water were falling onto my forehead, one drop at a time, until I felt like I could no longer bear it."

By the end of the direct examination, he had come across to the jury as the person he was, a man of quiet dignity who had temporarily cracked under pressure.

The cross-examination by the prosecutor was skilled and effective in showing that Steven understood the nature and consequences of his actions, but it did not shake our position that he was not in control of those actions. The one dramatic moment took place when the cross-examiner asked Steven if he thought he was insane at the time he robbed the bank. Steven, refusing to be stereotyped as a dangerous nut, said, "No, I was not crazy. But, I was not myself."

Closing argument was scheduled for the following day. In modern courts lengthy orations are a rarity. Judges, particularly federal judges, strictly enforce time limits on attorneys. The lengthy O. J. Simpson case was an aberration. Most criminal trials resemble an assembly line, with the judge as foreperson, pushing the attorneys to finish the case as fast as possible so he or she can crank out another case. Judge Weigel warned us to keep our closing arguments under an hour. Actually, this was not unfair. In a week-long case—most criminal trials take less than a week—forty-five minutes to an hour and a half is usually plenty of time. The idea is to communicate with the jurors, not to bore them.

There are many goals of a closing argument. Among the most important is organizing the evidence into a coherent whole that supports your theory of the case—your explanation of why the evidence points to the innocence of the defendant. Passion is also a component of a closing argument, but it should be combined with logic and common sense. You have to make the jurors *want* to decide in your client's favor. In Steven's case I knew that I had to create a desire in them to find him not guilty. I also knew that I had to give them reasons to acquit. Both desire and rational arguments were essential so that when they went into the cauldron of the small, uncomfortable jury room, the jurors who wanted to acquit would have logical reasons to use in persuading the other jurors.

Preparing a closing argument is an exciting part of the trial experience. A good lawyer will have developed a theory of the case well before the trial begins. She will also be familiar with the prospective witnesses and their testimony and will have inspected the physical evidence. Therefore, she can and should write 70 percent of the closing argument before the trial begins. After the testimony ends in the actual trial, the attorney can finalize the argument, making changes consistent with how the evidence was presented and capturing the tone of the trial in argument.

That night, after my family was asleep, I sat down at the dining room table and put on my music tapes labeled "For Closing Argument" to energize and inspire me. I listened to Paul Robeson, the man after whom I was named, sing folk songs like "Joe Hill" and "The Warsaw Ghetto." I played Jimmy Cliff's reggae beats "The Harder They Come" and "Born to Win," and George Winston's version of Bach's *Jesu, Joy of Man's Desiring*. By midnight, I had finished writing the argument out on my yellow legal pad. Then I stood up and practiced delivering it aloud. The argument was a little less than an hour long. I delivered it aloud in its entirety two times, and at two o'clock in the morning I went to bed, so exhausted that sleep quickly overcame my adrenalin.

The next morning tension filled the courtroom. The bank robbery, Steven's flight to Georgia, the attempted guilty plea, the two months of intense preparation, the week of witnesses and argument, the specter of five years in prison—all of the elements that make a criminal trial an authentic human drama came together the morning of closing arguments.

The U.S. attorney speaks twice; he goes first and last because in a criminal trial the state has the burden of proof. Sandwiched between his two speeches to the jury is the defense's one chance to persuade them. The prosecutor, John Milano, was excellent. The essence of his argument was that the rational, calm acts of the defendant in robbing the bank were indicative of preparation, knowledge, and purposeful thought, not a sign of insanity.

Prosecutors will often try to influence the jury's emotions by suggesting that if they acquit the defendant it will cause an increase in crime. The message is that they must find the individual defendant guilty in order to deter hordes of other criminals. This type of argument plays on the fears of the jurors and finds fertile ground in insanity cases. The prosecutor will tell the jurors that if they accept the logic of the defense, then all kinds of criminals will commit horrible crimes, claim insanity, and get off. This was just the kind of argument Van Buren made in the William Freeman trial. The U.S. attorney in Steven Robinson's case took the same tack. He forcefully argued that if the jurors accepted the defense's theory they would be exonerating all poor, angry, frustrated black men who rob banks.

Milano finished the first part of his closing and sat down next to the FBI agent.

Judge Weigel looked at me and said: "Mr. Harris, are you ready to proceed?" I had already stood up and was walking toward the jury box. I stood about six feet from the jurors and walked back and forth every once in a while as I talked to break up the monotony that comes with speaking to an audience for more than a few minutes. There are many outstanding speakers among trial lawyers, but few Sidney Poitiers or Richard Burtons. The idea is to be oneself, not to get lost in formal debating style. The idea is to communicate with those twelve people who are at the heart of our greatest democratic institution: the jury—twelve people chosen basically at random from the general community. Unlike many European systems where professionals trained in the law decide the case, the American jury consists of twelve lay people who are called upon and given the right to judge another human being.

I tried to speak to their common sense, logic, and compassion. "There is no such thing as 'black psychology,' " I said. "In order to examine Steven Robinson's behavior, we look at three factors. One, basic psychological principles which apply to all people regardless of skin color. Two, the historical experience of black Americans. Three, the unique, individual life experience of Steven Robinson. We must merge *all three* in our attempt to explain the actions of Steven.

"In order to truly understand this case we must understand the concept of black manhood. The black family was attacked by slavery. This was no accident; there was a conscious decision to separate families and separate people from the same tribes. In modern times, unemployment, the difficulty that black men in particular have in obtaining and keeping jobs, continues to weaken the family. Black manhood consists of providing for one's family, in succeeding in the outside world.[3] It is grounded in self-respect and self-worth.

"Steven taught at the Malcolm X School. Why is Malcolm X such a hero in the black community? Let me quote to you from actor Ossie Davis's eulogy at Malcolm X's funeral: 'Malcolm was a man! White folks do not need anybody to remind them that they are men. We do! . . . Protocol and common sense require that Negroes stand back and let the white man speak up for us. . . . But Malcolm said to hell with that! Get up off your knees and fight your own battles. That's the way to win back your self respect!' "

I walked to the far end of the jury box and continued. "Of course, self-respect is important to all people. Of course, providing for one's family is important to all of us regardless of the color of our skin. But for a black man, given America's racial past, it is an essential part of his identity. It defines him.

"The prosecutor has argued that by finding Steven Robinson not guilty you let all black bank robbers go free. This case is not about all black men who rob banks. You are listening to the evidence of that man's life who is sitting right over there. He is not a hypothetical person. He is real. People commit crimes for different reasons. Our defense is not a simplistic racial defense. You are sitting in judgment of one man, one individual.

"To some black men, the concepts of manhood and pride may not be crucial. But to Steven, it was the measuring stick of his life. Let's look at the evidence. Steven was too proud to let Elaine go on welfare. He had too much self-respect to return to Sacred Heart Church for charity. Elaine was too sick to work. She borrowed money from her parents, but could not tell Steven. Look at his continual attempts to find work, going to the Urban League over thirty times to find potential job interviews.

"Let us look at the evidence of Steven's relationship with his father. He loved his father so much. He identified with him, happy that people would comment on how much he looked like his dad. Yet he resented his father for leaving his mother and him and for never being able to provide for them. Remember how Steven, at thirteen years old, swore he would never fail to protect his family as his father had failed.

"Remember the bank manager's testimony. When the police were taking Steven out of the bank, he asked Steven if he could get him anything as his nose was bleeding. And what did Steven reply? He said 'No.' Then he looked right at Mr. Hanston and said, 'A man has got to try!'

"It is impossible to understand Steven or his act of bank robbery without understanding this interplay of black manhood with Steven's own personality."

I took a deep breath and reminded myself to slow down. The court reporter had already interrupted me once, telling me I was talking too fast for her to take down my words. I spent the next fifteen to twenty minutes dissecting the testimony of both psychiatrists and relating it to what the judge would instruct them was the applicable law of insanity. I ended that part of the argument by putting up a poster on an easel from the Malcolm X School that had earlier been admitted into evidence. I had made a motion to allow the jury to visit the school to see the difficult conditions it operated under and which had contributed to Steven's breakdown. Although the school was only eight blocks from the federal building, the judge had denied the motion. This was not considered a major trial, and judges almost never allow juries to visit crime scenes or any other relevant locations in regular trials. Even if a viewing would be helpful to the jury's deliberations, judges feel it takes too much time. There is often more concern for the administration of justice than for justice itself.

As a compromise, Judge Weigel allowed me to introduce three photos of the school building and the poster into evidence. On the poster was a poem by one of America's greatest poets, an African American named Langston Hughes. The poem was entitled "Raisin in the Sun." I recited the poem to the jury:

> What happens to a dream deferred?
> Does it dry up
> like a raisin in the sun?
> Or fester like a sore—
> And then run?
> Does it stink like rotten meat?
> Or crust and sugar over—
> like a syrupy sweet?
> Maybe it just sags
> like a heavy load.
> Or does it explode?

"On January 22, 1971," I said, "Steven Robinson exploded, and that explosion propelled him into the bank!"

I was nearing the end. I discussed the evidence that pointed to a conclusion that the robbery was an unconscious cry for help. I explained "reasonable doubt" and told the jury that the government had the burden of proving beyond a reasonable doubt that Steven was not insane at the time of the bank robbery. I told them that the prosecutor had the last word, but asked them to please think about what I would say in response if I was allowed to answer his arguments.

I then paused, looked into the eyes of the two or three jurors we thought were the most favorably inclined toward Steven, and began my final comments. "We hope that this trial has given you a window into the black experience. Unlike some people, we believe that you can begin to understand what it means to be black in America. Steven does not want your sympathy. If you are persuaded beyond a reasonable doubt that the government has proved he was not temporarily insane at the time of the robbery, then find him guilty. Steven asks not for sympathy, but for empathy. Empathy is when you understand another person.

"Looking at all the evidence in this case, can you say that the prosecution has proved, beyond a reasonable doubt, that Steven Robinson was in rational control of his actions when he robbed that bank? Can you say that?"

I sat down, feeling as if all my energy had been sucked out of me. Steven gave me a small smile of support. After the prosecutor's rebuttal the judge spent forty-five minutes reading the "jury instructions" to the jurors. These highly legalistic, formal rules are suppose to tell the jury how to apply the laws relevant to the facts of the case. Finally, when the jury instructions were over, the twelve people were led into the jury room. The case was now out of our control.

The jury deliberated for two days. Finally the jurors returned to the courtroom, Steven was brought down from the cells in the United States Marshal's office and we all congregated for that anxious moment when the clerk reads the verdict. Those few minutes are painfully intense. I often have wondered why I go through this pain time after time. Then the clerk read the verdict: "Not guilty." There was shocked silence on the prosecutor's side of the courtroom and a profound, quiet joy on ours.

In 1971, federal law in almost all jurisdictions did not require that a defendant acquitted by reason of insanity be put in a mental institution unless there was evidence that he was dangerous to himself or society. Since Steven's defense was based on temporary insanity, and there was no question that he was recovered, he should have walked out of the courtroom a free man. But he still had to face the charge for jumping bail, so he was taken back to jail. The judge set a date for a plea and sentencing on that charge in thirty days. Even this problem did not lessen his happiness, and the happiness of his wife and daughter.

The law students and I rushed to the elevator to try to get some feedback from the jurors. After a few minutes, I spoke to the young man who had held out so long for a guilty verdict. "Why did you change your vote?" I asked. The man replied, "Well, I wouldn't have done what he did, but I can see how he felt he was backed up against the wall." At that moment I knew we had broken through racial barriers. It was just one small case, with an unknown defendant and a young lawyer. But I felt that a foundation had been built for a defense that broke down racial walls by helping jurors understand another person's life experience.

Thirty days later we were back in court on the felony charge of failure to appear. The prosecutor adamantly argued for substantial prison time, but the judge had been favorably affected by the evidence in the trial, the defendant's testimony, and the jury verdict. The sentence was five years probation.

A few days later I called three of the jurors to find out what had taken place in their deliberations. They told me that the first vote was seven for guilty and five for not guilty. The foreperson, Susan Lowenstein, was one of those favoring acquittal. Lowenstein had been very moved by the trial, both intellectually and emotionally. She argued that Steven's testimony showed his remorse and that the crime was inconsistent with his prior life. The second vote was seven for not guilty, four for guilty, and one undecided.

On the second day some racial issues came up that had not been part of the trial. For example, it turned out that eleven of the jurors were against busing in order to achieve integration. But Lowenstein kept the focus on the case itself. Many of the jurors accepted our theme that the robbery was a cry for help. The third jury poll was nine for not guilty, one for guilty, and two undecided.

The one holdout admitted that his mother was a bank teller and had been held up twice. Lowenstein pointed out that he had not told the lawyers this fact on voir dire, and that it sounded like he was biased. Shortly thereafter there was another poll, which was unanimous for acquittal.

Months after the acquittal, one of the arresting police officers vented his frustrations in a publication of the Police Officers' Association. His article was picked up by a conservative columnist for a San Francisco newspaper. Under the heading "Caught Red-Handed" the columnist wrote, "The defense attorney argued that his client was innocent because of 'diminished capacity' caused by social pressures. These pressures seemed to be that he was black, out of a job and needed money. . . . He walked out a free man." The columnist followed up with another piece in which he printed letters he had received from readers who were outraged at the acquittal and blamed the judge and jury. Neither of these columns mentioned "black rage." I had felt it was presumptuous for a young white lawyer who had only completed two jury trials to give my defense a name, much less a name as controversial as "black rage." But other lawyers who heard of the trial began to refer to it as the "black rage defense."

I was a member of the National Lawyers Guild. One benefit of being active in an organization is that it puts you in touch with others in similar fields and spreads your ideas. The National Lawyers Guild began in 1937, partly as an integrated alternative to the racially segregated American Bar Association. The Guild had been a place for left and progressive lawyers, and by the time of the Steven Robinson case its membership included law students, legal workers, and jailhouse lawyers. Many people in the organization were enthusiastic about the Robinson trial, and with their encouragement I spoke at law schools throughout the Bay Area, using the phrase "black rage defense."

After completing two more black rage trials, I began to speak at a few legal education seminars and consult with other attorneys around the country. Very slowly, the concept of a black rage defense began to enter the country's courtrooms and the legal literature.

Years later, a Hollywood screenwriter interviewed most of the participants in the trial and wrote a screenplay. By that time Steven had successfully completed his probation and had left the Bay Area. By refusing to plead guilty to a white legal system he had been a catalyst for a defense that challenged that very system.

That Justice is a blind goddess
Is a thing to which we black are wise:
Her bandage hides two festering sores
That once perhaps were eyes.
—Langston Hughes, "Justice"

Chapter 3

The Law: Its Myths and Rituals

The black rage claim is a political defense because it confronts the myths of the law. It is a political defense because it injects race and class into a legal system that steadfastly avoids an honest and true discussion of these issues. Before we can fully understand the problems of raising and winning a black rage defense, it is helpful to analyze the legal culture in which we are immersed. This chapter examines the role of the law and three of the major underpinnings of the legal system: courtroom rituals, legal reasoning, and the pretense of colorblindness.

The law is the most powerful expression of a society's rules. The dominant purpose of the law in every country is to preserve the status quo, to protect people and institutions who have privilege and power, whether in government or in civil society. The law fulfills this purpose by the peaceful resolution of conflicts, but also by coercion. An example of the resolution of conflict through the legal system is the immense amount of time, money, and energy used in dealing with business arrangements. Politicians complain about criminal cases clogging up the courts, but in reality most lawyers' time and a large amount of litigation concern capitalist business deals and conflicts. A 1995 University of Wisconsin survey reported that only 3 percent of lawyers focus on criminal law. In San Francisco in 1995, the public defender's office had sixty-eight lawyers, eleven investigators, and thirty staff personnel. In contrast, one of the largest corporate law firms, Pillsbury, Madison, and Sutro, had 294 lawyers and 335 staff personnel in their San Francisco office alone. They also have ten other offices, including one in Hong Kong and one in Tokyo.

Criminal law gets most of the media attention, but corporate law is where billions of dollars are negotiated and litigated, and where decisions are being made which control our environment, our jobs, and the very quality of our lives. The law is necessary to facilitate and mediate these decisions, thereby avoiding an anarchy that would severely disrupt the free market and societal relations.

The law also mediates thousands of other conflicts in civil society, from landlord–tenant conflicts to consumer-related product liability suits; from simple car accident cases to major constitutional issues; from divorces to bankruptcy proceedings. In the United States in particular, law seems to surround us.

Peaceful resolution of conflict through the mutual acceptance of a judicial forum is one method of keeping society on an even keel. Another method is coercion—using the force of the state, or the threat of that force, on individuals in order to secure their obedience. And when they fail to obey, the state uses that force to inflict punishment. Robert Cover gets to the heart of the matter when he writes, "The Judges deal pain and death. That is not all they do. Perhaps that is not what they usually do. But they *do* deal death, and pain." [1]

If law's primary purpose is to protect the powerful and keep things as they are, in America its secondary purpose is to protect individual rights. The Bill of Rights is the cornerstone of these protections. Of course, the rights of free speech, the right not to be tortured into confessing, the right to abortion, the right not to be forced to go to a segregated school, the right to a jury trial—these, and all of our liberties, did not come to us as self-executing protections leaping off the parchment of the Constitution into our lives. People fought for these rights, in the courts and in the streets. It is because of the right of due process for people who are arrested that the black rage defense can be raised and developed. It is because the law is more than stark, brutal coercion that the black rage defense can exist and be used to free persons charged with crimes.

If human history teaches us anything, it is that governments cannot rule by force alone. In every period of history people have fought against tyranny. Whether in the form of men shooting rifles on Bunker Hill in colonial America, or women marching with signs protesting the disappearance of family members at the Plaza de Mayo in Buenos Aires, Argentina, or schoolchildren with their voices raised in song in the streets of Soweto, South Africa, people ultimately will attempt to organize and rebel against arbitrary and unjust state power. Therefore, for a government to continue to hold power it must create a legal system that has an image of justice and some sense of fairness. It must also win the psychological acceptance of the majority of its citizens. How it does this has been the subject of increasing academic scrutiny. One of more prevalent theories of this process is put forward by Peter Gabel, a founder of the Conference on Critical Legal Studies and the president of New College and New College School of Law:

> The principal role of the legal system within these societies is to create a political culture that can persuade people to accept both the legitimacy and the apparent inevitability of the existing hierarchical arrangement. The need for this legitimation arises because people will not accede to the subjugation of their souls through the deployment of force alone. They must be persuaded, even if it is only a "pseudo-persuasion," that the existing order is both just and fair, and that they themselves desire it. In particular, there must be a way of managing the intense interpersonal and intrapsychic conflict that a social order founded upon alienation and collective powerlessness repeatedly produces. "Democratic consent" to an inhumane social order can be fashioned only by finding ways to keep people in a state of passive compliance with the status quo, and this requires both the pacification of conflict and the provision of fantasy images of community that can compensate for the lack of real community that people experience in their everyday lives.[2]

Society fashions this "democratic consent" through what has begun to be referred to as *legal culture*. Law has a culture of its own, including education, training, rules of behavior, philosophy, folkways, habits, language, economics, tradition, and stories. The courtroom is one of the key elements of this culture. The structure and rituals of the courtroom are intended to communicate the "three M's" of the law: majesty, mystique, and might. The architecture of the courtroom divides the lawyers and the judge and his staff from the lay people. The judge's seat is elevated above everyone else. There is an American flag near the judge, who wears a large black robe. There is a bailiff, usually a law enforcement officer in uniform, who enforces the judge's rules for the courtroom. Sometimes these rules have no relationship to the process of justice. For example, some judges won't allow members of the public to chew gum. When I was a law student observing a regular trial in Oakland Superior Court, I was told to leave the courtroom for chewing an antacid tablet. In the O. J. Simpson trial, Judge Lance Ito called a reporter into chambers for sucking on a cough drop. A number of years ago, in the United States District Court in San Francisco, the chief judge had a standing order that children were not allowed in the courtroom. My client's wife was told by the bailiff to take her two children, aged ten and seven, out of the courtroom on the day their father was being sentenced to prison for five years. I refused to allow this clear violation of the Sixth Amendment's right to a public trial, the First Amendment's right of association, and the general constitutional right of privacy, which protects family relationships. Although the judge allowed the children to stay in my case, the standing order continued in force and lawyers continued to obey it.

Lawyers are coconspirators in perpetuating the alienation and symbolism of the legal culture and its message of power and authority. Let us travel through a typical proceeding with a criminal defendant and her lawyer. The defendant enters the courtroom through two large doors, stepping into a narrow aisle that leads to a half-sized pair of swinging doors through which she cannot walk unless accompanied by an officer of the court. She takes a seat in the pew-like benches behind the swinging doors. On the other side are large tables and fancy chairs. A podium stands in the center facing an impressive and elevated dais, and behind the dais is a marble wall covered in part by an immense American flag. A man in a uniform approaches those sitting in the pews, telling them to stop talking and reading newspapers. Then the lawyers, brandishing briefcases, enter the courtroom and take their places at the large tables. One of the attorneys nods at the defendant and she comes through the swinging doors to sit at the same table.

A man raps a gavel, crying "Hear ye, hear ye, all rise!" Another man wrapped in a flowing black robe enters through a door in the back of the courtroom and takes his place behind the podium in the dais. Only after he sits may the others be seated.

Names and numbers are called, passed, and continued for an interminable amount of time until the defendant finally hears her name. Her lawyer says he is filing a motion under section 1538.5. The district attorney says the charge is only a 415 and requests a conference in chambers. Court is then recessed for a discussion in the judge's chambers. Afterwards the lawyers return to court and the man in the robe, continually addressed as "Your Honor," asks the defendant a question. The defendant, finally part of the proceedings, succumbs to her attorney's coaching and quietly answers "nolo contendre." His Honor asks the attorney a question. The lawyer assures him of the repentance and good works of the defendant, which will be reflected in the presentencing report. Then the man in the robe dismisses all until the afternoon service.

As the defendant leaves the House of the Law she realizes that her case has been dependent on her attorney's ability to translate human experience into legal dogma. She also understands that her future will depend on the judge's acceptance of the defendant's confessional as translated by her probation officer and attorney.

The lawyer, like the priest, is the middleperson between life and judgment. He suffers the initiation rites of his calling, wears its vestments, legitimizes its authority, speaks its language, partakes of its rituals, and maintains a monopoly on its mystery.

For the client, the lawyer, and the public, the result of this courtroom process is an acceptance of authority and a conditioned submission to its philosophy and rules. People enjoy rituals and symbols. Watching the court process is frightening, but it can also be exciting for the public. They feel secure observing authority in action. They admire and identify with the judges and the people in power, while at the same time accepting their own position as lower in the hierarchy of societal relationships. Just as a formal church service legitimates established religion, the traditional courtroom ritual legitimates the legal system.

Another major structural support of the existing legal culture is legal reasoning. This is a form of thought that presupposes existing societal relations. It does not allow for questioning of the political decisions that have led to our institutions. It makes it seem as though our laws are the inevitable result of human nature. The assumptions of the status quo can be found in every area of the law. Torts and real property law provide us with examples.

"Torts" is a required first-year class in every law school. It is also a word that those wide-eyed students can never adequately explain to their parents and friends. Basically, a tort is a harmful act committed by a person or a legal entity for which you can sue them. It is a civil case, as opposed to a criminal case. For example, if a person gets in his car and runs into your car on purpose, that is a criminal case for which he can go to jail. If a person gets in his car and runs into your car by accident, that is a civil case for which you can sue him for money damages.

In American law you cannot sue anyone unless they owe you what the law calls "a duty." Drivers on the highway owe a duty to other people to drive safely. But in our country, an individual owes no legal duty to another individual solely because the two people live in a society together. Therefore, if you are at a public swimming pool and see a child drowning, you do not have to jump in to try to save him. Since you do not have a legal duty to this child, you do not even have to pick up the life preserver lying at your feet and throw it in the pool. You may have a moral obligation, but in America you have no legal obligation. If a lawyer brought a suit against someone at the pool for not throwing a life preserver to the child, the suit would be dismissed, probably without even a hearing in court. The law doesn't *have* to be that way. We could have a society where people do not see themselves as atomized, isolated individuals. In many countries a person would have a legal duty to try to save the child.

In China there can be actual criminal penalties for failure to help a fellow citizen in a life-threatening situation. In 1995, a motorist was sentenced to two years in jail when he refused the pleas of a man whose wife was dying. The motorist was flagged down by the woman's husband, who said she was gravely ill and pleaded with the driver to take her to the hospital. The motorist rejected the request and drove away. Under American tort law the motorist could not be sued, nor could he be prosecuted. In most law schools this example would not be discussed because our legal reasoning equates the isolated, nonresponsible human being with human nature.

Real property law affords another example of how legal reasoning presupposes the justice of existing societal relations. This area of law presupposes the unequal distribution of property, which is justified by the philosophical notions that in America everyone is free and that if a person has enough talent he or she can acquire property. If an individual fails to "make good," it is his or her own failure based on lack of merit. What is fascinating about the law is that it incorporates the existing system of inequality, but then the law itself is used as a rationale for legitimating the very system that is imbedded within it. In other words, the law enforces rules as the natural order, when in fact those rules *have already assumed* one set of philosophical tenets and rejected any alternatives.

The term *real property* refers to houses, buildings, and land, as contrasted to *personal property,* which includes most other things one owns. Real property law in the United States allows one to own all the houses, buildings, and land one can afford. A person can make a living sitting in his home and collecting money from other people living in their homes, which he owns. An individual can own a tree or a beach. This arrangement is called capitalism. If a lawyer brought a lawsuit in an American court on behalf of neighbors who wanted occasional access to a "private" beach, the lawsuit would be dismissed immediately. A judge would not allow legal arguments regarding the public nature of a beach and whether it should or should not be owned by an individual.

This legal result is not common to all societies. Historically, among many Native American tribes land could not be owned by an individual. There was no proprietary interest in the environment. One could no more own a beach than one could own the ocean. People made fun of the Indians for allegedly selling the island of Manhattan for a few beads. But in Native American legal thought people could not own Manhattan Island, and therefore they could not sell it.

In modern-day America a tenant cannot refuse to pay rent on the grounds that the landlord owns more homes than she needs. But in Cuba one could raise such an argument and win. The Cuban General Law on Housing adopted in 1988 provides as follows: "Personal property in housing must be understood . . . essentially as a right to enjoyment of the house by the owner and his/her family, without having to pay anything after paying its price, but in no case can this right of personal property in the house become a mechanism of enrichment or exploitation." In her 1994 book on Cuban law and society, *Revolution in the Balance,* Debra Evenson notes that the official interpretation of the Housing Law is that a person's home is to live in, not to make a living from. Cuban citizens may own a primary residence and a vacation home, but no more.

In the United States you have a Fourth Amendment constitutional right to have your home free from searches without a warrant. But you have no right *to* a home. Which right would the man sleeping under a Los Angeles freeway prefer? In Cuba, the Constitution states that the "socialist state strives to provide each family a comfortable place to live." Decent housing for all is a goal of the society, and that goal is expressed in the Constitution as a legal obligation of the government. This would raise an interesting legal question if the Cuban state tried to prosecute a homeless person for sleeping in a park. That person's lawyer should be able to defend the case on the grounds that the state failed to strive to provide a decent place to live according to Article 8(c) of the Constitution. Actually, the parks and streets of Cuba are not filled with homeless people, even under its present economic crisis. But if they were, the legal system would provide a possible defense for the homeless.

The result in America is totally different, because our legal reasoning presupposes that there is no legal obligation for a government to provide housing for its people. In fact, what is taking place in America is the *criminalization* of homelessness.

There are many cases around the country dealing with homelessness. In 1995 the California Supreme Court ruled in *Tobe v. City of Santa Ana* that the city could prosecute and send to jail for six months any person who camps out or stores their personal belongings (a shopping cart for example) in a public park, street, or area. Justice Stanley Mosk, in dissent, angrily criticized the city for arresting persons "whose sole 'crime' was to cover themselves with a blanket and rest in a public area." The decision noted the fact that the city provided shelters, but on any given night there were 2,500 more homeless people than there were beds in shelters. In Cuba, such a fact might be used as a defense, arguing that the government was failing to attempt in good faith to provide housing. But in the United States, this fact was considered *legally irrelevant* to the decision of the court. Is being poor legally irrelevant to a criminal defense? Is being black and suffering actual discrimination legally irrelevant to a criminal defense?

These are the questions with which the black rage defense confronts the law. (This confrontation will be explored in following chapters).

Another major factor in legal reasoning is the myth that the law is made up of neutral, fair rules. Rules are supposed to become evident to any educated and legally trained judge or lawyer who objectively analyzes the facts and the previous legal decisions. This myth was articulated perfectly by California Court of Appeals Judge Edward Wallin: "I am never troubled by making a decision. I just decide the way the law dictates."

The judge's statement assumes that reason and logic determine judicial results. It denies the influence of the judge's personal political views. The statement also carries the message that the "law" is just floating out there in space, majestically dictating the correct (fair and just) result. This denies the fact that judges must interpret conflicting arguments to arrive at a result, and that their interpretation is based on a myriad of factors that are rooted in present-day political conditions.

Anyone who does not believe that judges are influenced by public pressure, social movements, and their own prejudices and opinions should read *The Brethren* by Scott Armstrong and Bob Woodward, the journalist who helped uncover the Watergate story. This was the first popular book to go behind the black-robed mystique of the United States Supreme Court and expose the myth that judges interpret the law based on objective, neutral principles untainted by politics and predisposition.

One key legal concept supporting this myth is *stare decisis,* which says that judicial decisions flow from previous decisions, going back centuries to the beginning of English Common Law. Every lawyer searches musty old law books, or, these days, computer data bases, for "precedent" — that is, for judicial opinions that support her argument. Indeed, much of the skill of legal practice is taking those previous opinions and expanding or shrinking them to fit the facts of one's present case. We spend an enormous amount of time in law school learning how to distinguish cases from each other, and how to analogize the facts or law of previous decisions to the facts of the case at hand. This prompts our friends and spouses to remark irritably that law students can only speak in analogies.

Precedent is not just a concept, it has a real role in day-to-day litigation. I once appeared in front of a conservative federal judge on behalf of a radical union caucus. My clients had refused to stand and pledge allegiance to the flag at the beginning of union meetings. Their refusal was used as a ruse by the union officials to kick them out of meetings. I brought a claim under the civil rights section of the Landrum-Griffin Act. The judge had no sympathy for my clients—indeed, he was clearly hostile to their politics and their actions—but he felt he was bound by precedent. Therefore, he ruled in our favor, and then wished the other side success on appeal. We won the appeal and returned to the same lower court judge to receive attorney fees. However, he refused to authorize me the full amount of attorney fees I was due under the statute's provision for a successful outcome. In the area of attorney fees the judge has discretion, and though he liked me personally, he was so opposed to my clients' politics that he exercised his discretion against my reasonable claim for fees. It is typical for judges to find ways to exercise their discretion as their politics dictate. It is rare that precedent completely binds a judge. It would be foolish to deny the effect of precedent in determining outcomes, but it would be a bigger mistake to fall into the trap of believing that our legal system is controlled by this seemingly objective rule.

Critical legal theory writers have attempted to explain and expose the concepts of stare decisis and precedent. In his essay "Freedom of Speech," David Kairys looks at the history of the right to speak in a public park, a right we now take for granted.[3] However, in 1894 there was no such right, in spite of the First Amendment. Reverend William F. Davis, an opponent of slavery and discrimination, attempted to preach the Social Gospel, a religious doctrine that stressed social responsibility and criticized the corruption of local government. Davis was jailed the first time he attempted to preach on the Boston Commons and fined the second time. The case was eventually heard by the Massachusetts Supreme Court. In an opinion by the man who was later to become one of America's most famous Supreme Court Justices, Oliver Wendell Holmes, the court upheld the conviction.[4] It said that a city ordinance prohibiting a public address on public grounds without a Mayor's permit was constitutional:

> That such an ordinance is constitutional . . . does not appear to us open to doubt. . . . For the Legislature absolutely or conditionally to forbid public speaking in a highway or public park is no more an infringement of the rights of a member of the public than for the owner of a private house to forbid it in his house.

The U.S. Supreme Court unanimously affirmed, quoting Holmes's analogy to a private house.[5] The Court said that the government had a "right to absolutely exclude all right to use."

Forty years later, a case arose with similar circumstances. Labor organizers with the Congress of Industrial Organizations (CIO) wanted to speak and pass out leaflets in a public park in Jersey City. But Mayor Frank Hague, adamantly opposed to CIO labor organizers, refused any permits. One would think that precedent would win the day, and that the CIO would lose its case under the rule and rationale of *Davis*. But a completely different result occurred. In *Hague v. CIO* the Supreme Court ruled that the right to speak and hold assemblies in parks is protected by the First Amendment.

> Wherever the title of streets and parks may rest, they have immemorially been held in trust for the use of the public and, time out of mind, have been used for purposes of assembly, communicating thoughts between citizens, and discussing public questions. Such use of the streets and public places has, from ancient times, been a part of the privileges, immunities, rights, and liberties of citizens.

The Court's assertion that streets and parks have been held for the public "from ancient times" and from "time out of mind" is in direct contradiction to its own history, as just forty years earlier it had stated that the right to use public areas was dependent on the absolute will of the government. The Supreme Court made a political judgment based on changing social conditions—namely, the rise of a powerful labor movement that was organizing in streets and parks throughout the country. By the time the *Hague* decision was written, it was 1939 and the New Deal had been implemented. Labor had a legitimate place in America. Allowing old-time city political bosses like Frank Hague to boast "I am the Law" and to forbid labor organizing would eventually result in violent confrontations. The *Hague* decision fulfilled one of the more important functions of the Court: to make decisions that lead to the peaceful transition of power relations and promote social reform, not social revolution.

One method the courts use to engender social harmony is ideological storytelling. Instead of specifically overruling their prior decision in *Davis* and admitting they had rejected precedent, the Supreme Court distinguished the two cases from each other through tortured reasoning. In this way it did not have to repudiate the idea of the primacy of private property inherent in its rationale for the *Davis* decision. Therefore, it did not have to confess to the influence of social movements on the Court. By distinguishing the cases and telling a story about the liberty of the people to use the streets and parks from time immemorial, the Court maintained the legend that judicial decision-making is based on neutral, eternal, time-honored principles. The role of the people engaged in political struggle is masked by the myth of freedom of speech as extant in natural law. Therefore, there is no social context to the ruling. The impression given is that the Justices merely looked to existing principles of law and followed that path as any educated, objective, politically nonpartisan decision-maker would.

Throughout the history of American jurisprudence, judges have rejected precedent when it has served their politics to do so. This trend has become so obnoxious under the Rehnquist Supreme Court that even Justice Byron White, a conservative in the area of criminal law, has been outraged. In *Arizona v. Fulminante,* a case that shocked the criminal defense bar and the academic community, the Court changed the law of harmless error that had been in effect for twenty-four years. The previous decision was *Chapman v. California,* which held that in some instances errors of law made in a trial could be considered "harmless" and were not to be used as a basis to reverse a conviction. However, some constitutional protections were considered "so basic to a fair trial that their infraction can never be treated as harmless error." One example the Court gave in its *Chapman* decision was the admission into evidence of a coerced confession. But in *Fulminante,* in a five-to-four decision by Chief Justice William Rehnquist, the Court held exactly the opposite—that the use of a coerced confession could be considered harmless error. In his dissenting opinion, Justice White wrote, "Today, a majority of the Court, without any justification ... *overrules this vast body of precedent without a word,* and in so doing dislodges one of the fundamental tenets of our criminal justice system" (emphasis mine).

Justices Harry Blackmun, William Brennan, Thurgood Marshall, Stephen Breyer, David Souter, and John Paul Stevens have also unhappily noted the Rehnquist Court's disregard for precedent.[6] Justice Marshall described the process best when he wrote, "The majority chooses to pretend that it writes on a blank slate, ignoring precedent after precedent."[7] Although the false image of judges objectively following precedent does not have the strength it did in previous years, it still confuses the public discourse and enchants the public mind. The idea that judges are restricted by, and defer to, precedent continues to be a controlling notion in our legal system because it fits in with the ultimate myth of democracy—that we are "a country of laws, not men."

Proponents of traditional jurisprudence want us to believe that judges are bound by law, not politics. Rituals that condition the public to authority, legal reasoning that justifies existing inequality, and the myth that law is neutral all result in a legal culture that masks the existence of economic and racial conflict. But such conflict does exist. In fact, it has become so intense that it tears at the social fabric.

In opposition to these myths, the black rage defense attempts to discuss the reality of race. But it runs headfirst into a legal system that continually regurgitates the idea that the United States is a meritocracy, a country where any person can rise above his circumstances by hard work and merit. Certainly some individual members of minority groups have been able to rise above their initial circumstances, both economically and socially. But African Americans as a group are still drowning in a quagmire of poverty, and the law will not act as a life preserver.

Judicial decisions in the last fifteen years have made it increasingly difficult to win claims of racial discrimination. Current law focuses on the individual as a perpetrator of racial discrimination and rejects an analysis that would factor in societal patterns of racism or institutional practices that result in discrimination. Court decisions now require proof of intent to discriminate.[8]

This burden of proving a racist motive, purpose, and intent is almost impossible to meet. A good example is the 1981 U.S. Supreme Court opinion in *City of Memphis v. Greene.*[9] That case involved two neighborhoods—Hein Park, in which all the homes were owned by whites, and an adjacent community that was predominantly black. West Drive, a street about a half mile long, went through the center of Hein Park. The city, acting at the request of the white property owners, closed West Drive, which was the main thoroughfare for black residents, thereby forcing them to drive out of their way in order to get to their homes. The city actually put up a physical barrier at the point where the two neighborhoods intersected, at West Drive and Springdale Street. The Court of Appeals found a discriminatory intent in the erection of the barrier. But the U.S. Supreme Court reversed, holding that the city's justifications for traffic safety and tranquility were adequate to support a finding of no racist purpose. The residents of the all-white enclave wanted to stop "undesirable traffic." As Justice Marshall stated, "Too often in our Nation's history, statements such as these ['undesirable traffic'] have been little more than code phrases for racial discrimination." Yet the Court accepted this obvious subterfuge.

The Court's opinion also shows how the law interprets social reality in a manner that avoids recognizing racial discrimination.

> But the inconvenience of the drivers is a function of where they live and where they regularly drive—not a function of their race; the hazards and the inconvenience that the closing is intended to minimize are a function of the number of vehicles involved, not the race of their drivers or of the local residents.

Here, the Court closes its eyes and ears to segregated housing patterns, racial hostility, and the power of the white property owners to get the City of Memphis to do its racist bidding. Then, adding insult to injury, the Court tells the African American community to accept this racial oppression because it is their duty as citizens. Speaking of the burden of having to drive around Hein Park in order to get home, the Court says, "Proper respect for the dignity of the residents of any neighborhood requires that they accept the same burdens as well as the same benefits of citizenship regardless of their racial or ethnic origin."

A cogent and powerful attack on the racist nature of legal culture has come from men and women of color in the legal profession who make up an intellectual movement called *critical race theory*. An excellent description of the defining elements of this movement is found in the book *Words That Wound: Critical Race Theory, Assaultive Speech, and the First Amendment*.[10] The criticisms the authors list go to the heart of the prevailing legal culture:

> Critical race theory expresses skepticism toward dominant legal claims of neutrality, objectivity, color blindness, and meritocracy. These claims are central to an ideology of equal opportunity that presents race as an immu-

table characteristic devoid of social meaning and tells an ahistorical, abstracted story of racial inequality as a series of randomly occurring, intentional, and individualized acts.

Critical race theory challenges ahistoricism and insists on a contextual historical analysis of the law. Current inequalities and social/institutional practices are linked to earlier periods in which the intent and cultural meaning of such practices were clear. More important, as critical race theorists we adopt a stance that presumes that racism has contributed to all contemporary manifestations of group advantage and disadvantage along racial lines, including differences in income, imprisonment, health, housing, education, political representation, and military service. Our history calls for this presumption.

The black rage defense, like critical race theory, rejects the ahistorical interpretation of behavior in society. It puts criminal actions into a context that infuses those actions with the racial reality of culture, economics, and politics. Since black rage is a defense that is used at the trial stage, it must confront the assumption of the "colorblind courtroom." American law promotes the idea that every person, regardless of race, is treated fairly and equally once he or she steps inside the sacrosanct walls of the courtroom. The California Court of Appeals states this concept quite explicitly: "One of our guiding principles in this courtroom, indeed in every courtroom, is that race, creed, color, religion, national origin, none of these things counts for or against anybody. These are neutral factors."[11]

In chapter 1, we saw how the prosecutor and the judge in the William Freeman trial relied on this myth of equal treatment when arguing to the jury and when sentencing the defendant to death. In many ways the courtroom process has become more conducive to equal treatment than it was in 1846. Black, Chinese, and Native Americans are now allowed to testify against white people.[12] African Americans are no longer systematically and intentionally excluded from jury panels. There are many African American lawyers and judges. But for all these advances, the acceptance of the notion of a colorblind courtroom still impedes the abolition of racial inequality and makes it more difficult for a minority defendant to get a fair trial. Two areas that deserve further analysis are voir dire (the questioning of the jurors for bias) and the use of peremptory challenges to knock people off the jury.

In 1931 the Supreme Court ruled that lawyers could ask jurors questions about racial prejudice. But in actual practice, very few lawyers would ask white jurors about their possible prejudice because they were afraid it would stir up racial animosity. Most lawyers and judges accepted the assumption of the colorblind courtroom and held the mistaken belief that once people were seated in the courtroom they would be colorblind. Even as late as 1971 judges and lawyers would advise me not to ask racial questions because, they said, it called attention to my client's race, which would make race an issue in the trial and would result in an unfavorable verdict for the black or Latino defendant.

Such a strategy flies in the face of reality. People do notice the color of other people's skin and attach certain characteristics to those people. Often these perceptions are filled with negative stereotypes of people of color. These stereotypes become filters through which jurors will see and evaluate the evidence and the witnesses. It is essential to root out negative preconceptions and prejudices. Many of these prejudices are subconscious. Charles Lawrence suggests two basic reasons for this.[13] The first is the conflict between the stated principle that race prejudice is unacceptable, and the simultaneous existence in the national psyche of negative beliefs about other ethnic groups. When an individual experiences that conflict he feels the discomfort of guilt for his socially unacceptable ideas, and therefore the mind excludes his racism from his consciousness. In psychological language, the individual is in "denial" regarding his own racial prejudice.

The second aspect of Lawrence's analysis posits that we are often unaware of many of the stereotypes we have internalized because these beliefs are an integral part of our mass culture and the unspoken lessons we learn from interacting with the world around us. For example, the belief that blacks are not as intelligent as whites may not result from the indoctrination of racist ideology, but rather from the individual's observation of how the society, including his peers and his parents, treats black people. The "tacit understanding" in the culture that black people are not as intelligent or as qualified as white people is transmitted to the individual as a rational, believable concept. This belief becomes part of the person's world view, and he is never conscious that it is a racial stereotype borne of power relations, not a result of nature.

Voir dire can be a tool for uncovering preconceptions and subconscious stereotypes. However, judges interpreted the case that allowed racial questioning to mean that only one question was necessary, and, worst of all, the form of the question was so restricted as to make it almost useless. The courts allowed defense lawyers to phrase a question something like the following: "Do you have any prejudice against the defendant's race that would make you unable to give him a fair trial?" Now, what juror would answer yes to such an inquiry in a public courtroom?

The image of the colorblind courtroom was exploded by defense lawyer Charles Garry when he defended Black Panther leader Huey Newton for allegedly killing a policeman. The year was 1968, and historical events had created an opportunity for Garry, known as one of America's greatest criminal defense lawyers, to create a new, antiracist voir dire. The civil rights movement had awakened the country to the reality of racial oppression and had affected the consciousness of many white people, who now accepted the fact that the courtroom was not a place where blacks could expect equal justice. Combined with this new awareness was the fact that the Black Panther Party for Self Defense had made a powerful impact in the Bay Area. The black community of Oakland was closely watching Newton's trial. In this atmosphere, Garry was able to spend days probing and pushing prospective jurors to come to grips with their racial prejudices. His voir dire was compiled in a manual by long-time legal activist and scholar Ann Ginger of the Alexander Meiklejohn Civil Liberties Institute. The manual, entitled *Minimizing Racism in Jury Trials,* was distributed by the National Lawyers Guild to attorneys throughout the country. But when lawyers tried to use it they ran into the fear and conservatism of trial judges as they attempted to ask race-related questions. As I began my practice in 1970, I found that judges could be persuaded to allow a limited amount of questioning about race. In order to win the right to voir dire on race I would file a legal brief citing case law and would tell the judge in our very first meeting that I intended to ask the jurors about their racial preconceptions. I had to assure each judge I was not going to spend days doing voir dire. After all, I did not have the stature of Garry and my trials were not receiving national attention.

Although prosecutors usually objected to my brief, the state court judges would allow me to ask each juror a few open-ended questions regarding race, such as, "Have you ever had an unfortunate experience with a black person? How has that experience affected your view of black people? Would you feel uncomfortable listening to a witness in this case who speaks with a heavy accent? Would you feel anger at a person living in the United States who will testify in this case through a translator?" After I gained some experience, I was even able to ask the following questions: "Did you read the statement by J. Edgar Hoover, Director of the FBI, that he wasn't worried about a Mexican shooting the President, because 'they don't shoot straight, but if they come at you with a knife, beware.' Do you think this reinforces the stereotype of the knife-fighting Mexican, too stupid to shoot straight, but still violent?"

In federal court, the judge, not the lawyers, usually conducts the voir dire. However, twice I had the experience of judges admitting that they were uncomfortable asking jurors about race. This emphasized to me how much judges have internalized the idea of a colorblind courtroom. In those trials, one of which involved a Black Muslim defendant, the judges allowed me to ask the jurors a few open-ended questions about race, instead of asking the questions themselves.

Great progress has been made since Charles Garry's stunning voir dire in Huey Newton's trial, but it is disheartening to see so many judges still opposing an antiracist voir dire and restricting defense lawyers to a minimal amount of questions. Also, conservative politicians have led campaigns to have judges, instead of lawyers, do voir dire. They say that lawyers waste time and money, thereby impeding the efficiency of the administration of justice. They also blame voir dire as one of the reasons criminal defendants get acquitted. These arguments found a receptive ear among the California electorate, who voted to have judges *in criminal cases* conduct the voir dire. The result has been a limited, usually pro forma type of questioning regarding racial stereotyping. This type of superficial voir dire is an obstacle that must be combatted in a black rage defense.

Voir dire is obviously essential in a black rage case. Since this defense puts race on the table and confronts racist images, it is necessary to ask jurors questions that probe their racial unconscious. One purpose is to ferret out people whose prejudices make it unlikely that they can give the defendant a fair trial. An example of this is the juror in *People v. Ortiz* who proudly stated, "They better not take me on that jury, or I will hang that Mexican," or the juror in *State v. Russell* who said, "I don't like the Mexican race."[14] Those cases were in the 1920s. One result of the civil rights gains of the last thirty years is that overt racist comments are less socially acceptable in public. Today, therefore, it is harder to weed out racially prejudiced jurors. But an antiracist voir dire is also valuable in bringing stereotypes into the open and encouraging jurors to reflect on their private feelings. Once the jurors begin to recognize their own preconceptions, the defense has taken a significant step in combatting the racism engendered by those feelings. This is because most jurors want to be fair and want to feel that they are not acting in a prejudiced manner. Once they become *conscious* of their negative racial ideas, they will make a good faith effort either to overcome those beliefs or not to let them dominate their deliberations. An antiracist voir dire also strengthens the collective consciousness of the jurors to be sensitive to the perversion of ascribing negative qualities to blacks. This results in an atmosphere in the jury room conducive to the black rage defense.

The black rage defense attempts to interpret and explain the life experiences of African Americans so that a jury can understand the link between those experiences and the criminal act the defendant has committed. There should be black people on any jury that is judging a black man or woman. This is not because those jurors will be sure to acquit. In fact, most crimes committed by blacks are perpetrated on other black people. Karen Jo Koonan of the National Jury Project reported that in a recent voir dire in a murder case in the predominantly African American community of Compton, California, more than 50 percent of the jury pool of about sixty people either knew someone who was murdered or knew someone who had murdered someone else.

The issue is not who will acquit; the issue is how to obtain a group of jurors who will go into the jury room and conduct deliberations that evaluate the evidence from different points of view. My experience leads me to conclude that white jurors can empathize with the life and motivations of a black person. But it is also true that a jury diverse in race and class is more likely to have discussions that are open to the black rage defense. It is an unusual defense, and one that depends on the jurors rising above their stereotypes and expanding beyond their individual worlds. A multiracial jury can provide the context for the broadening of each person's world view and, in so doing, come closer to understanding the life of the defendant.

Unfortunately, the law regarding peremptory challenges does not adequately protect the defendant's right to a jury chosen from a cross-section of the community. There are two ways a lawyer is allowed to challenge a juror for bias. One is called a challenge for cause, the other is called a peremptory challenge. A challenge for cause takes place when the lawyer feels the juror has said something that indicates prejudgment of the case or some sort of bias against the defendant that would make it likely that she could not be fair in determining guilt or innocence. The lawyer makes a challenge either verbally or, in some situations, in writing, and the judge rules on the challenge, either dismissing the juror or allowing her to stay on the panel. Challenges for cause are unlimited in number. Peremptories are limited by statute—often ten each for the district attorney and defense, or twenty each in a capital case. Historically, a peremptory challenge could be made for any reason at all. The lawyer would not have to state the reason, and the juror was automatically discharged. It is beyond dispute that district attorneys used peremptories to knock black people off of juries. The Supreme Court noted this widespread and flagrant practice and in a 1986 case called *Batson v. Kentucky* ruled that peremptories could not be used for racial purposes.

However, the Court put forth a formula that left a huge loophole for prosecutors to continue their racist practices. The Court set up three steps: First, if it seems that there is a pattern of striking black jurors, the defense lawyer can object. If the judge feels a prima facie case of discrimination has taken place, he shifts the burden to the prosecutor. In the second step, the prosecutor must be able to explain adequately, in race-neutral terms, why he is kicking black people off the jury. In the third stage, the judge decides if there has been purposeful discrimination. If there is such a finding, the prosecutor's challenge is disallowed.

The problem is that it is very difficult to find purposeful discrimination. Judges do not like to interpret the prosecutor's state of mind as racist. And since judges believe in the colorblind courtroom, they end up accepting the most absurd explanations, for instance that a black juror wore his hair in a ponytail, that a black man was effeminate, or that a minority juror was a loner.[15] I was cocounsel in a high-profile first-degree murder case in which the defendant was African American. There were very few African Americans in the jury venire (the entire group of potential jurors that sit in the courtroom). The district attorney used his peremptory challenges to knock off two black jurors. He then challenged the only black male on the panel—in fact, the only black male under thirty in the entire venire. When chief counsel, Petra de Jesus, objected under the *Batson* rule, we went into chambers. The district attorney gave as his reason the fact that the young man had not voted in the last election and therefore did not take his obligations as a citizen seriously. The judge disregarded the fact that 60 percent of eligible voters chose not to vote, and that the district attorney asked only this black male juror if he voted. The judge ruled that the explanation was race-neutral and adequate. Because the defendant was acquitted, there was no appeal and therefore no decision of an appellate court. However, as we saw earlier in *City of Memphis v. Greene,* judges are willing to close their eyes to racism and allow subterfuge and mendacity.

Jeff Brand, a former public defender and current professor of law at the University of San Francisco, has persuasively traced the history of racism in jury selection, showing through both statistics and case analyses that *Batson* has basically been a failure.[16] Brand was not surprised when, shortly after his article was published, the Supreme Court further watered down *Batson*. In *Purkett v. Elem,* the court allowed the prosecutor to strike two black men for the following reasons:

> I struck number twenty-two because of his long hair. He had long curly hair. He had the longest hair than anybody on the panel by far. . . . Also, he had a mustache and a goatee-type beard. And juror number twenty-four also has a mustache and a goatee-type beard. Those are the only two people on the jury, numbers twenty-two and twenty-four, with facial hair of any kind of all the men and, of course, the women, those are the only two with the facial hair. And I don't like the way they looked, with the way the hair is cut, both of them. And the mustaches and the beards look suspicious to me.

Two Justices dissented, with Justice Stevens saying that the majority opinion now allows trial judges to accept "silly, fantastic and implausible explanations," and that the decision demeaned the equal protection values of their earlier opinions.

Lawyers employing the black rage defense must use all their skill and determination in obtaining a multiracial jury. For all its weaknesses, raising *Batson* objections is still one available tool. An antiracist voir dire is another. Most importantly, in all our strategy we must confront racism and not fall victim to the myth of equality and fairness represented by the statue of the Goddess of Justice.

People commit crimes at a fearful rate in America. Some of those crimes are direct results of racial and economic inequality. As long as the law is seen as something eternal, value-neutral, and objective, society will never come to terms with the consequences of the racial discrimination and economic oppression that can erupt in our streets, our banks, our auto plants, and even in the most frightening place—our homes.

The black rage defense tries to rip the blindfold off the eyes of the Goddess of Justice. It shouts out to Americans that their society's gross inequalities cause hopelessness and pain, which in turn cause some individuals to strike out. When the law defines that striking out as a criminal act and the legal system brings its awesome force down upon that individual, he should be able to defend himself by explaining the role of society in causing that explosion.

Please, Mr. Foreman, slow down you
  assembly line.
No, I don't mind working, but I do
  mind dyin!
—Joe L. Carter, autoworker and blues singer

Chapter 4

Black Rage 1971:
The Case of James Johnson, Jr.

In 1968 James Johnson got a job in the automobile plants of Detroit. That
meant it was more dangerous for him to go to work than to walk the
streets at night. Working men and women have received many benefits
from the industrial revolution. They have also paid an awful price in job-
related sickness, injury, and death. In 1972 the "President's Report on Occupational Safety and Health" made a conservative estimate that there
were 100,000 deaths every year traceable to working conditions. In addition, the report concluded that there were at least 390,000 new cases of
disabling occupational disease each year. Autoworkers in the 1960s and
1970s were particularly susceptible to injury and death. A 1973 report,
based on figures compiled by the National Institute of Occupational Safety
and Health, estimated that 16,000 autoworkers and retired autoworkers
died every year from job-related injuries and disease. In addition to can-
cers from poisonous materials and heart attacks from uncontrolled job
stress, every autoworker family knew someone who had been injured or
crippled in an accident while on the job.

An injury suffered by a worker named Brian T. Flannigan typifies the dangerous working conditions in the plants and the lack of proper medical care provided by the giant auto corporations. Flannigan had a summer job in 1969 at the Ford Rouge foundry, where he worked on a crankshaft table. He would pick up a mold as it came down the assembly line and then put it on the conveyor belt above his head. The conveyors were old; they would shake and jerk, and parts would fall off. The workers often complained of the danger of falling parts, but nothing changed. One day, two molds fell off the conveyor and hit Flannigan on the head, knocking him unconscious. He was taken to the company's medical office, where he received pain pills for his headache and was sent back to work, restricted to light duty. Flannigan complained to the union committeeman, who persuaded the general foreman to let the young man go home.

For the next two weeks Flannigan stayed home, in pain and losing feeling on the left side of his head. The company medical clinic never took cervical x-rays and suggested that his pain was psychosomatic. Finally, he went to his family's doctor, who sent him to a hospital for x-rays. The results showed his neck had been broken in three places. For eight weeks the company's doctors had misdiagnosed him, and Ford had withheld workers' compensation benefits and even failed to file the accident form required by state law.

In the 1974 book *Muscle and Blood* Rachel Scott documented, through powerful interviews, the human devastation caused by America's industrial might. Her description of the auto plants could be called "man as machine," as she exposed the companies' economic motivation for failing to keep the factories safe. The profit motive was the incentive for employers to hire lawyers to contest injury cases and doctors to downplay the workers' injuries and deny the work-related causes of long-term illnesses. Ultimately it was cheaper to pay the injured or sick worker the small amount due under the workers' compensation law than it was to make the plants safe.

Where was the union in this equation of company profits versus worker safety? Unfortunately, the United Auto Workers (UAW) was reluctant to take on the fight for safer conditions with the same militancy they had displayed in the struggle for higher wages. The movement to organize the auto plants was one of the proudest chapters in American labor history. In 1936, workers took over General Motors' Fisher Body Plant #1 in Flint,

Michigan. For forty days, two thousand strikers occupied the plant, setting up recreational activities, sanitation facilities, educational classes, and people's courts to maintain discipline. A court injunction was issued against the sit-in. In response, five thousand men and women encircled the plant. The police eventually attacked, wounding thirteen strikers. But the occupation of the plant continued, and the sit-down tactic spread to other General Motors factories. The company eventually gave in, signing a contract recognizing the union. The Flint strike and victory energized workers throughout America, and in 1937 there were close to five hundred sit-down strikes.

The UAW grew in strength and achieved real gains for workers. By the late 1960s, however, the UAW was out of touch with its past. George B. Morris, Jr., a General Motors vice president and director of labor relations, described the situation in *The Unions,* a 1972 book by Haynes Johnson and Nick Kotz: "I guess it was understandable when the unions were beginning to organize that they had to be militant and aggressive. . . . [They] inculcated into the minds of their constituents this idea of conflict, of war between the classes, between the worker and the employer. Hell, that day is gone. That's like nickel beer and button shoes. It's gone."

Two of the weakest aspects of organized labor were its failure to protect racial minorities and women against company exploitation and its failure to train and include them in the leadership of the union. In the late sixties at least 30 percent of the UAW was black, but of the twenty-six people on the executive board only two were black. In 1969, blacks had only seven of the one hundred key union staff positions. Women made up 14 percent of the UAW membership, but they had only one position on the executive board and no critical staff positions.

The UAW's inability to confront racism within its own organization left it in a weak position to fight the companies' racist practices. African Americans were always the last hired and first fired. During the labor shortages caused by World War II the plants hired many more blacks. For example, Chrysler had no black women employees in 1941, but had five thousand by 1945. However, the recessions of the fifties caused major cutbacks, and blacks were the first to go. With the auto industry's comeback in the early sixties, blacks were rehired. But they were often hired as temporary workers and fired before ninety days expired—the point at which the worker would have received the full protection of the union contract.

Within the plants, blacks got the noisiest, dirtiest, and most dangerous jobs. They worked in the foundries, the body shops, and the engine assembly lines. They were also limited in their upward mobility. The Dodge Main plant was typical: 95 percent of the foremen were white, 100 percent of the superintendents were white, 90 percent of the skilled tradesmen were white, and 90 percent of skilled apprentices were white. Class and race had always been boiling issues in the auto industry. Those issues were about to be affected by the agitation and politics of the sixties.

Detroit had suffered its share of race riots. Its history was stained by the actions of white mobs in 1833, 1863, and 1943. But in 1967 it was mainly black people who took to the streets. After a week of violence, 43 people were dead, 347 injured, and almost 4,000 had been arrested. Five thousand people were homeless due to the fires, and property damage was estimated at half a billion dollars. Within thirty days after the Michigan National Guard left the city, African American revolutionary leader H. Rap Brown spoke to a crowd of five thousand people approximately a mile from what had been the center of the rebellion. The sponsors of the event were black radicals who were putting together the first issue of a monthly newsletter called the *Inner City Voice*. The newsletter became a vehicle for exposing police brutality, slumlordism, and the exploitation of workers in the auto plants. It advocated class struggle and became a focal point for revolutionary activity, just as the Black Panther Party newspaper was doing in Oakland, California.

With the help of members of the *Inner City Voice*, a group calling itself the Dodge Revolutionary Union Movement (DRUM) organized a wildcat strike in May 1968 at the Dodge Main factory. Four thousand workers shut down the plant as a protest against speed-up—the demands of the company to work faster and faster to achieve higher production. DRUM concentrated its organizing among the black workers and put forth a program calling for worker control of the factories and the elimination of discrimination. Their program gained some adherents among white workers, but it was particularly attractive to blacks who labored at the worst jobs and felt left out of the union. DRUMS's model was followed at other plants. There was FRUM at Ford's River Rouge complex, JARUM at Chrysler's Jefferson Avenue Assembly plant, MARUM at the Mack Avenue plant, CADRUM at Cadillac's Fleetwood factory, MERUM at the Mound Road Engine plant, DRUM II at Dodge Truck, ELRUM at the Eldon Avenue Gear and Axle plant, and organizing units at six other plants. Some of these revolutionary union movements were small; the largest was at the Eldon Avenue plant where James Johnson worked.

In 1969 the radicals at *Inner City Voice* and DRUM coalesced in a group called the League of Revolutionary Black Workers. The League advocated socialism and was strongly influenced by the radical black nationalism that was prevalent throughout African American communities. Initially the League's primary focus was in-plant organizing, but it soon joined neighborhood struggles such as the campaign for community control of the public schools and the development of economic self-sufficiency. One member of the League's seven-man executive committee was a thirty-year-old lawyer named Ken Cockrel. Cockrel was a good-looking man, six feet tall, with a large Afro and a quick tongue. He had a sharp mind and a photographic memory, and he was a master of the English language. He considered himself a Marxist and a revolutionary. Cockrel was to have a profound impact on Detroit's legal culture.

Cockrel had grown up in Detroit. His parents, like so many black autoworkers, left the South during World War II for the promise of work in the auto plants. At first they lived in army barracks at the northern city limits, which were used to house the many blacks who had been recruited to work in the factories. Cockrel's parents died when he was twelve. He quit high school in the eleventh grade and later joined the Air Force, as his brother had done. After his discharge, Cockrel was admitted to Wayne State University in a special program for those who had not graduated from high school. After completing college, he went to Wayne State Law School and was admitted to the bar in 1968. His speaking ability, intellectual capacity, and overall charisma would catapult him into a leading role in the legal arena. Within a year after the legal incorporation of the League of Revolutionary Black Workers, Cockrel and a thirty-year-old Jewish radical lawyer named Justin Ravitz would be defending James Johnson on murder charges.

Who was James Johnson, why did he kill three people in the Eldon plant, and why were leaflets with the headline "Hail James Johnson" passed out at all the auto plants after the shootings?

James Johnson, Jr., was born in 1934 in Starkville, Mississippi. The dictionary defines "stark" as "desolate" and "rigid, as a corpse." These words aptly describe the conditions of Johnson's early life and his engulfing fear of death. He grew up on a plantation in Josie Creek. Like the other black children who lived on the white-owned plantation, he could go to school only four months of the year. This was because harvesting season started the same time as school, and eleven-year-old James had to be out in the fields working the cotton harvest. He lived with his parents, brothers, and sisters in a two-room shanty and rarely had adequate food or clothing. When asked at trial how he survived, his only answer was, "We just did without. We had no alternative but to do without."

James was a nervous, withdrawn child, with few friends. His mother was a loving, caring woman, his father a strict authoritarian who was abusive toward James's mother. When James was nine years old he saw the maimed and dismembered remains of his cousin Henry, who had been lynched. James's fear of death increased, and often he could not sleep because he feared that dead people would come for him. At the age of twelve or thirteen he began to have "spells," manifested by headaches and hallucinations, in which he would see the distorted and horrific faces of dead people. The faces would leer at him from the cracks in the walls and ceiling. He would scream out for his mother, who would comfort him. He also had auditory hallucinations in which voices would cry out to him. He viewed white people with suspicion and fear. He felt white people controlled the lives of black people and could do whatever they wanted. He developed stomach pains and was given medication for a "nervous condition."

When James was approximately eighteen he moved to Mt. Clemens, Michigan, to live with relatives. He continued to be a loner. His only social activities were singing in the high school glee club and attending church regularly. At twenty-two he joined the Army but was fearful of nighttime duty and felt persecuted by the white officers. On one occasion another soldier made sexual advances toward him, and he had what the psychiatrist at trial would term an "extreme homosexual panic" in which he worried that maybe he was homosexual. He continued to have hallucinations, during which he would break out in a profuse sweat and hear terrifying voices. He became more and more depressed and was finally discharged.

Returning to Mt. Clemens, James Johnson lived with his cousin and retreated into himself. He would look in the mirror and wish that his skin color was lighter. He fantasized about being a great singer. He was incapable of socializing. But he was always able to hold down a job.

While living with his cousin, Johnson found out that a man had died years earlier in the same room in which he slept. After that he could not stay in the house alone. He often felt people were picking on him. On two or three occasions he threatened or attacked people for slight provocations. In one instance he was fired from the Scotch and Sirloin Restaurant after stabbing a black waiter in a fight. Johnson believed that the waiter was being used by the white owners to provoke him in order to get him fired.

In 1965 Johnson lived in Detroit with one of his sisters. He spent his leisure time watching television, reading the Bible, and going to church. The constant in his life was a job. This time he worked in the City's Department of Purchasing and Supplies as a stock chaser and custodian. He contributed money to his sister's household, and regularly sent money to his divorced mother and younger siblings in Mississippi. After three years he lost his job in a general layoff. Almost immediately he obtained a job with Chrysler at the Eldon plant. The working conditions at this job would increase his paranoia and create intolerable stress on his fragile ego.

The Eldon Avenue Gear and Axle plant was responsible for machining metal parts for rear axles. It was the sole source of these axles, assembling them into the completed parts necessary for most Chrysler automobiles. It was a huge plant, over a million square feet, surrounded by an additional half-million square feet of storage and siding areas. It housed 2,600 machine tools of 170 different types. There were more than four thousand workers, 70 percent of whom were black. Blacks comprised most of the work force because Eldon was an industrial hellhole. Speed-up was a constant source of frustration and anger for the workers. They felt they were being pushed beyond the limits of human endurance and certainly beyond the limits of safety. In addition to the speed-up, people had to do compulsory overtime. This meant working nine to twelve hours a day, sometimes six to seven days a week. The companies called their methods efficient, modern automation. The black workers called it "niggermation."

In *Muscle and Blood,* the Eldon plant manager admits that the "requirements of the plant exceeded the capacity. We had to produce the axles for the entire corporation. . . . It becomes difficult then to maintain some of the standards you would like to maintain in a plant. . . . There are limits as to what maintenance you can perform when you are running on an all-out basis."

Unlike Japanese auto companies, where workers were encouraged to use their initiative and to contribute ideas to the manufacturing process, thereby creating a skilled and loyal work force, American companies viewed workers as unthinking, disposable machines. In their quest for immediate profits, the auto corporations ran down the workers and the plants. This economic nearsightedness was one of the primary reasons that American auto corporations were unable to compete with the Japanese. In 1979 Chrysler went bankrupt and had to go to the government for "welfare" payments in order to continue in business. But in the 1960s and 1970s Chrysler believed that its policies were the most efficient means of achieving optimal profits.

What was the impact of "niggermation" on the workers? Forklifts were in a state of disrepair, light fixtures fell down, and aisles were overcrowded. There was oil on the floors, on the stairs, and on the racks workers stood on to operate the machines. Ventilation was awful; a mist caused by the evaporation of an oil and water coolant pervaded the plant. Every day, James Johnson walked into a plant with thunderous noise attacking his ears, grease from the machines covering his hands, oil on the floor lapping at his feet, and a heavy blue mist clouding his eyes.

In *Muscle and Blood,* company attorneys admit that on a typical day at the Eldon plant ten to twelve workers were injured badly enough to have workers' compensation evaluations. A former workers' compensation adjuster for Chrysler agreed with a former union steward at Eldon that there were a number of cases in which workers had operations, even had their fingers cut off, and were sent back to work the same day. Another former workers' compensation lawyer for Chrysler corroborated that there was pressure to send injured workers back to work and to spend less money on safety: "Capitalism requires profits and the only way to keep on making profits is to speed up, cut down on expenditures." In their 1975 book *Detroit: I Do Mind Dying,* Dan Georgakas and Marvin Surkin analyze the 1960s and early 1970s in Detroit and argue persuasively that the auto industry's unrelenting greed for more and more profits directly resulted in the maiming, illness, and death of its workers and produced the intolerable conditions that explain the Johnson incident, as well as the support Johnson garnered among black autoworkers.

Johnson had been hired as a conveyor loader at Eldon. His primary task was to stand six to eight feet in front of a furnace where brake shoes were bonded with a lining. Wearing asbestos-lined gloves, he had to unload the hot, five-pound brake shoes from two conveyor lines at the production rate of one every ten seconds. Because of the heat and the time pressures of unloading two lines, this job was considered one of the worst in the plant.

Johnson's bosses considered him a good, hard, and reliable worker, and after ten months he was given a more desirable position as a line hanger in the cement room. He worked with five white men and was under the supervision of a production foreman named Owiesny. This foreman often assigned Johnson to work outside the cement room, sometimes making him do shifts at the brake oven. He called Johnson "nigger" and "boy." At times he assigned Johnson to a specific job without giving him adequate instructions. When Johnson would ask this foreman to explain things, Owiesny would say things such as "you niggers can't catch on to nothing" and "do this right now boy, and I mean right now boy."

In 1969, James Johnson's second year at Eldon, he lost a fingertip in an accident. A few months later Rose Logan, a black janitor, was struck by an overloaded jitney. Although her leg was broken she was told to return to work in a wheelchair and perform light duty in order to retain her job. Against her doctor's advice she returned to work, developed thrombophlebitis in her leg, and died. These and similar incidents increased Johnson's fears, both rational and irrational, of losing his job.

By the spring of 1970 the conflict between ELRUM's organizing and management's intransigence was reaching a boiling point. Although Johnson was not involved in the political activity taking place at the plant, his personal work experience reflected the strife at Eldon. On April 16, a wildcat strike took place after a worker got into an argument with his foreman. The foreman picked up a pinion gear and said, "I'll bash your brains out." The foreman was not disciplined, but the worker was fired. Johnson's union steward, a man with more than twenty years' seniority, helped lead the walkout.

May 1 is a day celebrated by workers around the world in honor of the historical struggle for the eight-hour workday. In the United States, "May Day" is officially designated and celebrated as "Law Day." On May 1, 1970, Eldon was shut down by another wildcat strike to protest speed-up, worsening safety conditions, and the firing of the stewards involved in the April walkout. Chrysler's response was to fire fourteen more union stewards, including Johnson's steward.

A week later Johnson was hurt in an auto accident unrelated to his job. After he had been off for one week he received a telegram directing him to return to work or be fired. Against his doctor's advice, fearful of losing his job, he went back to the cement room. But for some inexplicable reason the company did not pay him for the week he was off, as provided by his group insurance benefits, and actually canceled all his insurance benefits.

On May 14, Mamie Williams, a fifty-one-year-old black woman, was told by her doctors to stop working at Eldon for a while because of high blood pressure. She had worked for Chrysler for twenty-six years. The company sent her a telegram telling her to return to work or she would be fired and also lose her accumulated benefits. One week after returning to work she passed out on the assembly line and died the next day.

Less than two weeks later, a twenty-two-year-old Vietnam veteran named Gary Thompson was crushed to death when his forklift overturned and fell on top of him. When the UAW safety director investigated, he found that the emergency brake was broken and that the shift lever and steering wheel did not work properly. He found numerous problems with other trucks and noted in his report that the foremen would routinely pull repair tags off the trucks and put them back into service on the plant floor before they were repaired.

Another wildcat strike took place, and the next day many workers were fired. A year and a half later, a judge would rule that the firing of one of ELRUM's leaders, Fred Holsey, was based on racism and that at the time of the wildcat strikes, "safety conditions at the Eldon plant were abominable." Chrysler would admit that in 1970 there had been more than 167 separate safety violations at Eldon.

In the midst of this turmoil, which ELRUM leaders accurately called "class struggle," Johnson suffered from more discriminatory and dictatorial behavior. Two days after the second wildcat strike a totally stressed out James Johnson took a legally entitled vacation, approved by the black foreman Hugh Jones. When he returned a week later he found that his time card had been removed. In a panic he asked foreman Owiesny what the problem was. Owiesny replied that Johnson had been fired and then walked away without providing any explanation. Another worker told Johnson that he could continue to work at a different job using a "production card" instead of his missing time card. A few days later Johnson received by registered mail a Notice of Termination based on Owiesny's signed notice that Johnson had been "AWOL," when in fact he had been on his regularly scheduled vacation. For two weeks Johnson's anxiety mounted as he tried to clear up this obvious mistake. Finally, he was reinstated, but his coping defenses had been dealt a near fatal blow.

A week later, a white man and close personal friend of Owiesny's was given a job setter position even though Johnson had more experience and had been recommended for the promotion. A job setter received $5.00 an hour, while a conveyor loader received only $3.40 an hour. It was another example of the favoritism that white workers received, and the custom and practice of keeping black workers in their place, at inferior and more physically strenuous jobs. A worker active with ELRUM might have analyzed this event in the political context of the struggle between bosses and workers and tried to exert some organizing pressure. But James Johnson was unable to translate the discrimination into political action. He felt isolated and humiliated. His anger was barely under control, and his anxiety about losing his job caused him frightening nightmares. During the month of June there had been thirty-eight specific safety violations in the brake shoe department in which Johnson worked. He began to worry constantly about falling on the greasy, oily, and water-covered floors at work. He feared that gears and axles would fall on him from the overhead conveyors. His paranoia become severe; he was convinced that management disliked him and was "conspiring" to get rid of him.

One week after the white worker had been promoted over him, Johnson's rage grew beyond his control and he exploded in violence. On July 15, he began work in the cement room. Forty-five minutes later, foreman Hugh Jones sent him to the no. 2 oven. Johnson refused to work, saying that no asbestos gloves were available. He was called into the production office. There, the union steward attempted to plead Johnson's case. It seemed that the gloves were available, but that Johnson had been unable to face being sent back to a job he hated and which symbolized the demeaning way he had been treated during the previous four months. The general foreman announced that Johnson was suspended for insubordination. His badge was taken from him. He was escorted out of the plant and told to report the next day to the Chrysler labor relations office.

Johnson thought he had been fired. He believed management had finally manipulated him into a position where they were able to get rid of him for good. The anchor of his life—his ability to hold a decent job—had been ripped from its mooring. James Johnson, Jr., was afloat in a sea of rage and hopelessness. He went home, got his rifle, and returned to the plant. He would testify at his trial that he could recall entering the plant, but could not remember what happened inside. It is tragically clear from witnesses that Johnson repeatedly shot the foreman, Hugh Jones, fought with men who tried to pull the rifle away from him, went into another room and began randomly firing, killing Joseph Kowalski and Gary Hines and almost hitting Carl Tkachik. A few minutes later, as he stood outside the walls of Eldon, he was taken quietly into custody by the police. The violence of his rage had dissipated into pools of blood mixed with oil and grease on the plant floors.

When Cockrel and Ravitz interviewed James Johnson they realized an insanity defense was appropriate. But they knew that such a defense usually fails because the jury perceives the defendant as a dangerous person. Even though a defendant is mentally ill, the jury often feels more fear than sympathy. Jeffrey Dahmer, the Milwaukee man who killed and ate his victims, is the clearest example of the difficulty of winning an insanity case. Obviously, Dahmer was insane by any measuring stick, legal or medical. But the jury felt such repulsion and fear that they rejected the insanity defense and found him guilty. Cockrel and Ravitz recognized that Johnson was essentially a sympathetic person. He was a quiet man whose life consisted of going to church, saving money to buy a house for him and his sister, and going to his job every day. He wanted to work his sixty hours a week and be treated fairly and with a modicum of dignity. His mental health problems and his deprived childhood as a Mississippi sharecropper had left him with a fragile personality structure. At Eldon he had withstood all kinds of assaults on his psyche before he broke. Fortunately, he had two lawyers who understood his pain and knew how to convey his humanity to a jury.

Cockrel and Ravitz understood that they could not simply blame their client's awful crime on political and economic forces. There were two struggles going on: the political organizing in the plants and the legal battle in the court. Leaflets and articles were being circulated in the community and among autoworkers that blamed Chrysler and the UAW for causing the deaths. Johnson was seen as symbol for thousands of black workers. Cockrel and Ravitz were excellent lawyers, and they knew they could not win with a symbol. As political lawyers they also knew that the best chance of gaining an acquittal was by merging the political reality outside the courtroom with Johnson's individual life. The genius of these two young lawyers was in creating a strategy to help the jurors understand how race and class destroyed a fellow human being.

Cockrel and Ravitz rejected the traditional strategy, which relied primarily on a psychiatrist (often both a psychiatrist and a psychologist) to make the case for the defense. Instead, they sought to create a total environment that would allow for tying together Johnson's individual problems and societal problems. This meant balancing the expert psychiatric witness with lay witnesses, people who had known Johnson all his life, as well as fellow workers who would be able to breathe life into that part of the strategy Cockrel had articulated when he first took on the case: "We'll have to put *Chrysler on trial* for damages to this man caused by his working conditions."

Creating a total environment meant filling the courtroom with supporters. It meant conducting a voir dire that explored jurors' attitudes on race and on plant working conditions. It meant organizing the opening statement and closing argument around the theme of how institutional racism and worker exploitation intersected with Johnson's individual mental problems. Underlying this strategy was the necessity of getting jurors whose life experiences would allow them to hear the defense, as well as getting a judge that would not try to quash the defense.

The case was assigned to Judge Robert Colombo. He was considered a law-and-order judge, as he had been the attorney for the Police Officers Association. But he had also practiced as a criminal defense attorney, and as a judge he believed in letting both sides have their say. His politics were certainly opposed to the left politics of Cockrel and Ravitz, but he respected their legal abilities. The defense was confident he would give Johnson a fair trial.

If the case had been tried in 1968, there would have been an almost all-white jury. But a year before the Johnson incident Cockrel and Ravitz had been involved in another case, which had changed the jury selection process. The New Bethel Baptist Church was headed by Reverend C. L. Franklin, father of world-famous soul singer Aretha Franklin. A militant black nationalist organization named the Republic of New Africa was given permission to hold its first anniversary conference at the church. At the end of the celebration, as people were leaving, an armed confrontation took place in which one policeman was killed and one officer and four civilians were wounded. The police stormed the church, shooting it up and arresting 142 people. During jury selection in the ensuing trial of the men accused of killing Officer Czapski, Cockrel and Ravitz were confronted by the fact that the jury pool did not reflect the population of Detroit, as minorities, workers, and young people were disproportionally absent.

The defense team approached the jury commissioner and boldly demanded to see the questionnaires that prospective jurors were required to fill out before they were allowed into the pool of jurors. They found that the face sheets of the questionnaires had comments stating the basis for exclusion. In their arrogant exercise of power, the jury commissioner and staff had not even tried to hide their prejudices. Citizens had been excluded for reasons such as "long hair," "on welfare," "wears a mini-skirt," or "has an Afro." One teacher from Wayne State University was excluded because he had a beard. All people born in a foreign country were excluded, even if they were U.S. citizens. This screening process had resulted in a jury pool clearly skewed toward older, white, middle-class, conservative people. It was blatantly unconstitutional. The judge ordered a new jury panel, and a fair jury pool selection process was put into effect for all future trials. By the time the Johnson trial began the jury venire accurately reflected the population.

Trial lawyers are known to have strong egos. Many have an overblown sense of self-importance and an addiction to the spotlight. The backbiting and public disputes between O. J. Simpson's lawyers is only an exaggerated example of what often takes place in cases in which there is a lot of publicity. In order to work as an effective team, lawyers must keep their egos in check and treat each other with respect. Cockrel and Ravitz had proved to be a successful team in earlier cases, and they were sure they could do it again in Johnson's case. They split the trial responsibilities between them. Ravitz would give the opening statement; Cockrel would deliver the closing argument. Ravitz would take on the delicate task of the direct examination of Johnson; Cockrel would perform the difficult direct examination of the psychiatrist. Both agreed that Cockrel should do voir dire. No one could question a jury like Ken Cockrel.

The purpose of voir dire is to root out people with a bias from the jury. In the hands of a master, it also forces jurors to reflect on their stereotypes and not to let those preconceptions prejudice their view of evidence. Voir dire is the only opportunity for a lawyer to talk one-on-one with a juror. Therefore, an attorney who can create a rapport rapidly with a juror has an advantage over his opponent. An attorney will often question between twenty and sixty potential jurors. It is hard to stand up in a courtroom, worried about the district attorney's objections and the judge's restrictions, and still remember juror's names, where they live, what work they do, and what they said to the judge or the preceding lawyer that might indicate some hidden bias. Cockrel could do all of that. His photographic memory allowed him to remember each juror's name and the general background information initially elicited by the judge. He had an encyclopedic knowledge of Detroit. He seemed to know every neighborhood, even the names of the streets and schools. He not only knew the churches, he knew the names of the ministers at the churches. He knew every auto factory and the presidents of the local unions. This broad range of knowledge allowed him to plug into each juror's experience. He addressed each person by name, and in a totally natural manner built a bridge between himself and the juror. Although the judge kept the reins on the scope of the voir dire, Cockrel was able to do significant questioning on racism and working conditions.

In Johnson's case, the jury that remained after all the challenges by both sides consisted of eight women and four men, eight blacks and four whites, and included two autoworkers and three persons who were married to autoworkers. The defense was quite satisfied with the jury, but you can never really tell how those twelve individuals will vote once they are locked in the jury room.

The prosecution's case was straightforward. Witnesses from the plant described the shootings in detail, and a psychiatrist testified that Johnson was capable of knowing the difference between right and wrong at the time he committed the homicides. The defense responded by creating a favorable atmosphere for Johnson's testimony. For example, his mother testified that as a child he would have "spells" in which he would cry as he saw the faces of dead people beckoning to him, and she "would hold him in my arms and comfort him the best I could." His cousin was called to testify to how she found the body of her brother who had been lynched and mutilated and had seen the impact of that sight on a nine-year-old James. The defense also called witnesses from Eldon who testified to the unsafe working conditions and who gave detail and substance to Johnson's state of mind in the two months before his breakdown. By the time Johnson was called to the stand the groundwork had been laid so that the jurors were open to listening to him instead of demonizing him as an evil killer.

Traditional strategy dictates that you do not call the defendant to the stand in an insanity case. Attorneys are wary that the defendant will fall apart under cross-examination. They are afraid that the client will seem so crazy that he will scare the jury, or that he will be calm and rational and thereby undercut the insanity defense. Cockrel and Ravitz rejected the traditional approach because they correctly assessed the need for the jury to understand James Johnson as a fellow human being. The jurors needed to hear Johnson testify in order to have the empathy necessary for a not guilty verdict.

James Johnson walked quietly to the witness box. He was thirty-five years old, five feet nine inches tall, and approximately 130 pounds. He spoke quietly and had a calm demeanor. The direct examination was well organized and clear in its simplicity. Ravitz took Johnson through his life chronologically. Ravitz asked questions that brought out the racism and unsafe working conditions Johnson had endured, but he was careful not to have the witness justify his actions by blaming society. One of the more moving portions of the testimony took place when Johnson described a week-long revival at church when he was twelve years old. He explained how he had accepted Jesus Christ as his personal savior, and how he felt he had been cleansed of his sins. Ravitz then asked him if he had ever again experienced a similar feeling. Johnson answered that ever since the shooting he had been praying that he would be forgiven. For ten months he had prayed each day and night, and then two weeks before the trial he had a dream in which the healing came for the terrible thing he had done: "It was like a cleansing process and then after that it was like my soul was rejoicing, you know, and praising God for forgiveness."

Given the earlier uncontradicted testimony of Johnson's religious practice and devotion, this testimony seemed genuine and may have moved the religiously motivated jurors to feel that James Johnson was redeemable. There was no doubt that in this testimony, and in answer to other questions, Johnson's remorse was sincere. By the end of the direct examination Ravitz's confidence that his client would come across as a decent, vulnerable, troubled man instead of a menacing, treacherous criminal was proven right.

The task of the cross-examination was to show that Johnson was not insane because he understood the nature of his crime—that he had shot three men—and he knew at the time that such action was wrong. The strategy the prosecution embraced was two-fold: first, to show all the rational steps Johnson had taken in order to kill the three men, and second, to attack Johnson's credibility. Johnson testified that he had lost control of himself and could not remember what he had done, but that he was now no longer insane. Prosecutor Avery Weiswasser attempted to show that Johnson had acted in the same manner as any criminal planning a crime. His cross-examination was effective in this area:

Q. Let me ask you this, when you got back into the plant, why did you hide that gun inside your pants?

A. Why did I hide it inside my pants?

Q. Why did you hide the gun inside your pants?

A. I couldn't give you a concrete reason why I would hide it inside of my pants.

Q. Well, wasn't it because you didn't want people to see you walking in with a gun in your hand?

A. That could be one of the reasons, sir.

Q. So you used your own good common sense and you stuck it inside your pants?

A. That could have been one of the reasons.

Q. That could have been one of the reasons. And this was an hour after you left the plant, wasn't it?

A. I can imagine it was. It was somewhat in that area, sir, I didn't have a watch.

Q. What did you do in that hour?

A. Sir, I don't recall exactly what I done, specifically what I done in that hour.

Q. You got the gun amongst other things, didn't you?

A. Evidently, sir.

Q. You say you went home and got it, is that right?

A. I don't recall making that statement, sir.

Q. You didn't make that statement just a moment—a little while ago.

A. I don't recall.

Q. You don't recall. Did you happen to have any hallucinations during that hour?

A. Sir, I just stated that I don't recall what I—what—actually what all happened in that hour, so I wouldn't be aware of it.

Q. Isn't it a true statement when you are asked anything about those events, you just don't remember?

Even people who are suffering from severe mental illness when they commit a crime take rational steps in order to carry out the crime. That fact is always the strongest part of a prosecutor's case, and often when juries convict they will say that they were persuaded by the conscious and seemingly rational acts of the defendant. The cross-examination in Johnson's case was aimed at showing that while in an allegedly insane state of mind the defendant was capable of taking steps that were the acts of a man in control of his faculties and consciously planning a murder. The prosecutor continued the effective cross-examination by stressing his theory that Johnson had a violent temper and was not mentally "out-of-control."

Q. I still would like to know why you killed those three men?

A. Sir, I testified before, I lost control under the strain.

Q. In other words, you lost your temper?

A. I lost control.

Q. You lost your temper, didn't you?

A. I say I lost control, sir.

Q. What is the difference between losing your temper and losing control, what's the difference?

A. Sir, I don't know how to differentiate it. But I say I lost control and I was not conscious of what was going on until it was all over.

Q. I see.

A. Yes, sir.

Q. You lost control, you just turned the faucet off in your head and you were unconscious of what happened from then, is that right?

A. I didn't turn any faucets off. I just—

Q. What about the time you stabbed the man over at the Scotch and Sirloin, did you lose control the same way?

A. I will say so.

Q. What about the time you battered that door down in the incident involving your sister, did you lose control?

A. I will say so.

Q. And about the time they talked about in the opening statement, you attacking people down in Mississippi, when you lost your temper?

A. When I was a kid in Mississippi.

Q. Yes.

A. That's been a long time ago.

Q. You have had a bad temper all your life?

A. I wouldn't say so, no, sir.

Q. You would prefer to call it losing control?

A. I don't know what—I don't know what your terminology is.

Q. Your conversations with Defense Counsel and the psychiatrist having anything to do with your using the phrase losing control?

A. No, sir, nothing to do with it.

The foregoing cross-examination was outstanding, except for the last question. That question suggested that the defendant had contrived his insanity defense. In fact, the question also implied that Ravitz and the psychiatrist were part of the plan to put forth a phony defense. In their attempt to demonize the defendant some prosecutors will try to portray him as a devious person who has used psychiatric words to support his false defense. When using this tactic the prosecutor often looks for someone who helped give the defendant the ideas of an insanity defense. In chapter 1 we saw how the prosecutor suggested that William Freeman had watched a previous insanity defense of a black convict and then tailored his own defense to fit what the lawyers had argued in that case. In Johnson's trial, the prosecutor adopted a similar tactic. Unable to blame the lawyers, he tried to link Johnson's defense with the leftist organizations active in the plants. He asked Johnson if he read *Inner City Voice* and the *Eldon Wildcat* (a rank and file newspaper).

Q. As a result of reading the things that you read in the various newspapers, did that ever have any effect upon your attitude in your job?

A. The things that I read in the newspapers?

Q. Uh-huh.

A. The ones that was true. . . .

Q. You testified about this fellow Barney who didn't like your attitude?

A. Yes.

A. Was your attitude created in any way by the, some of the things you read in the newspapers?

A. No

Q. Or the *Eldon Wildcat?*

A. I will say this, I didn't have any particular attitude toward anything or anybody. I am an exceptionally quiet guy.

The prosecutor was not content to question Johnson about the newspapers. He also used the McCarthyite tactic of red-baiting by implying that Johnson was a member of a left organization:

Q. Did you ever belong to the League of Revolutionary Black Workers?

A. No, sir.

Q. You never did?

A. No, sir.

Q. Do you belong to any unions?

A. The U.A.W.—what's it, the U.A.W.

Q. C.I.O. But you didn't belong to DRUM?

A. No, sir.

Q. Didn't belong to ELDRUM?

A. No, sir.

These questions are irrelevant. Why didn't the defense object? Because they understood the cardinal rule governing objections: Do not object unless the questions and answers are hurting your case. Cockrel and Ravitz recognized that the prosecutor was exposing his own antiworker bias by these questions and was also showing the weakness of his case by the attempted red-smear. Also, Johnson's answers highlighted his nature as a passive, uninvolved man who was just trying to get his job done amid the turmoil at Eldon.

The most dramatic moment of the cross-examination occurred as follows:

Q. They [whites] just were picking on you?

A. Beg pardon?

Q. They were just picking on you?

A. There's been a lot of other people been subject to the same type of harassment.

Q. How do you know that?

A. I have seen it with my own eyes, sir.

Q. See it with your own eyes?

A. Right.

Q. And they are all black boys?

A. All that I ever seen.

Mr. Cockrel: I object to "black boys" your honor.

Mr. Weiswasser: Black men, I am sorry.

A. I am glad you asked that, all I have seen has been black. That's a fact.

People in the courtroom were stunned when they heard the prosecutor call black men "boys", just as James Johnson had testified he had been called by his white foreman. Cockrel's objection had highlighted the prosecutor's mistake. Weiswasser was Jewish, and by virtue of that should have been particularly sensitive to the use of the word "boy" when referring to grown men, because for hundreds of years anti-Semites have used the epitaph "Jew-boy" to humiliate and insult Jewish men. The prosecution's cross-examination had been compromised by Weiswasser's own prejudice and red-baiting.

The expert witness who testified on behalf of Johnson was an African American psychiatrist named Clemens Fitzgerald, Jr. Fitzgerald had excellent credentials and was conversant with the facts of the case and with Johnson's history. He also had a wide range of experience; the majority of his patients in private practice had been white, while the majority of patients at the county clinic he directed were poor blacks and Latinos. He had set up the psychiatric section of the City's T.A.P. (Total Action against Poverty) program, where he treated numerous autoworkers. He was certified as a diplomate by the American Board of Neurology and Psychiatry, was a clinical instructor at both Wayne State and the University of Michigan, and was the regional chairman of Black Psychiatrists of America.

Fitzgerald explained the emotional problems that autoworkers, regardless of their color, suffered due to their employment. He said that the high level of stress and tension caused mental conditions that led to alcoholism, drug usage, spousal abuse, and high rates of absenteeism. Under Cockrel's well-prepared questioning, the doctor then discussed the specific problems faced by black and Mexican autoworkers. He testified that the institutional racism of the auto companies meant that minority workers had "no opportunity of upward advancement," which produced frustration and despair. In addition, the demeaning treatment blacks were subjected to, such as thirty- or forty-year-old men being called "boy," caused feelings of anger that workers had to supress in order to retain their jobs.

Fitzgerald took his analysis further along the line of tying racism and mental illness together when he suggested that black people were more susceptible to certain types of stress. He postulated that blacks suffer a stress unknown to most white psychiatrists. This stress is caused by their lack of power in society and the relatively few successful black male figures for the young black man to identify with and emulate. Fitzgerald's testimony and his concept that black people lack the power to determine their lives goes to the core of the current debate about what constitutes "racism." Many commentators argue that Louis Farrakhan's prejudice toward whites can be equated with David Duke's prejudice toward blacks. This analysis holds that any negative stereotyping of a group of people based on their skin color or ethnicity is racism. In this view, when H. Rap Brown called a white person a "honkey," it was the same as when Mark Fuhrman called a black person a "nigger." The problem with such an analysis is that it leaves out the disparate power relationships between whites and blacks. Many radical authors and activists, both black and white, argue that it is misleading to talk in terms of black racism because blacks cannot impose their will on whites. This imbalance in power was at the heart of Fitzgerald's diagnosis of James Johnson. He testified that "the black person particularly is subject to the whims and capriciousness of the dominant forces in our society. Certainly that would be the white power structure!"

Fitzgerald was talking about the effects of *institutional* racism, not individual prejudice. Johnson, as a child, did not suffer economically and educationally because a few white people felt superior to blacks. He experienced hardship and faced the threat of white violence because of the institution of the plantation and the economic and social system of white supremacy that controlled life in Mississippi. As an adult, Johnson was forced to accept racial insults, was given the worst jobs, was not promoted, and was fired improperly because of the institutional racism of the auto companies, not because of the bigotry of one foreman.

The concepts of power and control are helpful in distinguishing between racism and prejudice. There are places in American society where blacks have carved out some control. African Americans control the basketball courts in college and in the National Basketball Association (NBA). They constitute an overwhelming majority of the players and have exhibited a clear dominance in skill level. The culture of the game, on the court, is black. In this culture whites sometimes find themselves victims of stereotypes. White players are considered slow of foot, even when they are quicker than many of the black players. Blacks complain that one or two white players are kept on teams just to make the fans happy. These white players are presumed to be less skilled players, just as blacks in law school are presumed to be less intelligent students. There are still only a handful of black coaches, very few black general managers or college athletic directors, and almost no black owners of NBA franchises. The institution of basketball, however, both on the college and the professional level, is controlled by whites. White money and power are the dominating forces, although one should not underestimate the growing influence and power of blacks. In this context, the racial stereotyping white players suffer is a form of prejudice based on race, but labeling it "racism" and equating it with white supremacy are not helpful in understanding the oppression of minorities in America.

Another example of race-based power and control, but one that is rarely discussed openly, takes place in the urban public schools. Black culture has gained hegemony among urban youth. Asian, white, and Latino boys and girls walk around with baseball caps turned backwards on their heads, shirts three sizes larger than their parents think they should wear, baggy pants, and athletic shoes with the laces often untied. This is considered cool. Black culture, whether it be jazz, blues, or hip hop, has always been perceived as cool. But on a deeper level, black culture is a culture of resistance, of maintaining one's soul against destructive forces. Young people recognize the authenticity of black culture and are drawn to its expression of heart in the face of adversity. That is why black culture dominates today's inner cities. Rap music, which focuses and expresses black rage, has found a huge audience among nonblacks. Its angry and rebellious poetry, its creative and energetic beats have struck a chord in young people of all races, and this is the music that pulsates throughout schools in urban America, pounding out of boom-boxes, the bass turned up so high that administrators' bones ache from the vibrations.

But despite this cultural phenomenon, blacks do not really have power in the public schools. Those creative, intelligent kids and their parents do not control the funding of public education. The white political structure not only has control, but it has spit upon the needs of the poor and exercised its power to strangle the schools. One of the finest components of democracy, the public school, is in danger of extinction. American capitalism has created an excellent private school system for those who can afford it, and is rapidly destroying the public system.

When a black teenager slugs a white teenager on a Chicago school playground and calls him a "bloodsucking Jew," it is certainly an example of racial prejudice and must be criticized. But we should differentiate that act from the institutional racism that leads Congress and state legislatures to abandon and, indeed, to directly attack our public schools.

School playgrounds and classes are filled with kids of different races playing together, helping each other, teaching each other, and loving each other. Walk into some of the schools in San Francisco and you would think you had walked into the United Nations. It is a vision of a diverse, beautiful America. But it is just that—a vision of the future. If we cannot identify the structures of white supremacy and expose and rectify institutional racism, then hateful, distorted ideas of prejudice will continue to infect all races, and individual acts of prejudice will hurt us all. Cockrel and Ravitz understood the need to expose the institutional racism of Mississippi's plantations and Chrysler's auto plants. Neither they nor Fitzgerald were blaming a few bad white people for Johnson's descent into temporary madness. They were trying to articulate society's responsibility for the awful events of July 15, 1970.

Michigan's law of insanity was fairly typical of the law in many states today. The defense had to produce evidence that, at the time of the crime, Johnson did not know right from wrong, and that he was not able to control his actions. Once that evidence had been produced the prosecution had to prove, beyond a reasonable doubt, that Johnson did know the difference between right and wrong. This test of insanity is very difficult for a defendant to satisfy. Many people who commit criminal acts while seriously mentally ill can distinguish right from wrong. In Johnson's case, Fitzgerald diagnosed him as having a "schizophrenic reaction, paranoid in type." As a result of this mental disease the doctor concluded that Johnson "was not capable of understanding the true nature of his act" and was acting under a temporary "delusional system" in which he felt he must attack the people who were out to get him. This testimony satisfied the legal requirement of producing evidence of insanity and had to be rebutted by the prosecution.

On a technical level, Weiswasser, the chief prosecutor in the trial, did a good job of weakening Fitzgerald's testimony regarding his diagnosis. Weiswasser was knowledgeable in the area of psychiatry and knew where the weaknesses lay in the doctor's presentation. His cross-examination was typical of the kind one will find in psychiatric cases. He brought out the fact that Fitzgerald had testified only a few times in criminal cases, that only two or three times had he been called upon to render an opinion regarding sanity, and that he had always testified for the defense. The cross-examination stressed that the doctor had not examined the defendant either right before or right after the time of the crime; that he first examined Johnson two and a half months after the murders; that he interviewed Johnson only twice, once for ninety minutes and once for two hours. This was not atypical; in the majority of cases the psychiatrist will have interviewed the defendant only one or two times and will not have had the opportunity to examine the accused near the time of the crime. The prosecution will always argue from these facts that the psychiatric testimony cannot be relied upon.

After showing the jury that the psychiatrist is trying to re-create the defendant's mental state months after the actual event, the competent prosecutor will attempt to show the rational acts that the defendant performed in committing the crime, in an effort to rebut the opinion that the accused was out of control. In Johnson's case the prosecutor asked a lengthy question that went to the weakness of the defense theory:

Q. During the delusional state, he went home, got the gun, knew how to get back, so forth. Doctor, how about the fact that after he shot three men—

before he shot those three men, before he even left the plant the first time when he was suspended, he told Hugh Jones that he had no right to put him on that job because there were other men with less seniority. And then more than an hour later after he had killed three men and was on his way out of the plant when other men stopped him, he said "I killed them because he was trying to put me on a job when other men had less seniority." So didn't he indicate there that he knew what he was doing, why he was doing it, that he remembered what he did, that he remembered why he did it? Because he did exactly what he did because of something that he explained why he was doing it. Now isn't that true, Doctor? And you say that this man is delusional?

A. A man can still be delusional and still carry out normal conversations in areas outside of his delusions. . . .

The prosecutor also hammered home the admitted evidence that Johnson had previous instances throughout his life in which he had threatened or attacked someone. This buttressed the state's theory that Johnson was a man with a violent temper who would "fly into rages when he didn't have his own way." At the end of this part of cross-examination it is fair to say that the prosecution had seriously weakened the psychiatric testimony.

Weiswasser also chose to attack Fitzgerald's theories that blacks suffer unusual stress and that racism had to be considered as one of the causes of Johnson's schizophrenia. The ensuing cross-examination was an example of a lawyer winning points but losing the case. Two typical errors lawyers make are to discredit the witness on points that are irrelevant to the main issue and to offend the jury's common sense. A glaring example of the former mistake was the prosecution's cross-examination of Laura McKinney in O. J. Simpson's murder trial. McKinney testified on direct exam that police officer Mark Fuhrman had used the word "nigger" more than forty times in his discussions with her. There was no way to impeach her testimony because the discussions were on tape, and two instances of Fuhrman's arrogance and racial hate were played in court. The district attorney, Christopher Darden, attacked McKinney, trying to show that she was hostile to the prosecution and that she had done something despicable by not stopping Fuhrman when he called African Americans "niggers." Failing in these attempts, Darden attacked her on the one issue to which she was vulnerable. McKinney had steadfastly denied that she was going to sell the Fuhrman tapes. But Darden finally got her to admit that her lawyers had shopped the tapes around. McKinney said this was solely to establish a "value" for the tapes, that it was done at her business lawyers' advice. She then weakly repeated that she was not going to sell the tapes. The result of this cross-examination was to injure McKinney's credibility somewhat regarding whether she was going to sell the tapes. But that was a pyrrhic victory because it had nothing whatsoever to do with the real issue—that Fuhrman used the word "nigger." The only explanation for Darden's cross-examination is that he and coprosecutor Marcia Clark viewed every witness called by the defense as an enemy and attacked them without fitting their cross-examination into an overall strategy. Facing the truth of the taped evidence and needing to show the state's abhorrence of Fuhrman's behavior, the prosecutor's cross-examination should have consisted of two sentences. Darden should have stood up and simply said, "Thank you Ms. McKinney for bringing Mark Fuhrman's racial bigotry to light. No questions."

The cross-examination of McKinney was not an aberration. Two other white witnesses testified that Fuhrman made bigoted and degrading references to African Americans, and one African American witness testified that Fuhrman called him a "nigger" to his face. It was obvious to the jurors that these people were telling the truth, yet each one was cross-examined in a hostile manner by Clark and Darden. The prosecutor's cross-examinations were contrary to what the jurors' common sense told them—that Los Angeles police officer Fuhrman was an extreme racist.

The prosecuting attorney in Johnson's trial made the same mistake. In front of an interracial, working-class jury, he tried to attack the psychiatrist's contention that race and economics play a role in mental illness. This tactic was consistent with the prosecutor's theme, announced at the beginning of the trial, that "race has no place in this case."

The prosecutor was well versed in the psychiatric literature and therefore was able to get Fitzgerald to admit that the primary textbook on schizophrenia did not distinguish between races. Fitzgerald countered by saying that this was a failing and that he and other black psychiatrists were in the process of writing articles and a new textbook addressing this oversight. However, the prosecutor did not back down. He asked question after question attempting to undermine the psychiatrist's opinion that race and socioeconomic conditions must be considered when diagnosing or treating a person. At one point the examination became intense, and Fitzgerald went on the offensive and actually started questioning the prosecutor:

> A. *[Dr. Fitzgerald:]* What I am saying is you have to understand socio-economic conditions.
> Q: *[Prosecutor:]* You mean all the poverty and depression is restricted to black people?
> A. I didn't say that.
> Q. There are black neurotics, aren't there?
> A. Certainly.
> Q. There are white neurotics.
> A. Yes.
> Q. Black psychopaths?
> A. Yes.
> Q. White psychopaths?
> A. Right. But I am talking about other factors such as second class citizenship. Such as being in the plant and seeing other people being given jobs when maybe you are qualified and the only reason you didn't get it is because you are black. Or are you aware of racism?
> Q. That's something you heard from the defendant?
> A. I am asking you, are you aware of racism? Are you saying this doesn't exist?
> Q. Oh, I know there is racism, by black people and by white people.
> A. We are talking about institutional racism, which is more prevalent against the most buyable object, that being the black person.

Here we see an attorney losing control of his cross-examination, and losing sight of how the jury is perceiving the case. The jurors' life experiences had taught them that race and class can have powerful effects on a person's life, and no amount of lawyerly cross-examination would overrule their common sense. The real issue was whether James Johnson—an individual, not a symbol—had been so wounded by racism that he had lost control of his rational thought processes. On that issue Fitzgerald's testimony had been helpful to the defense. But courtroom observers—particularly other lawyers and the press—felt that the psychiatric evidence would not determine the result.

The one event in the trial that had the most profound impact was the jury view of the Eldon plant. The defense made a motion for an on-site view of the plant on the grounds that it would help the jurors better understand the evidence by allowing them to see where events had taken place. Such a motion is left to the discretion of the judge. In this case there was no compelling legal reason to grant a jury view. But in a case where there is a great deal of publicity or where the community is politically organized in support of the defendant, there is pressure on the judge to provide a fair trial. Judges will react differently in these situations. In the Chicago 8 case, in which Dave Dellinger, Abbie Hoffman, Tom Hayden, Bobby Seale, and others were tried for conspiring to cross state lines to incite a riot during the 1968 Democratic National Convention, Judge Julius Hoffman's tactics were to do everything in his judicial power to restrict, hinder, and hurt the defense. Hoffman refused Black Panther leader Bobby Seale's request to have the case continued briefly so that the attorney of his choice, Charles Garry, could defend him. He had Seale bound and gagged in the courtroom. He constantly berated the defense lawyers and ruled against their motions. Although some of the defendants were convicted on some charges and the lawyers were given lengthy sentences for contempt, the judge's behavior was so outrageous that the Court of Appeals reversed the verdicts and the contempt sentences.

An opposite example was the trial of O. J. Simpson. Even though most of Judge Lance Ito's important legal rulings were for the state, he protected Simpson's right to a fair trial as he gave the defense attorneys wide latitude in their direct and cross-examination, allowed extensive voir dire, gave continuances to prepare essential motions and evidence, and granted an on-site jury view.

Judge Colombo reacted to the political context of the Johnson trial in the same principled manner as Judge Ito did in the Simpson case. He allowed the defense breathing space in the courtroom, thereby protecting Johnson's right under the Sixth Amendment to a fair trial. Such a course of behavior is, in the long run, beneficial to the power of the legal system because it legitimates the system. Judge Colombo was well aware of the black community's mistrust of the legal system in Detroit. His treatment of Johnson and the defense lawyers would send a message far beyond the confines of the Recorder's Court. In this context it is not surprising that he granted the motion to allow the jury to tour the auto plant. In so doing he showed that the court was not hiding from Detroit's economic and social conditions, symbolized historically, and in Johnson's case, by the auto plants. None of this political subtext was articulated in court. Cockrel and Ravitz's motion was based strictly on the existing case law, and their arguments did not refer to racism and injustice. That would be saved for closing argument. When the judge granted the motion he did not speak of the need to strengthen the legal system's credibility in times of social turmoil. But his favorable ruling demonstrated that judges, especially politically astute ones, understand their role in maintaining the legitimacy of the law.

The judge, jurors, lawyers, and defendant went to Eldon while the plant was in operation. They saw and felt the conditions under which Johnson had worked. But what turned out to be more important than viewing the inanimate objects and locations was seeing the solidarity the workers showed toward the defense. Johnson had killed three autoworkers; the reaction of the other workers could have been angry and hostile. Such a response would have undercut the theory of the defense and supported the prosecution's depiction of Johnson as a violent man, an evil murderer. But the workers raised clenched fists and nodded their heads in approval. Some quietly cried out, "Right on, Brother Johnson." Their acknowledgment of the defendant conveyed to the jury the validity of the defense. The oppression of the workers generally and James Johnson specifically was not some radical fantasy—it was a reality. As Justin Ravitz walked among the men, women, and machines of the Eldon plant he sensed that an acquittal was within their grasp.

Unfortunately, a transcript of Cockrel's closing argument does not exist. But a transcript would not show his commanding presence, his control of the courtroom. Courtroom observers remember his closing as a masterpiece, meshing race, class, law, and the moral responsibility of the jury into one persuasive whole. By the end of the closing he had succeeded in uncovering the soul of a man who had killed, and in exposing the society that had driven him to kill. Now it would rest in the hands of the jury.

The jury deliberations were at times so loud that their voices could be heard in the courtroom. Members of the press reported some of the comments they heard:

> "You weren't born in Mississippi and I was. You don't know what you're talking about."

"Did you see that cement room in the plant? Working there would drive anyone crazy."

"I've worked in a factory all my life, and I didn't kill anybody."

"He wasn't crazy. He hid the gun in his pants and looked for who he wanted to kill."

"The man needs help. You know he won't get it in prison. It's up to us to help him."

After a day of deliberation the jury found James Johnson not guilty by reason of insanity. When he heard the verdict, Johnson dropped his head between his knees and wept.

Johnson was sentenced to a mental hospital for the criminally insane. The three-week trial and verdict received national publicity, including a favorable article and photo in *Newsweek*. The term "black rage" was not used, but the defense rooted in the anger and despair produced by racism was clearly established.

Every year thousands of us are
maimed. The life of men and women
is so cheap and property is so sacred.
—Rose Schneiderman, organizer
for the Women's Trade Union
League, 1911

Chapter 5

James Johnson's
Workers' Compensation Case

The controversy over James Johnson did not end with the verdict in the
criminal case. A bright young lawyer who specialized in worker disability
cases had filed a workers' compensation claim on behalf of Johnson. The
lawyer, Ron Glotta, worked in the same law firm as Ken Cockrel and Justin
Ravitz and was active in the movement to organize autoworkers. He was
a cofounder of the Motor City Labor League, a group of white leftists
whose purpose was to organize among white workers and to support the
actions of the black radicals in the League of Revolutionary Black Workers,
DRUM, ELDRUM, and other such alternative union groupings. The Motor City Labor League recognized that black workers who spoke out for
radical change were isolated by the established union and were attacked
by management. They felt it was necessary for whites to give ideological
and concrete support to blacks who were leading the struggle for fundamental change. They believed that if the demands of the black workers
were satisfied the result would benefit all workers. In this context of racial
solidarity, Glotta became one of the attorneys for the League of Revolutionary Black Workers and offered his skills in the field of workers' compensation and labor law.

Glotta pursued a claim for workers' compensation on the grounds that Johnson had a nondisabling, preexisting psychiatric condition that was aggravated by racism and unsafe working conditions, and that this aggravation resulted in his breakdown. Chrysler's attorneys could not believe the audacity of trying to make the corporation liable for benefits to someone who had killed two foremen and a coworker. Even some plaintiff's attorneys doubted Glotta's judgment and warned him that he would "make bad law." But Glotta's theory was soundly based in the philosophy of workers' compensation and in previous rulings of law. He was just pushing the envelope—and pushing it hard.

The workers' compensation insurance system is a no-fault system of remuneration. That means a worker does not have to prove that the employer was negligent in order to win benefits. This is different from the system known as personal injury law. Under that system, when one person injures another person the plaintiff must prove that the defendant did not exercise reasonable care and thereby caused the injury. For example, if John Doe's restraining wall falls down during a normal storm and a ton of mud slides into Tom Smith's house and injures him, John Doe may be liable for damages. But he is liable only if Tom Smith can prove that a reasonable person would have foreseen a storm and built a stronger restraining wall. This is called the rule of negligence. It was the law in all factories in America until the early 1900s. So in the 1800s if a worker had his finger cut off by a conveyer belt, the worker would have to prove that the belt was functioning improperly and that the employer was responsible for the malfunction.

The consequence of the unequal power relations between capital and labor was that millions of workers were maimed and killed in job-related accidents but did not have resources to mount effective lawsuits against companies. They therefore received no compensation for their injuries, unless the owner was a benevolent capitalist who offered some form of charity to the worker or, in cases of death, to the surviving spouse and children.

The personal injury system also barred a worker from recovering money if the accident was his own fault. The problem with that rule was that it did not take into account that industrial work, in its normal course, produces accidents. Whether it is mills, mining, steel, auto making, or construction, no product can be produced without injuries. An example of this harsh reality is the building of the famous Golden Gate Bridge. Based on previous studies and construction projections, it was known that a number of workers would have accidents causing their deaths. Some of these accidents would be caused by employer negligence, some by worker negligence, but the bridge could not be built without accidental deaths. Even though strict safety precautions were taken, ten workers were killed.

The worker' compensation system was based on the recognition that men, women, and children would be injured, at times by the negligence of the boss, at times by the carelessness of the worker, and at times by the mere fact of working in an imperfect world. Regardless of the cause of the accident, the owner was making profits based on the labor of the worker. The humanitarian approach was to accept that disability and death were part of the profit process and to compensate the worker whether the injury was caused by employer negligence or by the actions of the worker. However, for decades capitalists around the world refused to allow such a system of compensation.

As the industrial revolution progressed, Germany developed a strong, politically conscious working class. The Bismarck government, fearing that the workers would turn to socialism, instituted the first workers' compensation system as part of a broad Social Insurance Plan. In 1897 England passed its workmens' compensation act, which by 1910 covered every kind of occupational injury. By the early 1900s a number of factors combined to persuade employers in the United States that a limited workers' compensation system would be in their own interest. Unions were beginning to exert organizational power, and it was necessary for the owners to make some compromises with labor to maintain industrial peace. Some workers had also been successful in bringing personal injury lawsuits. Since there was no cap on damages, potentially large jury verdicts became an unpredictable element in doing business.

Responding to the changing power relations between capital and labor, and to the economic benefits of a predictable insurance system, Maryland in 1902, Montana in 1909, and New York in 1910 passed legislation creating workers' compensation systems. However, not all employers were ready to accept the obligation to pay into an insurance system that would compensate their injured workers. State courts took a conservative view of the new laws and held them unconstitutional on various grounds, such as the infringement of freedom of contract and the deprivation of an employer's property (money) without due process of law.

The New York case *Ives v. South Buffalo Railway Company*[1] is a good example of the conflicting class forces present in workers' compensation law. The New York legislature had passed a law creating an insurance system limited to workers in the most dangerous jobs, such as building bridges, working on high scaffolds, using explosives, operating steam railroads, and constructing tunnels and subways. These jobs were determined to be "especially dangerous" in that the work itself contained "inherent, necessary, risks to the life and limb of the workmen." The legislature gave as its reasons for passing the law that the laissez-faire system was "economically unwise and unfair, and that in its operation it is wasteful, uncertain, and productive of antagonism between workmen and employers."

The New York Court of Appeals had no quarrel with the legislature's reasons. In its opinion the court accurately restated the theory of workers' compensation:

> It is based upon the proposition that the inherent risks of an employment should in justice be placed upon the shoulders of the employer, who can protect himself against loss by insurance and by such an addition to the price of his wares as to cast the burden ultimately upon the consumer; that indemnity to an injured employee should be as much a charge upon the business as the cost of replacing or repairing disabled or defective machinery, appliances, or tools; that, under our present system, the loss falls immediately upon the employee who is almost invariably unable to bear it, and ultimately upon the community which is taxed for the support of the indigent.

The court agreed that the law was supported by public sentiment and, although "plainly revolutionary," was based on sound principles. But it held that the law violated established laws protecting "the right of property." By holding the workmens' compensation law unconstitutional, the court's opinion suggested that if people wanted to institute such a system they would have to pass a constitutional amendment.

The struggle for fair and just treatment of working men, women, and children did not stop in face of this and other judicial decisions. The labor movement, social reformers, and enlightened capitalists combined to persuade other states to pass workers' compensation systems. As the tide grew stronger, courts found ways to interpret the law to hold such systems constitutional. California's plan was accepted as legal in 1913. It provided for specific, fixed benefits based on a formula that included a worker's age, job category, degree of disability, wages received in the months preceeding the injury, and other factors. The fact that the benefits were definite allowed an employer to estimate his costs for worker injuries, buy insurance, and thereby calculate that amount into his cost of doing business. All employers were compelled by law to have workers' compensation insurance.

The employers were able to win important concessions in this new program. The benefits were kept very low. There was no compensation for pain and suffering. Even if the injury was caused by the employer's negligence, the worker could not sue under the personal injury system. The worker was locked into the workers' compensation system. The difference in money received by the injured party in the two different systems was, and still is, enormous. If a thirty-year-old woman autoworker lost an eye due to the negligent driving of someone on the highway, she could recover hundreds of thousands of dollars. If the same woman, making an average wage in an auto plant, lost an eye due to the negligent maintenance of a fork lift in the plant, she would receive approximately $40,000. If she worked at a lower paying job, such as a file clerk, and in a state with less benefits than Michigan, she might only receive $10,000.

As unions became stronger, the interests of working people made their way into the law. One important new concept was the idea that the workplace should not make a person's health worse than it was before she began to work. Thus, if a healthy twenty-year-old woman begins work in the cotton mills and fifteen years later leaves with lung disease caused by her working conditions, she deserves to to compensated based on the fact that for fifteen years her labor power was producing profits for the owners. The next logical step was to protect people who were able to work with pre-existing health conditions, but because of job conditions became disabled. For example, a young man with a weak heart goes to work for General Motors, and twenty years later, due to the stress of the job, he dies of a heart attack. There are two reasons his family receives benefits: First, his weak heart had not kept him from being able to work (a nondisabling, pre-existing condition); second, conditions on the job aggravated that weak heart so that it finally gave out. In Michigan and other states, this rule of law was extended to cover pre-existing psychiatric conditions. In 1960 the Michigan Supreme Court ruled that a worker could recover benefits if the long-term pressures, requirements, and demands of the total work environment caused an injury or illness.

Glotta put all of these concepts together in Johnson's case. Many good lawyers could have done that. But Glotta's political insights and experience allowed him to take the black rage defense from the criminal trial and transform it into an offensive weapon in the civil case. Johnson's workers' compensation trial began in 1972. There is no jury in a workers' compensation case, so the hearing is held before a "referee." The rules of evidence apply, but the hearing is more informal than a criminal trial.

At the hearing James Johnson took the stand and testified. The referee found him to be a credible witness. The referee stated that "based on plaintiff's demeanor, manner of testifying, depth of feelings expressed, as though from the deepest recesses of his being at times, . . . [I find] his testimony to be worthy of . . . considerable credence and belief."

Fitzgerald had examined Johnson at the Ionia State Hospital four months after the not guilty verdict. At the compensation hearing, he testified to the same conclusions he had made at the criminal trial and added that Johnson was still suffering a disabling mental illness that was job related. At Chrysler's request, a Dr. Forrer examined Johnson once and testified that Johnson's breakdown could "in no conceivable way be attributable to his working condition." However, under cross-examination by Glotta, Forrer conceded that when Johnson was fired he lost his coping mechanisms.

The referee found that Fitzgerald's testimony was more convincing that Forrer's. He also pointed out that when Forrer had said that "it was incredible that someone had filed a Workmen's Compensation Petition on Plaintiff's behalf" he had indicated a negative predisposition, which probably explained why he had trouble eliciting information from Johnson.

Glotta's strategy was to show that Chrysler had created a "plant culture" that would lead inevitably to a worker exploding in violence—the only question was which worker would be the first to crack. He argued that "Chrysler had pulled the trigger," a phrase which would earn him criticism in politically moderate circles, but which captured the heart of the legal argument and the spirit of the community support for Johnson.

As the hearing proceeded, it was clear that Chrysler's attorneys had been thrown off balance by Glotta's creative strategy and were unable to mount an effective defense. Referee Conley ruled in favor of Johnson and made the following findings of fact and law in favor of Johnson: (1) The plaintiff had a pre-existing mental tendency toward schizophrenia and paranoia, but this mental condition was "nondisabling"—that is, Johnson was able to perform his job adequately; (2) his condition was significantly aggravated by the long-term work environment, including being unfairly assigned undesirable work at the oven, being passed over for a better job for which he was qualified, being addressed by a foreman as "nigger" and "boy," being denied his medical benefits, being suspended improperly for taking a legal vacation, and being suspended under clouded circumstances; (3) these job-related actions caused his breakdown on July 15, 1970; (4) Johnson still suffered a disability resulting from the occupationally related injury and therefore was entitled to workers' compensation benefits of seventy-five dollars per week starting July 16, 1970, and continuing until he recovered from the job-related disability.[2]

The establishment media was outraged by the decision. The *Detroit News* editorialized that the concept of holding the employer responsible for the aggravation of personality problems caused by the "typical rat race of employment" would deluge the system with false claims. One columnist, writing for a suburban paper, blamed the whole incident on the fact that after the 1967 riots Johnson and "many others of his race" were hired because "industrial firms were prevailed upon to hired the jobless and disadvantaged to ease the inflammatory conditions of the city." The columnist alleged that the "expedited" hiring process meant that applicants were not asked the "usual inquiries about fitness for the job," allowing Johnson to hide his mental illness.

Under public pressure the director of the Bureau of Workers' Compensation said that his office had "agonized" over the decision, and he issued a formal statement: "What will probably seem appalling and shocking to most people is that it appears the state is giving cash to a criminal. We are not condoning his crimes, which are serious indeed. But we are saying that this man was mentally disabled, in part, due to his job."

The decision had legitimated the claims that the automobile corporations practiced racism and allowed unsafe environments in their plants. It also legitimated the cry that workers suffered mental illnesses and breakdowns because of the conditions under which they were forced to work. A liberal view of the Johnson cases, both criminal and civil, would say that they were examples of how law in a democratic nation can bring about social change. But radical lawyers such as Glotta, Cockrel, and Ravitz would have argued that though these cases were important victories, real social change would take place only when workers were politically conscious, had achieved racial unity, and were organized to force a change in capitalist work relations and its unjust distribution of income.

That legal victories cannot be relied on to ensure lasting social change was made apparent in the early 1980s when workers' compensation law was rewritten by the Michigan legislature. Using the Johnson case as a stalking-horse, business interests successfully argued that worker abuse of the system was a major cause of their economic problems. The laws regarding emotional disability and cardiac illnesses were rewritten to exclude more workers from the compensation system.

Unlike many of their peers, Glotta, Ravitz, and Cockrel were not coopted in the ensuing years. Glotta was listed in *Who's Who in American Law* after winning a number of significant workers' compensation trials. He broadened his expertise, litigating and lecturing in such areas as law and discrimination, polio and social security disability, and compensation for asbestos-related diseases. He maintains a progressive approach to legal strategy as he continues to advocate on behalf of workers.

In addition to the acquittals Ravitz and Cockrel won in the New Bethel and Johnson cases, Ravitz had a string of victories in political cases. He successfully defended antiwar demonstrators and won a victory for welfare mothers arrested for demonstrating at the Bureau of Social Services. He was part of a team of lawyers that sued to improve conditions at the Wayne County Jail. He also brought suit against the STRESS unit of the Detroit police, a secret, elite assault section that was responsible for Detroit's police killing more civilians per capita than any other American police department.

In 1972, a portion of Detroit's political left decided to enter the arena of electoral politics. Justin Ravitz was put forth as a candidate for a position as judge in the Recorder's Court. One of the main coordinators of the campaign described its overview of the electoral process: "The Ravitz Campaign understood that we can neither litigate nor elect our way to liberation, but selective and serious entries into each arena can advance the building of a socialist society."[3]

The day of the primary election returns, the *Detroit News* ran a front-page story with a photo of Ravitz and Cockrel under the headline "Radical Tops Court Nominees." With the help of more than four hundred volunteer poll workers and a grassroots campaign, Ravitz came in second among the seven judges elected.

Ravitz understood the psychologically oppressive role ritual and mystification play in the legal system. In small but symbolic ways he tried to diminish the authoritarianism of the courtroom. He did not wear a judicial robe, nor would he exhibit the American flag in his courtroom. Ravitz had taken the bench at the height of the Vietnam War, when for many the flag symbolized American imperialism in the third world and the use of military violence in the rice paddies of the Mekong Delta, as well as the use of police violence in the streets of Detroit. However, the legal system would not countenance this assault on its symbols of power and legitimacy. The Michigan Supreme Court issued a ruling that all judges had to wear robes and exhibit the flag in order to maintain a "proper" judicial atmosphere.

Ravitz complied with the ruling but continued his attempts to demystify the legal system. He and another progressive judge drafted a letter that was sent to defendants explaining the role of the preliminary hearing, emphasizing that they had a right to this important procedure, and warning them against waiving that right. He accepted numerous speaking engagements to explain the law in terms people understood, and he gave a series of seminars held in his courtroom on Saturdays to discuss how the legal system really functioned. He rejected the false concepts that the law was colorblind and that it treated rich and poor alike. The following words, written by Ravitz in 1974, are an example of critical legal theory, before that term was invented:

> The rawness of white racism in this country is only a part of the real message. The law is not only not "color blind," but it more than "tolerates

classes among citizens." It is designed to tolerate and perpetuate class division. The law serves the dominant class in a class society.[4]

In 1983, Judge Ravitz ran for reelection and won easily. When he retired from the bench in 1986, an article in the *Detroit Monthly* stated that "Ravitz has earned a reputation as one of the finest legal minds in the state." Returning to private practice, he showed the breadth of his intellectual ability by developing a varied caseload in an era of specialization. Ravitz does trial and appellate work, and his practice includes civil rights, police and government misconduct, employment discrimination, and personal injury. He has maintained his passion for social justice and tries to practice in a manner consistent with his belief that all people are entitled as "birthrights" to a dignified job, adequate housing, medical care, and equal educational opportunities.

From the civil rights movement of the early sixties through 1975, lawyers were constantly representing people who were organizing and demonstrating for social change. Some cases, such as the Chicago 8 trial, the prosecutions of Native Americans after the Wounded Knee shootout with FBI agents, and the prosecutions of prisoners after the Attica rebellion, garnered national attention. The National Lawyers Guild, considered the legal fist of the movement, quadrupled in size and was attacked by FBI Director J. Edgar Hoover as "more dangerous than the people throwing the bombs." Kenny Cockrel was one of the better-known lawyers of this generation who were spied upon by the FBI. He exemplified the kind of lawyer who was described by the United States Attorney for the Northern District of California as "movement attorneys. They do more than just advise. They're part of the revolution."[5]

Cockrel could have jumped into the role of super-lawyer, flying around the country handling one high-profile case after another, but he was somewhat critical of all the money and energy that go into big, national cases. He believed it was necessary to build power on a local level, and consequently he focused his attention on the Detroit area. One incident that did thrust him into the national spotlight took place during the New Bethel case. Although one of the defendants, Alfred Hibbit, had voluntarily surrendered when he appeared at the pretrial hearing, Judge Joseph Maher doubled his bail to an amount that was unattainable for Hibbit.

An outraged Cockrel was quoted by the media as calling the judge a "honkey dog fool" and a "lawless, racist, rogue, bandit, thief, pirate." Judge Maher called for Cockrel's disbarment and the State Bar instituted disciplinary proceedings. Distinguished lawyers, white and black, rallied to Cockrel's side. He would not back down and apologize. Instead, an offensive strategy was developed. The arguments were threefold. First, his choice of language had expressed the sentiments of the black community in colloquial terms used by that community. Second, the allegations were true: the raising of bail without just cause was "thievery and piracy." Third, lawyers had a First Amendment right and an obligation to inform the public about what was happening in court, particularly about issues of political importance. The first day of Cockrel's hearing, hundreds of people tried to get into the courtroom. A door was broken down, a court reporter fainted, and court was adjourned. After a week's continuance the proceedings against Cockrel were dismissed. Judge Maher reduced the bail from $50,000 to a more reasonable $10,000. Eventually Hibbit was found not guilty of the murder charge.

Cockrel continued to represent political activists. A police officer admitted years later that some officers "might have wasted Kenny if they had had the chance." Cockrel at times carried a gun for self-protection, and Ravitz recalled that a bomb was thrown onto the balcony of their law office. By the late 1970s, however, the confrontations between the community and the state had taken less direct and less violent forms. The Vietnam War had ended with a defeat for American aggression, and the extreme abuses of prosecutorial power by the Nixon administration had terminated with Richard Nixon's resignation and Attorney General John Mitchell's criminal conviction. Police departments were integrating and were no longer seen as a white occupation army in minority neighborhoods. Blacks were exercising the right to vote and were entering the electoral field. In Detroit, Coleman Young, a liberal African American, had been elected mayor.

By this time, criminal lawyers were no longer in the forefront of the legal struggle to change the landscape of America. Most of the legal battles were taking place in the arena of civil law. Unfair employment practices, sex and race discrimination suits, corporate abuses, and environmental protection—these were the areas receiving the attention of public interest attorneys. Immigration law and Central American solidarity groups had replaced criminal procedure and mass defense committees. In this changing context, Cockrel decided to run for public office, and in 1977 he was elected to the Detroit City Council. During his term he shook up the council and advocated for social reform. After four years he returned to private law practice, and in 1988 he joined the large firm where his old friend Justin Ravitz practiced. Just a year later, Cockrel died from a sudden heart attack. U.S. Congressman George Crockett, Jr., articulated the thoughts of many when he said, "I had sort of hoped that one day Ken would become mayor of Detroit. I think he had all it took to occupy that job. . . . I don't think the City Council has been the same since Ken left."[6]

Ken Cockrel was only fifty years old when he died. When his wife, Sheila Murphy, a former community organizer and currently a city councilwoman, was asked how she would want him to be remembered, she answered for hundreds of his clients and friends: "I would like him to be remembered as a man with a passion for justice and an impeccable integrity. And that he believed in making things better for working people and poor people with his whole heart and soul."[7]

Dr. Clemens Fitzgerald, Jr., who had testified in behalf of James Johnson, was murdered seven or eight years after the case was over. His car was found abandoned at the airport, with his body stuffed in the trunk. The killers were never caught and still remain unknown.

In most cases involving noncelebrities, when the case is over the defendant fades into the background. James Johnson was sent to Ionia State Hospital for the Criminally Insane. Judge Robert Colombo wrote a letter to Ionia, which he released at a press conference, recommending that Johnson be kept in custody for the rest of his life, stating that if he were ever released he would kill again. The judge was wrong on both counts. Johnson was incarcerated for five years. Upon his release he lived quietly with his sister in Detroit. Three years later he was interviewed by a reporter for the *Detroit Free Press*. The forty-five-year-old Johnson recounted his feelings about what had happened: "I think your mind has something like a release valve, like a pressure cooker on a stove. If it doesn't get released, it'll explode, blow up the kitchen and you with it. I don't know why mine didn't get released, I just lost control completely."[8]

While James Johnson was in jail awaiting trial, he was shown literature depicting him as a hero. He had responded with simple words that should sear the heart of corporate America: "I'm no hero. I never wanted to be a hero. All I wanted to do was to go to work, come home, and get my paycheck once a week. It was either that job or welfare."[9]

James Johnson has not killed again; Steven Robinson has not robbed another bank. Both men have receded into the background. These men were not political heroes like civil rights leader Medgar Evers who was assassinated by a white supremacist in Mississippi, or Black Panther leader Fred Hampton who was assassinated by police in Chicago. Johnson and Robinson represent the hundreds of thousands of men and women working in factories or standing in unemployment lines whose anguish, desperation, and rage are welling up inside them. The great majority of them will control that rage and lead productive lives free of criminal acts. But for the few, or the many, who lose control, lawyers have the obligation to consider the black rage defense, as well as a responsibility not to misuse it.

There emerged from the depths of
my tormented being a deep groan
like the rumbling thunder of a
gloomy rain—or the jarring sound
of a thousand exploding guns or the
obscene roar of a prowling, hungry
lion. Only Allah knows the acute
hurt of my scarred soul.
—Raage Ugaas, Somali poet

Chapter 6

Racism, Rage,
and Criminal Defenses

The environmental defense took a step forward in the case of *United States v. Alexander*.[1] The U.S. Court of Appeals for the D.C. Circuit heard the *Alexander* case in 1972, just one year after the acquittals of Steven Robinson and James Johnson. Ironically, the decision has had a lasting impact because of the *dissenting* opinion. Judge David Bazelon, America's foremost jurist in the field of law and psychiatry, wrote a penetrating dissent suggesting that severe socioeconomic hardship should be allowed as a defense to a criminal charge. Two thought-provoking articles have continued the discussion of whether an environmental defense, and by analogy a black rage defense, could fit within the traditional framework of criminal law and, if not, whether a new defense should be crafted.

The *Alexander* case began one night in June 1968, two months after Martin Luther King, Jr., was assassinated. Five white U.S. Marine lieutenants stationed in Quantico, Virginia, drove into Washington, D.C., to celebrate their near-completion of basic officers' training. On their way to a nightclub with a young woman named Barbara Kelly they stopped at a hamburger shop, around three o'clock in the morning. As they stood by the take-out counter, the five Marines in their formal dress white uniforms, they exchanged hostile stares with three black men at the other end of the counter. At the subsequent trial, Lieutenant Ellsworth Kramer would describe the black men in a way that showed his prejudice: "Their hair was in Afro-bush [sic] cut, wearing medallions, jersey knit shirts, sport jackets. . . . They were what I consider in eccentric dress."

The three black men were named Murdock Benjamin, Gordon Alexander, and Cornelius Frazier. After a few minutes Frazier and Benjamin walked out of the shop, and as Alexander followed them he had words with Lt. Kramer. As the two men challenged each other to step outside and fight, Lieutenant William King walked over and, according to the government witnesses at the trial, said, "What do you want, dirty nigger bastard?" "Get out of here nigger." "What you god-damn niggers want?" and "What do you want, you nigger?" In response, Alexander drew a .38 caliber revolver, cocked it, pointed it at King, and said, "I will show you what I want." Benjamin had come back into the shop and, seeing what was happening, began shooting. The Marines were unarmed. When the shooting stopped King and Lieutenant Thaddeus Lesnick were dead, Kramer was wounded in the head, and Kelly was wounded in the hip. As Benjamin, Alexander, and Frazier drove off, Benjamin stuck his gun out of the car window and fired three shots at the hamburger shop. A police car in the vicinity stopped them within a few blocks and arrested them.

At the conclusion of the trial both sides agreed that Alexander had not fired his gun. He was convicted of carrying a dangerous weapon and four counts of assault for pointing his gun. The Court of Appeals reduced the four counts to one count of assault.

Murdock Benjamin was indicted and tried under the incorrect name of Benjamin Murdock. Therefore, in the legal literature his case is known as the *Murdock* case and he is referred to as Murdock. (Here I shall use his correct surname.)

Benjamin argued that he heard someone say, "Get out, you black bastards," and that the Marines advanced on him. He said he shot when one of the Marines was one foot away from him, and he thought he was going to be killed. However, the jury believed the testimony of the other witnesses in the shop, who said that the Marines and Kelly were standing still after Alexander pulled his gun, and that Benjamin emptied his fully loaded revolver into them. He was convicted of the weapons charges and second-degree murder. After the verdict, Benjamin was entitled to a second trial on the issue of insanity. In insanity cases sometimes the same jury would hear the insanity evidence, sometimes a new jury would be empaneled. In Benjamin's case the same jury heard testimony regarding Benjamin's mental state at the time of the shootings.

Three psychiatrists examined Benjamin and testified at trial. A doctor from St. Elizabeth Hospital concluded that he had "predisposing factors" that led him to "overreact" to possible physical threats, but that he had the ability to control his behavior. The doctor appointed at the government's request admitted that every person is influenced by his or her background, but concluded that Benjamin suffered from no more than mild "neurotic symptoms."

The psychiatrist who testified for the defense was Dr. E. Y. Williams, a professor at Howard University Medical School. He found Benjamin delusional, "preoccupied with the unfair treatment of Negroes in this country and the idea that racial war was inevitable." He testified that these emotional disorders had their roots in Benjamin's childhood in the Watts ghetto of Los Angeles. Benjamin was deserted by his father, and he grew up in a large poor family where he received little love or attention. Williams concluded that because of his abnormal psychological condition, Benjamin probably had an irresistible impulse to shoot when the Marine called his friend a nigger and him a black bastard. Unfortunately for the defense, Williams gave his personal opinion of what constituted a "mental illness," an opinion that was devastating to the insanity defense and contrary to the law. The doctor testified that Benjamin was suffering from an abnormal mental condition that substantially impaired his behavior control, but since it was not a psychotic reaction he did not consider it a mental illness. Benjamin's lawyer was left with a situation in which his own expert witness had weakened the claim of insanity.

The problem was that the legal definition of insanity and the various psychiatric definitions of insanity do not always fit. Williams's definition clashed with the legal definition. Changing fashions in psychiatry, as well as the philosophies of individual psychiatrists, affect the medical definition. Political changes also affect the legal definition. In 1968, in federal jurisdictions the law was clear that a mental illness included *any* abnormal condition of the mind that substantially affected mental or emotional processes and substantially impaired behavior control. Legally, mental illness was not limited to psychosis.

Benjamin's lawyer did his best, given that his psychiatrist had decimated his case. In his closing argument, he used a variant of the black rage defense without calling it by that name. The lawyer tried to explain Benjamin's abnormality by pointing to the difficulty of his childhood environment.

> Dr. Williams premised his conclusion on the fact that this man had had what we might call a rotten social background. Now we know that most people survive rotten social backgrounds. But most people are not now here at this time on trial. The question is whether the rotten social background was a causative factor and prevented his keeping control at that critical moment.

The phrase "rotten social background" was a poor choice, probably reflecting the lawyer's paternalism toward his client. It places the speaker on a higher level than the person growing up in a poor, single-parent family in Watts. "Rotten" is defined as "morally corrupt," "decayed," and "foul smelling." It is a pejorative term, and by using it the attorney associated Benjamin with negatively charged images. A positive and sympathetic way of describing Benjamin's early life would have been to say he came from a disadvantaged, traumatic, or painful background. It would also have been important to find some positive, redeeming factors in his life and express them in a positive way to the jury. Every client I've ever represented has had redeeming qualities, which I found when I took the time and energy to connect with him or her.

Benjamin's lawyer, in a quandary after Williams's testimony, correctly tried to focus on whether or not Benjamin could control his behavior the night of the shootings.

> At the critical moment when he stepped back in the Little Tavern restaurant and he was faced with five whites, with all of his social background, with all of his concepts, rightly or wrongly, as to whether white people were the bogeymen that he considered them to be, the question at this moment is whether he can control himself. . . . Now you have got to take the trip back through his lifetime with him and look at the effect that his lifetime had on

him at that moment and determine whether he could control himself or not.

Although this was a good argument, again the lawyer's choice of words was counterproductive and may reflect a subtle prejudice. "Bogeymen" are not real. Racists are real. A bogeyman is a figment of one's terrified imagination. The Marine who hurled racial epithets at Benjamin was an actual person, standing just a few feet from him, spewing hateful invectives. Benjamin may have responded with excessive force, but he didn't imagine the threat. Only two paragraphs of the closing argument were published, so it is hard to analyze it, but the use of terms like "bogeyman" and "rotten social conditions" indicate a closing that was apologetic in approach, and a lawyer who was not in sync politically and emotionally with his client's background.

We'll never know how persuasive the jury found the defense argument to be because the trial judge completely undercut Benjamin's defense. The judge instructed the jurors that they were not to concern themselves with the issue of how a "rotten social background" affected Benjamin. The judge had allowed the psychiatrist to testify to Benjamin's childhood because it was proper evidence for a doctor to consider when making a mental diagnosis. He allowed the defense lawyer to discuss it in his closing argument because it was a proper comment on the evidence. However, after closing arguments the judge became agitated and refused to allow the jury to consider the social and economic environment of the defendant. His colloquy with the defense counsel outside the jury's presence shows the judge's determination to keep race and poverty out of the jury's decision-making process. It is also an example of a judge reinforcing the myth of the colorblind courtroom.

The Court: I will tell them it is not in any way a question of his rotten social background.
Counsel: I object.
The Court: You may.
Counsel: May I state my reasons?
The Court: You may.
Counsel: I was talking in terms of the cause of his condition.
The Court: No, you weren't sir. You were appealing in the most direct way

to something that I am going to keep out of the courtroom, if I stay a Judge. I am not going to permit it to come in here.

After Benjamin was found guilty of second-degree murder, the case was appealed. In a two-to-one decision the Court of Appeals upheld the verdict. The majority implied that the trial judge made a mistake in his jury instruction, but held that in the context of all the instructions and the evidence he had allowed, there was no reversible error. Feeling uneasy about their decision and attempting to meet the concerns articulated in Judge Bazelon's dissent, the majority opinion stated that the ultimate responsibility for the deaths was society's inability "to eliminate explosive racial tensions" and "to deny easy access to guns." The judges then rationalized their failure to rule that the jury should have been allowed, in clear terms, to consider the racial and economic evidence by repeating the old standby that the court's role is limited and that it cannot be concerned with broad issues of justice.

Some lawyers believe the most important variable in winning or losing a trial is the judge. This is an overstatement, but as the Benjamin trial showed it contains a lot of truth. Judges can influence the outcome of a jury trial in three significant ways. First, their attitude toward the witnesses and the integrity of the physical evidence impacts on the jurors. When a judge gives off signals that he believes the prosecution's witnesses and evidence, this carries substantial weight with the jurors. Second, a judge's negative attitude toward the defense lawyer can make it difficult to present an effective case. Judges will sometimes interrupt, castigate, and ridicule defense attorneys. They will put immense pressure on the attorneys to "move the case along." The speed-up assembly line model of work is not limited to the auto plants. Criminal trial lawyers are often treated like production workers. The judge, acting like a boss or foreman, pushes the attorney to finish the case with only one goal in mind, getting the case off the assembly line and the next one into production. There is often little regard to justice.

If the lawyer stands up to the judge, jurors can become aware of the conflict between a fair trial and administrative efficiency. A jury may react negatively to a judge who rides a defense lawyer. After one acquittal, a juror told me that the jury actually discussed the judge's bullying behavior during deliberations and felt sympathetic toward me. After another successful trial, two jurors asked me why the judge did not want to give the defendant a fair trial. Although handling a case before a hostile judge is technically difficult and an emotionally unpleasant experience, I try to follow the example of that spirited, fictional English barrister, Rumpole of the Bailey, who once said, "On the Day of Judgment I shall probably be up on my hind legs putting a few impertinent questions to the Prosecution."

The third and by far most crucial way in which a judge molds the trial is by her rulings on evidence and testimony. Judges can determine what questions may be asked a witness and in what form the questions are asked. They control the time allowed for examination and for opening and closing arguments. Judges also rule on what pieces of physical evidence are admissible and which testimonial evidence (words of a witness or defendant) will be heard by the jury. These decisions can make or break a case. In Benjamin's case, the trial judge's instructions to the jury to disregard the influence of the environment on the defendant had an overwhelming effect on what the jury could consider. As Judge Bazelon said in his dissent, "Such an instruction is contrary to law, and it clearly undermined Murdock's approach to the insanity defense in this case."

Bazelon's dissent encouraged some of those responsible for the criminal justice system to look at "the root causes of crime." He wrote that the legal system would never be able to deal justly with crime unless it understood the relationship between environment and mental illness.

> We sacrifice a great deal by discouraging Murdock's responsibility defense. If we could remove the practical impediments to the free flow of information we might begin to learn something about the causes of crime. We might discover, for example, that there is a significant causal relationship between violent criminal behavior and a "rotten social background." That realization would require us to consider, for example, whether income redistribution and social reconstruction are indispensable first steps toward solving the problem of violent crime.

Bazelon's opinion reverberated through the legal community. It found a warm reception amoung judges and lawyers who saw the need to publicly debate the responsibility of society for crime. Bazelon hoped that the debate would lead to measures to alleviate poverty and thereby strike at the root of crime.

Almost a decade after Bazelon's article, Richard Delgado questioned whether the criminal law should allow a defense based on adverse social conditions. In an article the title of which alludes to the *Alexander* case, " 'Rotten Social Background': Should the Criminal Law Recognize a Defense of Severe Environmental Deprivation?"[2] Delgado makes a lengthy and persuasive argument that environmental adversity, primarily poverty, is a root cause of crime.

> There is also a strong relationship between environmental adversity and criminal behavior. Of course, not all poor persons violate the law and not all those from privileged backgrounds are law-abiding; it remains, however, that of more than one million offenders entangled in the correctional system, the vast majority are members of the poorest class. Unless we are prepared to argue that offenders are poor because they are criminal, we should be open to the possibility that many turn to crime because of their poverty—that poverty is, for many, a determinant of criminal behavior.

Delgado then asks the essential question with which this book concerns itself: Assuming that poverty and racism cause criminal behavior, then should not that fact mitigate criminal responsibility? But English and American jurisprudence historically has been rooted in the concept of individual responsibility. This doctrine is identified with the capitalist myth that every person has free choice, unconstrained by class, race, religion, or gender. The notion of free choice is found in all areas of law. For example, until the reforms of the New Deal, child labor laws were held unconstitutional as a violation of the right of the worker (a child) to bargain freely with the employer. Until fairly recently, consumers and tenants were legally defined as free to bargain *on equal terms* with monopoly corporations and large landlords. Therefore, if a consumer signed an unfair contract or a tenant signed an unfair lease, she was held to the terms of the agreement because under the law's mythology she had made a free choice when she signed the document.

Historically, in criminal law poverty has not been an excuse for crime, nor has it mitigated the penalties. Peasants who lost their lands were hanged for shooting deer to feed their families. In *Les Misérables,* Jean Valjean is sentenced to five years in prison for breaking a window and stealing a loaf of bread. The fact that his sister and her seven children suffer from extreme hunger is no defense. The law has not changed much in hundreds of years. The story of Valjean may have been successful on Broadway, but hungry, homeless people are still prosecuted and jailed under trespass and disturbing-the-peace laws. In San Francisco in the fiscal year 1993–94, eleven thousand homeless men and women were arrested or criminally cited for nuisance-type crimes. Economic deprivation is still not allowed as a defense. The fiction that all people are capable of free choice unencumbered by race, class, and gender still dominates American jurisprudence.

The law does recognize certain situations in which criminal behavior is excused or legally justified. The rationale is that where individual choice is absent there is no moral basis to punish. The doctrine is ably articulated by H. L. A. Hart: "We should restrict even punishment designed as 'preventive' to those who at the time of their offense had the capacity and a fair opportunity or chance to obey the law: and we should do this out of considerations of fairness and justice to those whom we punish. This is an intelligible ideal of justice to the individual."[3] Although this doctrine would seem to include the homeless or the racially oppressed, if they could make a persuasive case that they had no "fair opportunity" to obey the law, neither the penal statutes nor common law has allowed for such an interpretation. There are two classifications carved out of the criminal law to protect people when there is no "moral blameworthiness": *excuse* and *justification.* Under excuse, the largest category is insanity. The theory is that an insane person has lost free choice and therefore should not be held criminally responsible for his actions, although he may be locked up in a hospital to protect the public.

Until the 1980s, states were moving to a liberal—that is, a broader, more inclusive—definition of legal insanity. This inclusive definition was represented by the law in all federal jurisdictions. A person would be held not guilty if he had a mental disease or defect that caused him to lack substantial capacity to understand the wrongfulness of his conduct *or* to conform his conduct to law. However, the law-and-order politics of the Reagan years combined with a high-profile case resulted in a restrictive rule of insanity. After John Hinckley was acquitted of shooting President Reagan on the grounds of insanity, Congress passed the Insanity Defense Reform Act. The Act was basically a throwback to 1843, when the English House of Lords in the M'Naghten case established a rule referred to as the "right-wrong test"—that is, the defendant is insane only if he did not know his act was wrong. The Act also provided a commitment procedure in which a defendant found not guilty by reason of insanity is confined to an institution for the criminally insane. The most significant change was to shift the burden of proof from the prosecution to the defense. Instead of the state having to prove the defendant is not insane beyond a reasonable doubt, the defense must now prove insanity by "clear and convincing" evidence. This change definitely makes it more difficult to win a black rage case in all federal jurisdictions.

The federal courts were not the only ones to change from a liberal to a conservative view of insanity law. Even before the Hinckley case, there was a movement to make it more difficult to obtain not guilty insanity verdicts in state courts. The movement gained momentum after Hinckley's acquittal. By the end of the Reagan era, Idaho, Montana, and Utah had abolished the insanity defense and thirty-four states had passed new laws restricting its use. Thirteen states enacted various forms of a "guilty but mentally ill" defense. The harshest version mandates that persons found not guilty but mentally ill are to be sent to regular prisons for the maximum term authorized for the crime and may, but need not, be offered psychiatric treatment. The U.S. Supreme Court has ruled that state laws that adopt a restrictive definition of insanity, shift the burden of proof to the defense, provide for commitment in a hospital or prison, or completely abolish the insanity defense are constitutional.

The law of diminished capacity has fared somewhat better in the onslaught against the insanity defense. This defense was introduced successfully into American law in 1949 and 1960 by Charles Garry (later to gain fame as chief counsel for the Black Panthers). With the help of his partner, Benjamin Dreyfus, Garry persuaded the California Supreme Court to rule that psychiatric evidence was admissible in determining whether an accused was capable of the mental state of premeditation or malice required for a murder conviction. The court, under the stewardship of the greatly respected and forward-thinking Chief Justice Roger Traynor and influenced by Justices Raymond E. Peters and Mathew O. Tobriner, established a rule of law which by 1975 was followed by approximately twenty-five states and came to be known as "diminished capacity." Under this doctrine, if a person knows the difference between right and wrong but is suffering from a mental illness that affects his ability to follow the law, the degree of his crime is reduced. For example, first-degree murder would be reduced to second-degree murder or manslaughter. The defendant would not be judged insane but rather to have a diminished capacity to control his behavior, which means he is considered not as morally blameworthy as the normal, healthy individual. Diminished capacity can also be used to negate the element of specific intent. In many crimes the law requires the proof of a conscious choice to commit the designated crime. For example, in burglary it must be proved that the defendant entered with a specific intent to commit a felony. In assault it must be proved that there was a specific intent to cause great bodily injury. A failure to prove the required mental state reduces the degree of the crime, usually from a felony to a misdemeanor. Since the black rage defense seeks to explain the defendant's mental state, the doctrine of diminished capacity is well suited to these cases.

Although many states allow some form of diminished capacity defense, the deluge of law-and-order statutes threatens to make this defense an endangered species. A sad example of that trend is found in California, where the combination of a high-profile case and the politics of blaming the courts for crime created the same dynamic that led Congress to enact the Insanity Defense Reform Act.

In 1978, Dan White, a conservative San Francisco supervisor (city councilman) killed the liberal mayor, George Moscone, and the first gay supervisor, Harvey Milk, shooting them in their respective City Hall offices. White's attorney put forth an excellent diminished capacity defense, and White was convicted of manslaughter instead of first- or second-degree murder. The night after the verdict was announced there were riots outside of the City Hall in which police cars were burned, protesters were beaten, and many people were arrested. White was sentenced to approximately eight years in prison. Conservative politicians were able to harness gay and liberal outrage surrounding the verdict in order to pass a law abolishing the diminished capacity defense in California state courts. The California example reminds us that the future of the black rage defense will be fought out in the political arena as well as in the courtroom.

In addition to insanity, the category of excuse includes duress, mistake, accident, and provocation. Duress is a legitimate defense when a person commits a criminal act because she is threatened with imminent death or serious injury. For example, F. Lee Bailey used this defense in the case of newspaper heiress Patty Hearst. Hearst was kidnapped by a very small group called the Symbionese Liberation Army. Months after her abduction she took part with the group in an armed bank robbery. Bailey argued she was under duress when she helped rob the bank.

All of these excuse defenses involve a two-step process. First, the judge must be persuaded that all the legal elements of the defense are present. For example, in the duress situation there must be evidence of an *imminent* danger. If the judge agrees that the legal requirements are fulfilled, she allows the evidence into the trial and later instructs the jurors that they may consider the duress defense. The second step is the actual weighing of the evidence by the jury during deliberations. In the Hearst case, the judge found that there was enough evidence of duress to instruct the jury that they could entertain that defense. The jury found the argument, as well as the brainwashing defense, unpersuasive and convicted Hearst.

Delgado suggests that a judge might find that living in desperate socio-economic conditions creates the legal elements of a duress defense. However, it is unlikely that most judges would find *imminent* harm, and therefore they would refuse to instruct the jury that a duress defense is permissible. With the right facts, however, a judge such as Bazelon who is open to the connection between poverty and crime might give a duress instruction. If so, a creative lawyer would be able to use a black rage strategy to gain an acquittal.

Another excuse category is provocation, which is the killing of another person while under the influence of a reasonably incurred emotional disturbance. This is not a complete defense—it only reduces murder to manslaughter by negating the element of malice. Provocation, commonly referred to as "heat of passion," has often been used in cases where a husband comes home to find his wife in bed with a lover and kills one or both of them.

The doctrine of provocation would also fit a situation in which a person acts violently after being insulted with racial epithets. An example of black rage exploding into violence when a man is provoked by racial insults can be found in the classic American novel *Invisible Man*. Echoing Dostoevsky's *Notes from Underground,* Ralph Ellison created an African American protagonist who lives undiscovered in the basement of an apartment building restricted to whites and goes through life with his hopes, his needs, his pains—his entire being—virtually invisible to an uncaring white society. In one powerful scene the main character is insulted by a white man and reacts with an awful fury.

> One night I accidentally bumped into a man, and perhaps because of the near darkness he saw me and called me an insulting name. I sprang at him, seized his coat lapels and demanded that he apologize. He was a tall blond man, and as my face came close to his he looked insolently out of his blue eyes and cursed me, his breath hot in my face as he struggled. I pulled his chin down sharp upon the crown of my head, butting him as I had seen the West Indians do, and I felt his flesh tear and the blood gush out, and I yelled, "Apologize! Apologize!" . . . And in my outrage I got out my knife and prepared to slit his throat . . . when it occurred to me that the man had not *seen* me. . . . And I stopped the blade, slicing the air as I pushed him away, letting him fall back to the street. I stared at him hard as the lights of a car stabbed through the darkness. He lay there, moaning on the asphalt; a man almost killed by a phantom. It unnerved me. I was both disgusted and ashamed. . . . The next day I saw his picture in the *Daily News,* beneath a caption stating that he had been "mugged." Poor fool, poor blind fool, I thought with sincere compassion, mugged by an invisible man!

Reading Ellison's words, we may wonder whether that's how Murdock Benjamin felt when the Marine called him and Alexander a "black bastard" and a "dirty nigger bastard."

There are two problems with using provocation as a defense. First, many jurisdictions hold that words alone do not justify a response of violence. Second, the rule in most states is that the personal history of the defendant is not allowed in assessing whether his response was "reasonable" in light of the provocation. Even with these limitations, a black rage provocation defense is viable in the less restrictive jurisdictions. With the right facts and a sympathetic client, this defense could be used in all jurisdictions.

The other rule of law that allows a person to commit an act that otherwise would be a crime is called *justification.* Justification encompasses cases in which the social value of the act outweighs its moral blameworthiness. The two categories of justification are self-defense (including defense of another person) and necessity. Necessity is a defense when one must break a law in order to prevent a greater harm, such as a driver who breaks the speed limit in order to get a critically injured person to the hospital. In the 1970s lawyers were successful in defending protesters at nuclear power plants on the grounds of necessity. Lawyers argued that the protesters' criminal trespass was a reasonable action to prevent the danger of radiation discharges and meltdowns. However, many appellate courts responded by making the elements of the defense more restrictive, so that it was extremely difficult to use the necessity defense in civil disobedience actions at nuclear plants or cases in which protesters destroyed weapons at military bases. The necessity defense has been used successfully in cases of people engaged in programs to prevent AIDS by allowing addicts to exchange used needles for clean ones.

Necessity cannot be used if there is an adequate alternative. Therefore, a woman cannot steal food to feed her children if welfare is available. Also, the harm caused by the act cannot be greater than the harm it seeks to avoid. It would be hard to justify violent acts in most situations. It is difficult to envision a court giving a necessity instruction in a black rage case because it would, by definition, justify criminal responses to racial oppression.

Self-defense is fertile ground for the black rage defense. Chapter 8 discusses how Clarence Darrow used a form of the black rage defense in the context of the law of self-defense. Chapter 13 discusses how a form of Native American rage also fit into the traditional rule of self-defense. An analysis of those cases would lead one to agree with Delgado that self-defense is a more effective means of putting forth the socioeconomic defense than insanity, duress, or provocation.

Delgado suggests four new models of excuse that would allow an extreme environmental deprivation defense. These models are also theoretically appropriate for the black rage defense. In two categories, involuntary rage ("automatic behavior") and inability to control conduct, he develops liberalized variants of established insanity law. However, since Delgado wrote his article the political atmosphere has become even more hostile to broadening the insanity defense, so his models will have to await a more propitious time.

Delgado puts forth a third model, which he calls "isolation from dominant culture." In this model a person who could show that due to his extreme cultural isolation he did not internalize the values of the larger society or was pressured into adopting the norms of a deviant subculture would be allowed to argue this as a defense. At first glance, such a defense seems totally unrealistic. But Delgado's model foreshadowed a defense used in a 1994 Fort Worth, Texas, murder case. That case received national publicity, not because of the facts or the people involved but because defense lawyers David Bays and Bill Lane used the term "urban survival syndrome." The defendant, a seventeen-year-old black teenager, had been harassed and threatened by two other black men, aged twenty-eight and nineteen, over a year-long period. The defendant, Daimion Osby, was forced into a fistfight with the two men in a parking lot. Osby told the police that he was scared and pulled out a gun and shot and killed both men, who were unarmed but had a gun in their car.

The defense attorneys raised a self-defense claim and argued that Osby had a reasonable fear for his life even though the two men were unarmed. In order to support the element of reasonableness they focused on the danger in the community. An author who had written on race relations was allowed to give expert testimony on statistics showing that southeast Fort Worth was a dangerous high-crime area. FBI statistics were used to prove that the two victims fit the FBI profile of the most dangerous men in America. The lawyers argued that Osby lived in a world where he had to use a gun in order to protect himself from these two men. According to the norms, customs, and reality of his environment, his fear of his assailants was reasonable and he was legally entitled to use deadly force.

The prosecutor was Renee Harris, an African American woman who graduated from the same high school Osby dropped out of. She aggressively attacked the theory of urban survival syndrome, arguing that no such syndrome exists in the entire field of psychiatry and that Osby's actions could not be excused legally or morally. The jury, which consisted of nine whites and three blacks, hung eleven to one for conviction. The lone dissenter, a fifty-three-year-old black man who actually lived in southeast Fort Worth, told the other jurors that they did not understand the neighborhood this shooting took place in or the people who lived there. Six jurors who were interviewed by a newspaper said they ignored the defense, considering it either a publicity tactic or just a far-fetched theory.

A group of black ministers held a press conference in which they called the defense racist and untrue. Reverend Michael Bell said, "Southeast Fort Worth is not a free-fire zone. We refuse to let the word go forth that our community is so gripped by anarchy and lawlessness that everyone has to tote a gun and shoot first and ask questions later."[4] The ministers' reaction reveals the weakness of any defense that relies on a set of values and violent rules of behavior as a replacement for the norms of the dominant society.[5]

Delgado's final model is based on his persuasive argument that crime is in part society's fault. The "societal fault" defense would be used in sentencing in order to mitigate the punishment. In fact, when making a sentencing determination some judges already take into consideration the socioeconomic hardships an individual defendant has suffered. Delgado suggests that this issue should go to a jury. Analogizing to civil law, where juries are allowed to apportion damages based on the comparative negligence of the parties, Delgado argues that a jury should apportion the blame for the crime between the defendant and society. The judge would then reduce the sentence by the proportion of fault allotted to society. Actually, in some jurisdictions, such as Texas, the jury does decide the sentence, but it does not use Delgado's formula. In death penalty cases in all jurisdictions, after a finding of guilt there is a penalty phase in which the jury is allowed to hear evidence regarding the personal hardships of the defendant, including family abuse and social, racial, and economic deprivation. These factors are weighed by the jury in determining whether the defendant should spend the rest of his life in prison or should be executed. Delgado's societal fault model could certainly be useful in sentencing. However, there has been a move in criminology toward harsh mandatory sentences, which take discretion out of the hands of judges. Such mandatory sentencing laws have flooded the federal prisons with first-time drug offenders. Recently, I sat in federal court and watched a judge apologize to a defendant for giving him five years in prison. He had no prior arrests, had a family and a job, and was convicted of selling marijuana. The judge explained that under federal law she had no discretion to lower his sentence. Three-strike laws and lengthy mandatory sentences are being passed in many states, making moot Delgado's proposal to mitigate sentences of persons who act as a partial result of the hopelessness, anguish, misery, and fury caused by a dysfunctional society.

By holding the present criminal law system up to the light, Bazelon and Delgado allow us to see its weaknesses and injustices. One can poke holes in their proposals, but their models help us to see that there can be alternatives to the fiction of free choice and the failure of the penal system to recognized the role of racism and poverty. The black rage defense attempts to focus attention on what Bazelon calls the "root causes of crime." It is a means of forcing the decision-making process to factor in the results of chronic unemployment, lack of opportunity, racial harassment, and discrimination. It is an alternative to the predominant jurisprudence in the country with its assembly line of guilty pleas. It is an alternative that has worked.

As authors, scholars, and lawyers develop the black rage defense, however, we must be careful not to restrict its meaning or its usage. The most recent law-related article about black rage unfortunately does just that. In a law review comment entitled *Black Rage and the Criminal Law: A Principled Approach to a Polarized Debate,* University of Pennsylvania law student Judd Sneirson misinterprets black rage and ends up limiting its meaning and potential as a trial defense or a sentencing mitigator.[6] Sneirson uses the Colin Ferguson case as a jumping-off point to propose that black rage be recognized as a mental disease, but that it only be allowed as a partial excuse in criminal trials. That is, it should be restricted to use as a diminished capacity defense, not as a full-blown insanity defense. Sneirson writes,

> External forces ranging from racist environments to witnessing adultery can trigger profound human responses. By reducing the degree of moral responsibility to below that of a calculating killer while refusing to exculpate entirely, diminished capacity recognizes human weakness, holding individuals accountable only for controlling their responses to external forces. In this respect, diminished capacity consigns external forces and internal responsibility each to the respective role that befits them.

Analogizing black rage to the anger of a husband who kills his adulterous wife or her lover is problematic. Although racist environments and witnessing adultery can both cause violent responses, allowing them as defenses will yield quite different results. In modern times, a diminished capacity defense in an adultery situation is no longer intended as a social message that sexual relations outside of marriage are immoral and worthy of death. Rather, it is simply a recognition that a person who kills when confronted visually with the act of adultery is not in a rational frame of mind, and thereby a jury can find him guilty of manslaughter instead of murder. In a black rage case, however, there is a message being sent to the public: Society's tolerance of racism causes criminal acts. This societal fault is the philosophical basis of the defense. Snierson argues that the jury should not be allowed to acquit a person raising a black rage defense because we must maintain a balance between "individual and societal responsibility." He says that this satisfies "the traditional goals of criminal law." We have seen, however, that traditional criminal law hides social reality with fables of colorblind courtrooms, equality of opportunity, absolute free choice, and fair administration of the law. We should be trying to develop defenses that go beyond conventional rules, not confining our strategies to the restrictions of a criminal law system that perpetuates racism.

As a former law review editor, I am well aware of the pressure on students to write "balanced" articles. When writing about black power and the First Amendment, I had to get permission from my faculty editor to use the word "black" instead of "Negro." Law reviews often suffer from an emphasis on academic scholarship instead of practical application. Sneirson's comment falls prey to the pressures of compromise and the mistake of putting theory ahead of practice. It has no discussion of actual black rage trials in the text and mentions *United States v. Robertson* and *United States v. Alexander* only in footnotes.

Let's look at real cases. Accepting Sneirson's proposal would mean that Steven Robinson would have had no defense at all; his only option would have been to plead guilty. Was it "unprincipled" to argue that Robinson was not guilty by reason of temporary insanity? Did the jury violate some sacred convention of criminal law by acquitting him? Would society be better off if Robinson had gone to prison for five years? What about James Johnson? Under Sneirson's proposal he also would not have been allowed a complete defense. These are real human beings. Their crimes were caused in substantial part by the effects of racism. Legally and morally, these men deserved a chance to argue their circumstances, and a jury deserved a chance to find them not guilty. The black rage defense gave them that opportunity.

Sneirson has written a genuine and well-meaning article, but he makes a crucial error when he defines black rage as a mental disease and goes on to argue "that black rage is a form of legal insanity that criminal law should recognize." He bases this interpretation in part on the book *Black Rage* by William Grier and Price Cobbs. Describing their book as a "seminal sociological and psychiatric study," he incorrectly states that the authors "treat black rage as a mental disease independent of an underlying mental condition." Grier, in a newspaper interview regarding the Colin Ferguson case, said very clearly that "black rage is not a psychiatric diagnosis." [7]

In *Black Rage,* Grier and Cobbs are explicit in their position that the principles of psychological function are universal:

> There is nothing reported in the literature or in the experience of any clinician known to the authors that suggests that black people *function* differently psychologically from anyone else. Black men's mental functioning is governed by the same *rules* as that of any other group of men. Psychological principles understood first in the study of white men are true no matter what the man's color.

The book emphasizes how the "*experiences* of black people in this country are unique." The authors devote numerous chapters to explaining how those experiences cause mental illness. Though the experiences are race-based, the illnesses are the same ones that whites, Asians, and Latinos suffer. For example, they show how the black experience results in a significantly higher rate of paranoid symptoms among mentally ill blacks than among mentally ill whites. But the category of "paranoia" is the same for both races. This point was driven home to me when I spoke with jurors after the Robinson acquittal. One conservative young white man said that he would not have robbed a bank under similar pressures, but he understood how the experiences of Robinson as a black man caused him to crack up temporarily. The juror appreciated that a white person or a black person could suffer from a transient situational disturbance. He also comprehended that experiences *unique* to a black man had driven Robinson over the edge.

James Johnson suffered from the mental disease of paranoid schizophrenia. He did not have a mental disease called "black rage." The black rage component of the trial was critical because it explained the societal experiences that inflamed Johnson's mental illness and caused him to kill in a blinding fury.

Grier and Cobbs show that in order to treat black people effectively, it is necessary to distinguish between normal adaptive behavior and pathology. An example they use is their description of "cultural paranoia":

> We submit that it is necessary for a blackman in America to develop a profound distrust of his white fellow citizens and of the nation. He must be on guard to protect himself against physical hurt. He must cushion himself against cheating, slander, humiliation, and outright mistreatment by the official representatives of society. If he does not so protect himself, he will live a life of such pain and shock as to find life itself unbearable. For his own survival, then, he must develop a *cultural paranoia* in which every whiteman is a potential enemy unless proved otherwise and every social system is set against him unless he personally finds out differently.

Sneirson quotes much of this same passage, but he uses it to buttress his misinterpretation that "black rage describes a mental disturbance caused by long-term exposure to racism." In contrast, Grier and Cobbs follow up their example by explaining that cultural paranoia, along with cultural depression and cultural masochism, are the norms for black America, not mental diseases. "They are no more pathological than the compulsive manner in which a diver checks his equipment before a dive or a pilot his parachute." This distinction is critical to the treating therapist because her job is to differentiate between normal adaptive behavior and mental illness. Grier and Cobbs warn therapists treating black people that they "must first total all that appears to represent illness and then subtract the Black Norm. What remains is illness and a proper subject for therapeutic endeavor." To use psychiatry to treat the healthy norm of black rage would be ineffective and destructive, some would say genocidal.

Identifying black rage as insanity is not only a psychiatric error, it also has negative political consequences. Bell hooks addresses this issue in her 1995 book *Killing Rage, Ending Racism*. She explains how rage is a necessary and usually healthy response to white supremacy. She describes a sequence of racially discriminatory incidents against black women that took place at an airport, which served to intensify her rage against the white man sitting next to her. She writes, "I felt a 'killing rage.' I wanted to stab him softly, to shoot him with the gun I wished I had in my purse. . . . With no outlet, my rage turned to grief and I began to weep, covering my face with my hands."

Bell hooks uses her rage to write insightful and forceful books about race, gender, class, and culture. Black people have always tapped into their rage to achieve in the sciences, in the arts, in the law, and in their daily struggle to survive. Justified rage against racial and economic oppression fueled the civil rights movement. Its fury kept the young men and women of the Student Nonviolent Coordinating Committee (SNCC) warm as they filled the jails of the South. Rage was turned into the eloquence of Malcolm X as he educated white and black alike. It became the eloquent poetry and prose of Maya Angelou. Without such appropriate rage, there would be only depression, dejection, and inaction.

Grier and Cobbs are aware of the distinction between pathological and normative rage. Published in the tumultuous year 1968, the majority of their book is a psychological treatment of race and mental illnesses. Their last chapter, entitled "Black Rage," is a political polemic. They describe the painful reality of black men, raising themes reiterated over twenty-five years later at the Million Man March in Washington, D.C.:

> The grief and depression caused by the condition of black men in America is an unpopular reality to the sufferers. They would rather see themselves in a more heroic posture and chide a disconsolate brother. They would like to point to their achievements (which in fact have been staggering); they would rather point to virtue (which has been shown in magnificent form by some blacks); they would point to bravery, fidelity, prudence, brilliance, creativity, all of which dark men have shown in abundance. But the overriding experience of the black American has been grief and sorrow and no man can change that fact.

They echo the insights of Algerian psychiatrist Frantz Fanon when they say that it is healthy for one to move from grief to rage. When anger and self-hatred are redirected, they aim at the oppressor. Sometimes rage is redirected into political struggle, sometimes into blind violence. Grier and Cobb's concluding chapter, like James Baldwin's *The Fire Next Time*, warn white Americans that if they do not end racial oppression there will terrible, "apocalyptic and final" outbreak of black rage. They are not talking about a few individuals such as Murdock Benjamin pathologically killing individual white people. They are invoking the images of the Watts riots and the Detroit uprising. They are saying that rage is good, that it is necessary to a healthy people. They contrast the collective anger of black people with the collective acceptance of despair and assert that African Americans "will never swallow their rage and go back to blind hopelessness."

The authors' political point is echoed in the book's introduction by U.S. Senator Fred Harris, who was a member of the National Advisory Commission on Civil Disorders. Harris tells white Americans that "black rage is the result of our failure." Like Grier and Cobbs, Harris warns that the "root cause of the black wrath that now threatens to destroy this nation is the unwillingness of white Americans to accept Negroes as fellow human beings."

Black rage is much more than an insanity defense. It has a political as well as a psychiatric meaning. It has positive as well as negative aspects. Therefore, it is necessary for lawyers and legal workers to think through a black rage defense and to use it in a way that does not demean or stereotype black people. In the next chapter, I will analyze some cases in which lawyers failed in that responsibility.

I shall hate you
Like a dart of singing steel
Shot through still air
At even-tide.
—Gwendolyn Bennett, "Hatred"

Chapter 7

To Use or Not to Use
The Black Rage Defense

In most legal cases the lawyer has only one concern: the interests of the client. Unfortunately, the legal community has defined the interests of the client in the narrowest terms possible—the client's best interests equal winning the case. A broader view would include preserving the client's dignity and empowering her. This broader view is essential in a black rage defense, in which the client's painful personal history is revealed to the public.

Many cases go through the assembly line that passes for our criminal justice system, but very few of those cases send a message to the public. Most cases are isolated instances where the state punishes behavior that violates society's legal norms. But in black rage cases, the very nature of the defense sends a message to the public about race relations. Even in a nonpublicized case, the message will be heard by the jury, the judge, the court staff, the state, the families and friends, the institutions involved in the crime, the defendant, and the defense bar. In a highly publicized case like James Johnson's, the message will be heard throughout the country. Attorneys must be clear about the content of the messages they are delivering, because they are affecting the way people think about and act toward each other. The choice of whether or not to use the black rage defense is therefore both a political and a legal one.

Two cases can help provide us with guidelines on when to use a black rage defense. Both cases are ones in which this defense was rejected by the *clients*. The first case is *United States v. Robertson,* in which the defendant was convicted of second-degree murder and assault with intent to kill.[1] The second case involves Colin Ferguson, who was convicted of murdering six and wounding nineteen passengers on a Long Island commuter train. An analysis of these cases shows the pitfalls of a racial defense and points toward the situations that do merit use of a black rage strategy.

Thomas Robertson was raised in Washington, D.C., where as a young man he was arrested for a federal drug-related offense and sent to prison. At the prison he was described as "belligerent" and a "racial agitator." He assaulted two caseworkers and stabbed an inmate during a fight. He spent much of his time in maximum security and solitary confinement in six different prisons. Years later, in August 1971, Robertson got hurt in a fight at a Washington poolhall. A half-hour later he returned to the poolhall and shot a man he did not know in the shoulder. Running out of the poolhall he jumped into his car, went the wrong way on a one-way street, and crashed into some parked cars. He got out with his gun in his hand and talked briefly to the black people in the vehicle behind him. He then walked to where a man named Robert Aleshire was inspecting the damage done to his car. Aleshire was a white man who was active in the general struggle for social justice and was helping to develop strategies for improving the central city. Robertson walked up to Aleshire, whom he did not know, and without a word shot him three times at point-blank range. Robertson then ran down the street cursing "white sons-of-bitches." When he saw a police officer he shouted, "You are doing it; why can't I? Yes, I shot the white honkey son-of-a-bitch. What are you all going to do about it?"

Robertson was arrested and charged. At the preliminary examination he was ordered to be committed to a hospital for a psychiatric evaluation. At the hearing he made the following statement to the judge:

> I'm not going to get justice, I realize this perfectly. See, I'm one who is well versed in whiteness. . . . You won't get your white vengeance. . . . I have

never been guilty of nothing but being born black in a white America—
racist white America. . . . But, I am not going to let you think that I do not
realize who I am and who you are. You are the beast and I am a man. You
say I killed a man. I have killed no man in my whole life.

Robertson was examined by a court-appointed psychiatrist and also by
a psychiatrist and psychologist requested by the defense. All three found
him competent to stand trial. The two defense experts also concluded that
at the time of the crimes he had been insane. The defense lawyer wanted
to interpose an insanity defense, but Robertson absolutely refused. He
went to trial and was convicted. What took place next is a somewhat
confusing journey through the wonderland of criminal procedure, but it
shows how the black rage insanity defense can erode a defendant's dignity.

Under the law applicable in the Washington, D.C., federal courts, a
defendant with an insanity claim could have a bifurcated trial. The first
trial determined whether or not he was guilty; the second determined
whether or not he was insane at the time of the crime. If he was found to
have been insane, then he was committed to a hospital for the criminally
insane. Robertson adamantly denied that he was crazy and forbade his
lawyer to ask for a second trial. However, if it was determined that there
was enough evidence of insanity, then the judge was required, *on his own
motion,* to convene the second trial. The judge held a hearing to determine
whether a second trial was necessary in Robertson's case. This hearing
allows us the opportunity to see four differing views of what clearly was a
form of black rage. Looking first at the defendant, Thomas Robertson, we
see a man who blamed society for causing him to kill. Robertson stated
that he "was under a lot of pressure on that day. The tension was due to
the circumstances of my birth." Robertson was described as extremely
articulate, well read, and knowledgeable about the black power movement
and the Black Muslims. He adopted the vocabulary of Malcolm X in distinguishing between the weakness of the "negro" and the manhood of the
"black." In an essay written in jail entitled "In Search of an Identity in
Racist White America," he described the difference thusly, "The negro has
a limited degree of manhood. He can be one-third man. A Black Man is
unlimited. I am *a* man. I am the man you think you are. This is a trial for
my extinction. They don't want too many me's running around." Robert-

son had been greatly influenced by the writings of Algerian psychiatrist Frantz Fanon, who wrote about the mental illnesses suffered by black and brown people under the domination of white colonial countries. In *Wretched of the Earth* Fanon analyzed, quite profoundly, the causes of violence by Algerians against other Algerians, and also violence by Algerians against the French. Robertson attempted to use Fanon's insights to justify his acts, saying that "murder is no different than war. If a black man kills a white man, it is not a crime. It is getting oppression off his neck."

Robertson's essay and statements lead to the conclusion that he felt he had committed a political act. But the two psychiatrists testifying for the government had a far different view of his motivations. Both stated that Robertson had an "anti-social personality," that he was "grossly selfish, callous, irresponsible, impulsive and unable to feel guilt or to learn from experience and punishment." They relied in part on the staff report from Saint Elizabeth's Hospital, to which he was committed after the crime. In the report, Robertson's mother said that a few months before the crime he had "disrobed and for the better part of the night terrorized the family, but did not hurt them and made numerous statements of his manhood." After that frightening incident his brother had tried unsuccessfully to have him committed. The staff psychiatrist described this as an isolated incident, probably attributable to a drug reaction rather than a mental disease. The staff report also stated that many times at the hospital Robertson would quote from the "literature of black culture" as a means to "reinforce his manhood." The psychiatrists concluded that Robertson was not insane when he committed the homicide.

Since Robertson was refusing an insanity defense, he directed his lawyer not to contest the conclusions of the report, not to cross-examine the two psychiatrists, and not to call the two defense psychiatric experts to the stand. However, the judge, under his own authority, took the defense experts' reports into consideration. These experts, a psychologist and a psychiatrist, gave a third perspective on Robertson's behavior. They agreed with the government psychiatrist that he was obsessed with his sexual identity as a black man in a white society. They found that his crime was a result of "schizophrenia, schizo-affective type," that he was "delusional," and that he projected his pathological identity problems onto whites by blaming and hating them.

The fourth and final perspective came from the judge, a black man named Aubrey Robinson, who had a very different view from that of the psychiatrists. He felt that as a black man, a lawyer, and a judge of considerable experience, he understood Robertson, and that the crime was not a result of insanity. He disregarded the white doctors who had testified for the government, stating that Robertson lived in "a world they don't understand. It is a world that they are not a part of. It is a world that they only relate to through books." He acknowledged that Dr. Alyce Gullattee, the black defense psychiatrist, talked the "same language as this defendant" and knew the "defendant in a way that Dr. Marland and the other doctor will never know him." But he rejected her conclusion that Robertson suffered from a mental disease.

> He knows that I know that he is not crazy. . . . And he knows that I understand him—because I have dealt with Robertsons over the years, little Robertsons and big Robertsons.
> And I know everything about the condition of life that made him exactly what he is and what he is going to be. . . . The public at large will never understand. But there are people who do. Now, there is no basis for me to raise the insanity plea in this case, the insanity defense.
> Do you see what he is saying to his lawyers and what he is saying to the community? "I won't cop out."

The judge seems to be saying that the racist conditions of life that Robertson faced were one of the causes of his crime, and that the white public does not understand this tragedy. He, as a black man, understands the rage that caused Robertson to kill. He also understands the pride that caused Robertson to refuse an insanity defense. Judge Robinson may have been wrong about whether or not the defendant was suffering from a mental disease, but he certainly understood why Robertson could not plead insanity. The judge knew that an insanity trial would have exposed Robertson's life in excruciatingly painful ways to a jury. Questions of his sexual identity, his problems of not feeling confident and secure as a black man, and his treatment of his own mother and siblings would have been revealed and debated in the context of whether he was crazy. Robertson wanted a public discussion on the substance of his philosophy—that white oppression could only be stopped through violence. He wanted to argue that his killing of Aleshire was the sane act of a man at war. Robertson feared that a finding of insanity would signify a defect in his character and would impeach his philosophy. Therefore, he had to reject any attempt to raise a defense couched in terms of insanity.

At the sentencing hearing, the defense lawyer argued that Robertson needed help, not a long prison sentence. The judge's response showed his awareness of racism and his genuine regard for the defendant.

> Don't you understand Mr. Robertson doesn't want your help. He doesn't need it because the only help that can be offered is help that he completely rejected. That is what he is telling you. . . . He would make it on his terms in his good time. That is what he has said. That is what his life has said. . . . He has the capacity for insight. And he has a sensitivity, too, the likes of which few defendants have about his predicament, not just his personal predicament, but his predicament generally.

The judge went on to indicate that if Robertson's behavior in prison showed a change for the better he would reduce the sentence.

The case was appealed, and the Court of Appeals for the District of Columbia ordered that the trial court judge should supplement the record by conducting a full hearing on the issue of insanity. The opinion was written by Chief Judge David Bazelon. Judge Bazelon said that given the substantial indications of mental disease, the court should have appointed another lawyer as amicus curiae to act as the court's representative. That lawyer could have cross-examined the government psychiatrists and called witnesses in behalf of Robertson, in spite of the defendant's objections. Judge Bazelon was cognizant of the racially charged issues. He cited two books, including *Black Rage* by Grier and Cobbs, to support the contention that "white American psychiatry has its . . . racist stereotypes about the black psychiatric patient." He said that in the context of this case it was particularly important for the only black psychiatrist involved to testify in court. The case was sent back to Judge Robinson for further proceedings.

Robertson had a new attorney and consented to an insanity defense. However, once the jury was seated and voir dire began, Robertson could not go through with it and told the judge that he refused an insanity defense "for personal reasons of a quasi-political nature." He went on to state the following: "I still say I am not insane. So, I cannot in good faith and honor of the United States Constitution pursue an insanity defense. . . . As a Black man, I made a stand . . . whether or not I am right in the eyes of the law."

Judge Robinson conducted a full hearing, listening to the testimony of Gullattee as well as numerous other psychiatrists, all of whom were cross-examined. Although they disagreed on the insanity issue, they all agreed that Robertson was competent to decide his own defense. The judge stated the defendant's "crimes arose in part out of protest . . . and [he] believes that exposition of the insanity issue would denigrate that protest." Taking all the testimony into consideration, relying on his own personal experiences, and giving great weight to Robertson's personal choice, the judge concluded that there was no basis for interjecting the insanity issue in the face of the defendant's opposition.[2] Robertson went back to prison to continue serving his original sentence for murder and assault with intent to kill.

What did Thomas Robertson mean when he said he rejected the insanity plea for "personal reasons of a quasi-political nature"? This is a man whom the judge described as having an unusual sensitivity and capacity for insight. Robertson had been in prison for almost six years from the time of the murder to the time he made the above statement. During that period it is possible that he more clearly understood the dual causes of his crime. On the one hand, he was responding to the domination of a white racist world, and on the other, he was being propelled by his private demons. He must have recognized that killing a stranger because that man had white skin was not an articulated political act. But also understanding the cumulative effects that racism had on him, he described it as "quasi-political."

Thomas Robertson's case lacked an important element that was present in the two successful cases that were discussed earlier: In James Johnson's and Steven Robinson's cases there was a context of political support around the defendants. The League of Revolutionary Black Workers and the Motor City Labor league helped build a defense committee for Johnson, and the Malcolm X School provided group support for Robinson. Also, both defendants had lawyers committed to exposing and explaining the quasi-political nature of their crimes. In Johnson's case, his lawyers clearly targeted the institutions of the Mississippi plantation and the Detroit auto corporations. In Robinson's case, I spent hours with my client explaining the black rage defense and promising him that I would not allow the trial to degenerate into a debate between psychiatrists on whether or not he was crazy enough to be legally insane. One has to sit in court and actually watch a personality be peeled away layer by layer— exposing the sores and hidden demons—to appreciate how traumatic an insanity defense is for the defendant. Johnson and Robinson went into their trials confident that their dignity as black men would be respected and protected even in the framework of an insanity defense. Robertson did not have this faith. We do not know whether this was due to the lack of a defense committee or support group, the failure of his court-appointed attorneys, or his expressed distrust of the legal system. For whatever reasons, he made a reasonable choice. A black rage defense would have had little chance of succeeding, and if not done carefully it would have left him with no self-esteem and no sense of manhood, both of which he would need to survive the many years he would serve in prison.

The second case that helps us analyze when a black rage defense is appropriate is the heavily publicized and controversial Long Island commuter train massacre. On December 7, 1993, Colin Ferguson, a thirty-seven-year-old Jamaican immigrant, boarded a commuter train going from Manhattan to Long Island. After the train had crossed the border into suburban Long Island, he got out of his seat and put a bullet into the back of the head of a middle-aged man. Then he walked down the aisle firing his nine-millimeter semi-automatic pistol into passengers. He fired twenty-five bullets before three passengers were able to disarm him. He had killed six people and wounded nineteen. As he lay on the floor of the train he said, "Oh, my God, what have I done?"

Notes found on Ferguson and in his home showed a man obsessed with race and his religious mission. The previous year, he had written a letter expressing his sense of martyrdom: "I am not the Christ but will suffer death to the delight of many who are offended by the truth which I speak; for I have dared to challenge the integrity of a brutal and unjust system and in doing so have also offended the slaves of the system." A note found in his pocket after the arrest blamed racism for his action. He wrote that his "reasons for this [were] Adelphi University racism, EEOC racism, Workmen's Compensation Board, and racism of Governor

Cuomo's staff. . . . Additional reasons for this: Racism by Caucasians and Uncle Tom Negroes." He also blamed "Chinese racism," "so called civil rights leaders," "the sloppy running of the number 2 train," and "corrupt 'Black' attorneys who not only refused to help me but tried to steal my car." He said that he had "spared" New York City out of "respect for Mayor David Dinkins."

Due to a combination of factors, the Ferguson case exploded into the headlines. First of all, it was a mass, random killing. These types of shootings always receive extensive news coverage, usually sensational in nature. Second, it took place in New York, the media capital of the world. Third, unlike almost all previous mass slayings, which were perpetrated by white men, this one was done by a black man who specifically targeted white people. Indeed, much of the news coverage said Ferguson had shot only white people, although his victims included Asians and one black woman. The shooting evoked a fear that lies dormant in the white population, a fear that someday black people are going to turn on them in mass retribution for years of slavery and discrimination. Into this already feverish mix of race, fear, and media competition stepped attorney William Kunstler. Kunstler, who recently passed away at the age of seventy-six, was America's most recognizable radical lawyer. His long history of high-profile cases and his eloquence, brilliance, wit, and passionate commitment to social justice made him a favorite of the media. The fact that he practiced out of a New York office and was a master of sound bites increased his visibility with the press. He and his younger partner, Ronald Kuby, began to represent Ferguson.

At a press conference Kunstler said he was going to use a "black rage" defense. Later, Kunstler admitted that he was shocked by the level of outrage his comment had caused: "I never realized how sensitive those two words were. Many people, black and white took the position that we were saying that any black guy that had rage in his heart because of the treatment of blacks in this country could kill with impunity, which is not what we meant at all."[3]

Kunstler's words sparked a national debate over the legitimacy of such a defense. He appeared on national television and in national magazines. Psychiatrists, social welfare workers, counselors, police officers, lawyers, professors, columnists, and reporters all weighed in with their critiques.

The benefit was that this defense received an exposure and a recognition that were long overdue. The downside was that most of the debate was superficial and negative. Bell hooks described the "carnivalesque aura [that] surrounds the public debate around black rage" and harshly criticized Kunstler and Kuby. In *Killing Rage, Ending Racism,* she accused the two defense lawyers of using a defense that made *all* black rage pathological. That is, in her eyes, Kunstler and Kuby were saying that black rage is an illness—it is legal insanity. This denigrates the legitimate feelings of black anger at injustice.

In addition, white commentators repeatedly argued that the black rage defense was a misguided justification of group violence. In an exchange of letters to the editor in the *New York Times,* an outraged writer complained that the defense vindicated violence based on being a member of an oppressed group and therefore could be used to justify Jews killing Arabs, or Indians killing whites. Kunstler and Kuby responded:

> What we are mounting is a traditional insanity defense, long recognized in our law, with "black rage" triggering December's massacre. Our approach is similar to the utilization of the battered women's syndrome, the post-traumatic stress syndrome and the child abuse syndrome in other cases to negate criminal accountability. . . .
>
> Our suggestion to [those] others who misrepresent or distort, either deliberately or out of ignorance, is that they await the expert testimony to be presented by both sides at Mr. Ferguson's trial before springing to ill-formed conclusions. If . . . "freedom lies in acknowledging responsibility," it also lies in waiting for all the facts.

Kunstler and Kuby never meant to suggest that all black anger and rage is evidence of insanity. Unfortunately, no one heard the black rage defense in the complexity with which they would have presented it at a trial. It was never heard because their client wanted nothing to do with it and fired them. Ferguson wrote a letter to the judge in which he said, "I will represent myself *pro se,* henceforth at all future hearings. I again state that I have never accepted an insanity defense, and certainly not the so-called 'black rage' insanity defense." He refused to meet with the defense psychiatrist and accused his lawyers of conspiring against him.

Kunstler asked the judge to reconsider his ruling that Ferguson was competent to stand trial, stating that the defendant had grown more delusional, paranoid, and obsessive, believed he received messages directly from God, and claimed he was not involved in the shooting on the train. However crazy Ferguson seemed, the court ruled that he satisfied the requirements of competency: (1) he understood the proceedings against him, and (2) he could assist in his own defense. Ferguson eventually represented himself, as was his constitutional right. The court appointed an attorney to aid him throughout the proceedings. At trial Ferguson denied that he had shot anyone, stating that an unidentified white man stole a pistol out of his bag as he slept on the train. Of course, the Nassau County jury found him guilty.

The day after the verdict—in a turnabout indicating Ferguson's mental instability—he asked Kunstler and Kuby to represent him on appeal. Kunstler said he would argue that Ferguson had been incompetent to stand trial, and that the trial showed that he could not mount a coherent defense. Kunstler went on to say that Ferguson understood that "black rage is no longer an issue" in the case, but that the issue of insanity would be the basis for the appeal.

The Ferguson case is a good example of why a black rage defense should not be used every time an angry, mentally unbalanced black person commits a crime. Many people, both black and white, initially viewed Ferguson's crime as a reaction to racial oppression. Given the American experience, this was not an unreasonable interpretation of the awful crime. However, as more facts came to light it became clear that Ferguson's case lacked an essential ingredient a trial lawyer looks for—the potential for empathy.

The first element a lawyer looks at in a black rage psychiatric defense is the nature of the crime. Colin Ferguson committed a violent act. His was not a crime against property, it was a mass murder. Although such an act suggests insanity, it also terrifies jurors and makes any chance of acquittal a longshot.

The second element to analyze is the object of the crime. Here, the shootings were essentially random. True, the victims were chosen primarily because they were white. But they were still random shootings in that none of the victims had any prior relationship with the defendant. In their letter to the editor, Kunstler and Kuby analogized their defense to the battered woman defense and the child abuse defense. But those defenses are based on the defendant's striking out at the actual person who has harmed her. In fact, in those defenses the defendants have been physically and/or sexually abused by the person they attack. That logical and powerful nexus is missing in Ferguson's mass attack on people he did not know.

The third element to weigh is whether or not there is a *concrete* connection between the crime and racial oppression. In James Johnson's situation, the institutional racism of Chrysler Corporation manifested itself in concrete acts of discrimination against Johnson, and he responded by shooting people at the very workplace where he had suffered humiliation and injustice. Maybe Kunstler would have unearthed particular and persuasive instances of racial discrimination against Ferguson, but there did not seem to be any discussed in the media coverage. Some of the "reasons" Ferguson gave for the shootings, such as the racism of Adelphi University and the Workers' Compensation Board, were never backed up with facts. Even Kunstler was circumspect about the so-called discrimination, describing it as "real or imagined." It is a fact that America is a white-dominated society, and study after study has shown that African Americans are subjected to acts of disrespect and discrimination in ways and with a frequency that white people just do not fathom. But when a man kills six people and wounds nineteen others, a lawyer cannot expect to rely on the general racism of society to explain the act.

A fourth element in determining whether to use a black rage defense is the client's personal life. In the successful trial of Steven Robinson, we saw a man who refused to consider himself a victim, who refused welfare, who related well to people, and who tried over and over again to succeed before he temporarily cracked up and robbed a bank. Ferguson's background seems to be one in which he blamed his failures on everything and everyone but himself. One former landlady described him as follows: "Colin had a problem with people in general. I wouldn't call it black rage. He had a problem with people who could achieve things in life that he couldn't. . . . Other people's successes were his failures. I don't think it mattered if you were black or white." A coworker said he "just didn't like anybody" and that he called Mexicans "wetbacks," Asians "rice eaters," and a black woman dating a white man a "nigger-bitch." Ferguson's notes expressed his hatred of other people and his inability to accept responsibility for his problems. A lawyer arguing for Ferguson might say that this hatred and blaming of others are evidence of his paranoia and insanity. Although that is true, it is not evidence of racial oppression. And it is certainly not the kind of client a jury or the public can identify with. Using a black rage defense for a man such as Ferguson sends a message that an individual has no responsibility for his criminal behavior. It is a superficial, wrong-headed, blame-everything-on-racism message. This is just the kind of message that blacks as well as whites reject.

Another negative factor in Ferguson's personal history was that he did not fit the model of a disadvantaged person struggling to survive in the face of racism. He was born into an upper-class family in Jamaica. His Cuban-born father, Von Herman Ferguson, was managing director of a multimillion-dollar pharmaceutical company. Ferguson went to one of the finest private high schools in Jamaica. After his father died in a car crash, Ferguson was unable to succeed at the pharmaceutical company. Feeling that his brother had received special treatment and that he had been cut out of the business, he left for the United States.

One basis for his black rage defense might have been the stress Jamaican immigrants feel when coming from a black society into a white-dominated society. A study by Jamaican psychiatrist Fredrick Hickling documented the unusually high incidence of schizophrenia found in Jamaicans who lived in the United States and Great Britain and concluded that "institutional racism" was a major factor in the illnesses. But since Ferguson rejected the insanity defense, the public only heard of Hickling's work in passing. The overwhelming perception was that because Ferguson came from a privileged background he had no justifiable cause to complain.

A fifth and crucial element is whether or not the client can testify. In Robinson's and Johnson's cases the clients agreed with the defense, were capable of testifying, and were able to elicit positive feelings from the jurors. In William Freeman's case, he had become so mentally deteriorated that he could not testify and may not have even understood what was taking place. Ferguson's paranoia and delusions made him an unlikely candidate to testify. Kunstler and Kuby therefore faced the unenviable task of putting forth a defense with political implications without the help of their client.

The end result was a client who was totally opposed to his lawyers' strategy and antagonistic toward them. It is not unusual for paranoid defendants to project their fears onto their lawyers and to accuse the lawyers of railroading them or conspiring with the district attorney to convict them. Lawyers have even been physically attacked by defendants they are representing. These are problems dedicated attorneys must face when representing insane people. But if a client is too crazy to help the lawyers put together a black rage defense, this should be a neon warning sign that maybe this defense is inappropriate.

Reviewing the factors in Ferguson's case, we see a defendant who considered himself a victim, blamed everyone else for his failings, came from a highly privileged background, could not point to concrete, persuasive instances of racial discrimination, had shot twenty-five people who had no specific relationship to his suffering, and was hostile to an insanity plea. All the elements weighed in favor of not using a black rage defense. Such a defense would have failed in the courtroom. However, this critique should not imply agreement with the trial judge's decision to allow Ferguson, a demented soul, to represent himself. He was entitled to be defended by an attorney who could have raised a traditional insanity claim.

How the black rage defense and Ferguson's case played out in the court of public opinion is harder to assess. There were reports of African American students cheering speakers who favorably described Ferguson's action as an outburst against racism. Many commentators supported the idea of a black rage defense. A survey by the *National Law Journal* showed that 68 percent of blacks and 45 percent of whites believed that a "compelling" defense could be made based on the rage caused by racism. Other minorities were able to relate to the defense. For example, Sheridan Murphy, director of the Florida chapter of the American Indian Movement, was quoted as saying, "If things don't begin to turn around, I think we will see a lot more acts of black rage, Indian rage and Chicano rage in this country."[4]

But the negative comments and editorials outweighed the positive. The African American and Jamaican communities both seemed to be split, with many people fearing that the defense would play into stereotypes about their criminality and would be seen as justification by those who refused to take individual responsibility for their actions. The fact that much of the media was negative should not lead to the conclusion that the defense was wrong. Any strategy that challenges established dogma will receive harsh criticism. But the fact that the African American community generally was not supportive of Ferguson is more problematic. This failure of support indicates a flaw in the defense. The black rage defense is supposed to educate and enlighten. It is a way of exposing racism and showing the terrible effects it has on the human psyche. If the facts of the crime and of the defendant's life blind people to the message that racial oppression is a catalyst to crime, then the defense is counterproductive.

Defending people who commit criminal acts is usually an unpopular undertaking. The strategy a lawyer employs in defending a person who has killed, whether it be James Johnson or Colin Ferguson, should not be determined by newspaper editorials or popularity polls. But the level of public support and the nature of criticism must be given serious consideration in deciding whether to use a black rage defense. In Johnson's case there was strong, visible, organized support in the black community and in the auto plants. This support reflected people's gut-level understanding of how racism had affected Johnson specifically. It also reflected the sophistication of the defense, which was able to open people's minds to the effects of race and class oppression. When the defense, prosecution, judge, and jury walked through the Eldon plant and saw autoworkers visibly express their support of Johnson, it confirmed for them the truth of his black rage defense. In contrast, there was no such truth in Ferguson's case.

There were two typical reactions to Ferguson's crime. Many thought he was just a crazy person who went berserk. Others believed he had planned to kill white people as a way of dealing with his hate and his own failures. Neither reaction saw racism as a significant causal factor. Although there was a certain level of sympathy in the black community, it did not translate into support.

Further impediments were caused by the media frenzy around the case, which made it difficult to communicate a meaningful black rage defense. As bell hooks noted, "A complex understanding of black rage will not emerge with this case as spectacle, it is already being designed to invalidate the reality of black response to racism." Most cases do not afford the opportunity to publicize the defense strategy. But an incident like the Long Island commuter train shootings creates pressure on the attorneys to enter into a sick symbiotic relationship with the media in which the attorneys receive airtime and press coverage but must produce shallow sound bites and controversial statements. For example, Kuby was widely quoted as saying, "The more the white community fears African Americans, the better." This is a foolish trial strategy. A jury that fears the defendant in a black rage case is a jury that will convict. It is also a counterproductive political philosophy. An electorate that fears blacks will vote for "three strikes and you're out" laws, nonunanimous juries, and law-and-order public officials. A white community that fears African Americans will build prisons instead of schools. Maybe Kuby's quote was taken out of context, but that is the danger of playing the media game in the middle of a controversial case.

Lawyers should step back from the media furor. A lawyer must first establish a strong relationship with the client, one that wins over the client's confidence and allows the attorney to delve deeply into the client's life and unearth his or her authentic, lived experiences of racial oppression. Then the psychiatric expert can be brought in to examine the client and determine whether there is a sound psychological basis for the black rage defense. After these steps are accomplished, a fact-oriented, individualized, sympathetic strategy may be possible. If it is, then the lawyer can consider releasing the concept of a black rage defense to the media, and can explain the defense in that specific case to community activists.

An alternative, which should be considered seriously, is to avoid the media, maintain the element of surprise, and test the strategy in the crucible of the courtroom. Throwing the media the bone of "black rage" instead of preparing a thorough, personalized strategy based on the potential for empathy will result in a spectacle that cheapens the black rage defense and sets back the cause of racial understanding and equality.

No one ever judges any one else
without finding him guilty, no one
ever *understands* another without
being in sympathy with [him].
—Clarence Darrow, *The Story of My Life*

Chapter 8

Race, Class, and the Trials
of Clarence Darrow

In the preceding chapters we have seen how the black rage defense has
been used in a psychiatric context. It can also be a vehicle for a self-defense
claim. The law of self-defense is one of those instances in a criminal case
where the state of mind of the defendant is considered relevant to the
charges. For example, a person charged with murder can argue that the
killing was justifiable homicide and that he is therefore not guilty. In order
to justify the killing, the defendant must believe (1) that there was an
imminent danger that the other person would kill him or cause him great
bodily injury, and (2) that it was necessary under the circumstances to kill
the other person to prevent death or great bodily injury. The law puts two
limiting conditions on this rule. First, the defendant's belief must be an
honest one. In other words, you cannot plan to kill an enemy and then
pretend you were suddenly afraid for your life. Second, the belief must be
reasonable. You cannot walk down the street and shoot a homeless man
because he "looked" dangerous, even if you were afraid. Of course, in a
self-defense case the issues of imminent harm, reasonable belief, and what
is necessary under the circumstances are hotly debated. Ultimately, these
are questions of factual determination for the jury.

In order to determine if a person has an honest and reasonable belief that her life is in danger, one must, to some extent, look into the mind of the defendant and the social conditions surrounding the crime. In the hypothetical case of a person shooting a homeless man, the defendant could introduce as evidence of her honest belief the fact that on two previous occasions she had been attacked by homeless people and therefore was afraid when confronted by a dangerous-looking street person. The defendant could also introduce evidence regarding the reasonableness of her fear. She could show that many assaults had recently taken place on that street; that women, in particular, had been victims; and that some of the attacks had come with no warning whatsoever. Without more evidence, a jury would be almost sure to reject her argument that her shooting a homeless man walking toward her was a reasonable act of self-defense. What is important for our discussion is that the beliefs of the defendant and the social context of the crime are allowed into evidence.

This chapter focuses on two 1925 cases in which the realities of racial prejudice and housing segregation were thrust into the courtroom by Clarence Darrow as part of a self-defense strategy. By the time Darrow defended Dr. Ossian Sweet in 1925, he had spent years forcing the American legal system to confront class and race issues, as well as advocating for religious liberty and abolition of the death penalty. Darrow's fifty-five years of legal practice included some of the most controversial cases in history. Although there are many talented lawyers in American history, and many lawyers whose cases gave them national notoriety, Darrow's reputation has been the most enduring.

The admiration and fame Darrow still enjoys are a testament to that strain of the American democratic tradition which finds compassion for the underdog and respects those who stand up for the rights of others. It is fascinating, in a society which has always condemned crime, that the most positive symbol of a lawyer is not a corporate attorney, not a prosecutor, not an attorney general, but a criminal defense lawyer. I suggest that part of the explanation for this lies in the people's abiding belief in the right of every person to defend her liberty. Even in times such as today, when law-and-order hysteria sweeps through the nation, defense lawyers can take heart from Darrow's legend and know that when they raise a black rage defense, they too are attempting to tap into that compassion, desire for equality, and respect for liberty that has always found a place in the American spirit.

Darrow was born in the little village of Kinsman, Ohio, in the year 1857. He was the fifth of eight children. His parents were people of modest means whose house was awash in books. Darrow credits those books and his insatiable desire to read for his philosophical development. He spent one year in law school, one year as a legal apprentice, and then became a self-described "country lawyer." After eight years of practice and a developing interest in politics he moved to Chicago, where he eventually became assistant corporate counsel for the mighty Chicago and North-Western Railway Company.

In 1894 an event took place that changed Darrow's life forever—the great railroad strike. Eugene Debs, a famous American radical, led the American Railway Union in a massive strike for better wages and working conditions. Darrow, influenced by his readings and moved by his compassionate nature, sympathized with the goals of working people and unions. In his autobiography, *Story of My Life,* Darrow professed a sympathy for socialism, although he had grave reservations about its compatibility with individual liberty. As the strike developed, he was shocked by the tactics of his corporate employer, who was determined to break the union. He was upset that the company was able to bring its considerable political power to bear in order to have federal troops brought into the Chicago train-yards to suppress the striking workers by force. Once he realized that the company was not interested in a peaceful settlement, he resigned as corporate counsel and became an attorney for the union.

Eventually, the strike was lost and the American Railway Union destroyed. Debs and other union leaders were put on trial for criminal conspiracy. It was a period in our history when almost all attempts at labor organizing were met by the state's legal power in the form of criminal conspiracy and criminal syndicalism indictments. Darrow, along with a former president of the American Bar Association, defended Debs. The trial ended in a hung jury, eleven to one for acquittal. A mistrial was declared and the charges were dismissed. However, Debs's problems did not end there, nor did Darrow's practical education. A federal prosecution was instituted, charging Debs with violating the court injunction against striking. No jury trial was allowed on this type of charge, and a judge found Debs guilty and sentenced him to six months in jail. Darrow visited Debs in jail and was moved politically and emotionally by this man whom he called the kindest, bravest, and most generous man he had ever known.

In 1906, now strongly aligned with the struggles of the working class, Darrow was called upon by the Western Federation of Miners to defend one of the most militant and charismatic labor leaders in the country, Big Bill Haywood. Haywood and two others were charged with the murder of a former governor of Idaho. The killing came during intense strikes in Colorado, Utah, Nevada, Montana, and Idaho. Frank Steunenberg, while governor of Idaho, had declared martial law and called in federal troops to be used against the striking mine workers, a tactic that was used throughout the country to break the union movement. Even after Steunenberg left office he remained a visible symbol of union busting. He was killed when he opened the gate to his house and a bomb attached to the hinges blew him up. A man named Harry Orchard was arrested for setting the bomb that killed Steunenberg, and Orchard claimed that Big Bill Haywood and another union leader had given him money to carry out the murder. Haywood's trial was viewed as symbolic of the government's attempts to stop union organizing throughout the country. When the jury brought in a verdict of not guilty, working people rejoiced and Darrow's reputation grew as a powerful advocate for the oppressed.

Darrow's unrelenting defense of the labor movement got him into serious trouble in 1911. He was indicted for attempting to bribe a juror in the case of the McNamara brothers, two union men who eventually admitted they had dynamited the Times Building in Los Angeles during a citywide unionizing effort. Darrow was defended by the flamboyant Earl Rogers, Horace Appel, and a young man named Jerry Geisler, who many years later gained fame representing Hollywood movie stars. When it came time for closing arguments, Rogers and Appel gave brief recitations after which Darrow rose to give what was hailed as one of finest summations ever delivered in any American courtroom. As Darrow spoke the following words observers in the courtroom wept: "I have committed one crime . . . I have stood for the weak and the poor. I have stood for the men who toil."[1] By the end of his closing, two jurors were crying. The jury was out thirty-four minutes before bringing in a verdict of not guilty.

Darrow's acquittal strengthened his reputation and fortified his resolve. He continued to defend workers, Communists, and common people charged with crimes. In 1924 he was again thrust into the national spotlight when he was hired to defend Leopold and Loeb. Richard Loeb, the eighteen-year-old son of a vice-president of Sears, Roebuck, and Company, was the youngest person ever to have graduated from the University of Michigan. His close friend, Nathan Leopold, Jr., the son of a millionaire, at nineteen was the youngest person ever to have graduated from the University of Chicago and had already passed his exam to be admitted to Harvard Law School. Loeb said he wanted to commit the "perfect crime." Together, they kidnapped a fourteen-year-old boy, Bobby Franks. The two young men killed Franks fifteen minutes after luring him into their car, and then tried to extract a ransom from the boy's father. When they were caught, they confessed, saying they had committed the crime for the thrill of it.

Darrow startled everyone when, on the opening day of trial, he had the youths plead guilty. His strategy was to try to avoid the death penalty by explaining the life of these young men to the judge, arguing that although they were not legally insane, they were "mentally diseased."

After a number of alienists (psychiatrists) testified for both sides, it was time for Darrow's summation. His oratory caused a riot in and out of the courtroom. Newspaper headlines read, "Darrow Pleads for Mercy: Mobs Riot." A subheadline was just as incendiary: "Bailiff's Arm Broken and Woman Faints as Frenzied Mob Storms Past Guards; Judge Calls for 20 Police; Fears Some Will Be Killed."

Darrow's argument was a masterful discussion of two subjects: human psychology and the illegitimacy of capital punishment. He had looked into the souls of these two sick, selfish, spoiled young men and had found some humanity. He then translated their humanity to the judge.

Darrow wove the specifics of Loeb's and Leopold's lives into a powerful indictment of capital punishment. He laid bare the vengeance, hate, and uselessness of the state's ritual hanging of people. Darrow argued and lectured for twelve hours. Although he was sixty-eight years old, his energy and passion had not been diminished by the years. A newspaper reporter described how he looked, writing that the lines in his face were "deeper, the eyes haggard. But there was no sign of physical weariness in the speech, only a spiritual weariness with the cruelties of the world."

The prosecutor summed up for two days. The judge granted life imprisonment. The press and public were divided over the sentence, some praising the judge's show of mercy, others damning him and Darrow. The boys went to Joliet penitentiary. Twelve years later Loeb, the ardent admirer of Nietzsche's superman, was killed in a prison fight. Leopold used his years behind bars to help establish an educational system for men in prison.

One year after the Leopold and Loeb case, Darrow was involved in a trial that still resonates. He defended a young high school teacher, Thomas Scopes, who had taught the theory of evolution in his class. This was in violation of the Tennessee law that made it a crime to teach "any theory that denies the story of the divine creation of man as taught in the Bible, and to teach instead that man has descended from a lower order of animals." Darrow and his opponent, the famous orator William Jennings Bryan, used the trial as a platform to debate the theory of evolution. The case became known as the "Monkey-trial" and was memorialized in the Oscar-winning movie *Inherit the Wind,* with Spencer Tracy playing Clarence Darrow. Although Scopes was convicted, he was only fined one hundred dollars, and the conviction was reversed on appeal.

One year later, Darrow was asked to defend Dr. Ossian Sweet, his wife, and nine relatives and friends. They had all been charged with murder after a few of them fired into a white mob that was attacking Dr. Sweet's home in an attempt to force him out of the neighborhood. Darrow's own history had prepared him to put racial prejudice on trial in this case. His father had been an abolitionist, and his home in Kinsman, Ohio, was a link in the Underground Railway that helped escaped slaves reach freedom in the North. When Clarence was five years old, John Brown himself visited the Darrow home to discuss the Railway with Clarence's father, Amirus. The famous abolitionist put his hand on the small boy's head and said, "The Negro has too few friends; you and I must never desert him." [2] When he grew up, Darrow joined the leading Negro civil rights organization, the National Association for the Advancement of Colored People (NAACP). He often lectured on the evils of discrimination, and he prepared a well-known lecture on John Brown which he delivered throughout the country. A few lines from it show Darrow's hatred of racial oppression and give an insight into his own philosophy:

> The war was not between men, but between two systems old as the human race—freedom and slavery. Then, as ever, officials and power and wealth were with slavery, and the dreamer and idealist with liberty. . . . The earth

needs and will always need its Browns; these poor, sensitive, prophetic souls, feeling the suffering of the world, and taking its sorrows on their burdened backs. It sorely needs the prophets who look far out into the dark, and through the long and painful vigils of the night, wait for the coming day.

William Freeman's father had been a slave in New York, but slavery had never existed in Michigan because the state had been part of the slave-free Northwest Territory. Detroit had been the last station for escaped slaves riding the Underground Railway to freedom in Windsor, Canada. Eight months before his historic raid at Harper's Ferry, Brown had gone to Detroit to meet with Frederick Douglass and a group of local abolitionists to plan a strategy to destroy slavery. But Detroit was not free of racism. In 1863, during the Civil War, white workers burned the "colored section" of town after they read newspaper reports that freed slaves would descend upon Detroit and take away their jobs. A few years later, when the first national organization of workers, the National Labor Union, established its headquarters in Detroit, it refused to allow black workers to be members.

In 1910 only six thousand blacks lived in Detroit. As heavy industry and the auto industry grew, so did the demand for labor power. The manufacturers set up employment centers around the country, particularly in the South. There, they recruited poor whites and blacks who were drawn north by higher wages and the promise of a better life. When blacks came to Detroit, they were required almost without exception to live in three districts. By 1924 there were approximately seventy thousand black people in Detroit, living in segregated, overcrowded housing.

As white laborers migrated from the South to fill the industrial labor pool, many brought with them their extreme prejudices. In 1924 the Detroit Klan was so powerful that its write-in candidate for mayor won the election with well over one hundred thousand votes. The mayor-elect was prevented from taking office, however, because seventeen thousand of his votes were disallowed. In 1925 at a Klan Convention hundreds cheered as the speaker castigated "Catholics, Jews, and niggers."

When blacks attempted to move out of the "colored sections" of town they were met by opposition, openly organized by the Klan. They were also met by whites who did not want to be part of the Ku Klux Klan but desired the same result—total and complete housing segregation. These people organized into groups with names such as "The Improvement Club" and the "Neighborhood Association." They put restrictive covenants into their real estate papers, so that no one could sell his house to a nonwhite buyer. These racial covenants were widespread in America, and they were not held illegal by the U.S. Supreme Court until its 1968 decision in *Jones v. Mayer.* The neighborhood associations did not limit their racial hostility to the use of legal documents. They also used threats and violence to intimidate liberal whites and any blacks who might consider moving out of the large, overcrowded ghettos.

Ossian Sweet was not a man who could be intimidated.[3] Sweet was born in Orlando, Florida. His father was a Methodist preacher. He had nine brothers and sisters. At twelve years old he left home and worked as a bellboy and a waiter. Later he took other jobs open to a black man, such as a janitor and a Pullman porter on the trains. With persistence and talent he worked his way through Wilberforce Academy in Ohio and then through medical school, receiving his degree from Howard University. In 1921 he opened his practice in Detroit, where he met Gladys Mitchell. Gladys's father was a professional musician, and she grew up with the small advantages of the black middle class. She was an intelligent, cultured woman who had graduated from Detroit Teachers College. Gladys and Ossian got married and a year later traveled to Paris, where Dr. Sweet worked with the world-famous Marie Curie studying the effects of radium in the treatment of cancer. The Sweets then went to Vienna, Austria, where the doctor took postgraduate courses in gynecology and pediatrics at the Eiselbury Clinic.

Returning to Michigan, the Sweets lived with Gladys's parents in the ghetto and Dr. Sweet set up a medical office. He was so well respected as a physician that occasionally white patients would cross the color line to be treated at his office. After the birth of their daughter, the Sweets felt they needed a home of their own and bought a house in a white neighborhood bordering on the ghetto.

Word spread rapidly through the area around the house at Garland and Charlevoix Streets that a "nigger" family was moving in. The residents formed an organization called the Water Works Park Improvement Association. They held a large meeting at the Howe Schoolhouse, directly across from the building into which Dr. Sweet was to move. At the meeting a representative of the Tireman Avenue Improvement Association gave a speech describing how their organization had driven a black doctor named Turner out of their neighborhood and exhorted the crowd to use force to get rid of the Sweets. The crowd responded with loud applause and cheers. When Dr. Sweet heard of the association's activity, he asked for police protection, which was reluctantly promised by city officials.

On September 8, 1925, Dr. Sweet, his wife, and his twenty-year-old brother Henry moved into the large house. Leaving their two-year-old child with Gladys Sweet's parents for safety, they brought their furniture, along with ten guns and ammunition for protection. The police stood nearby and detachedly observed the situation. Dr. Sweet had another brother, Otis, who was a dentist. Otis and seven male friends joined the Sweet family later that day. As night approached and the street became dark, a crowd of well over five hundred whites gathered at the schoolhouse and on the two streets that bordered the two-story house. The Sweets turned off all the lights, and each man took a gun and placed himself at a window. The angry crowd stayed for hours before melting away into the darkness.

Tired and tense from having stayed up most of the night, some of the men tried to nap, while others paced the house restlessly. At all times the windows were guarded by armed sentries. The streets were roped off for two blocks by the police, and eight to ten officers were posted near the house. But by evening people again filled the area, sitting on each other's porches, milling in the streets, laughing, yelling, drinking, and cursing. As the hours passed the crowd deteriorated from a "neighborhood association" into a hateful mob. At around eleven o'clock Otis Sweet and a pharmacist named William Davis arrived back at the house in a taxi. They had to run from the taxi into the house as the mob threw stones and bricks and yelled, "Get the niggers!" The crowd swarmed toward the house, throwing rocks. The police stood by. (Darrow would later describe them as "ornaments.") Two windows were shattered. Glass showered Dr. Sweet who, exhausted and demoralized, was lying on a bed upstairs. Shots rang out from the house, forcing the mob back. Immediately, the police rushed into the house and arrested everyone. As they exited the house the crowd was enraged. One white man had been killed and another seriously wounded.

Dr. Sweet, his wife, his two brothers, and seven friends were taken in handcuffs to the police station. Their request for a lawyer was denied, and they were interrogated fiercely without counsel present. Under police pressure they gave contradictory statements. Henry Sweet said he had shot at the mob.

The publicity surrounding the incident was intense. Mayor John Smith wrote a public letter in support of the police commissioner, in which he first denied that any race problem existed and then blamed the victims for exercising their legal rights:

> For almost three score years there have lived in Detroit thousands of colored persons, liked, admired and respected by the entire community. . . . These colored men and women, who were long residents of this city, decided their own problems with the realization of their legal rights, modified by their own common sense. It does not always do for any man to demand, to its fullest, the right which the law gives him.

The mayor continued his letter by chastising the Sweets and calling upon the respectable leaders of the black community to step in and stop other blacks from trying to move out of the ghettos.

> I believe that any colored person who endangers life and property, simply to gratify his personal pride, is an enemy of his race as well as an incitant of riot and murder. . . . I feel that it lies with the real leaders of the colored race in Detroit to dissipate this murderous pride. This seems to exist chiefly in a very few colored persons who are unwilling to live in sections of the city where members of their race predominate, but who are willing to rely on the natural racial pride of the rest of their people to protect them when they move into districts where their presence may be resented.[4]

This same type of rhetoric resurfaced during the civil rights movement of the sixties. When blacks and whites broke established conventions and thereby caused violent responses by racists, the demonstrators themselves were blamed. When civil rights activists held a sit-in at a downtown San Francisco hotel protesting job discrimination, the establishment reacted just as Mayor Smith had, castigating the activists as individual trouble-makers and calling on the respectable Negro community to avoid agitation. A lead editorial in the *San Francisco Examiner* expressed the typical politics of established power in face of racial protest. The editorial was written in 1964 as a reaction to a *nonviolent* sit-in of fifteen hundred young people, black and white, but its call to law and order echoes the calls of the Detroit establishment in 1925 and the rhetoric of the Right in 1997.

> San Francisco has been brushed by the sinister force of mob rule. For many hours over the weekend a shrieking horde of young men and women proclaimed contempt for the law and the courts.
>
> This was not a civil rights demonstration. It was naked lawlessness. It was irresponsibility gone rampant. It reflected instability and immaturity.
>
> The Negro community had only minuscule part in the disorders. Responsible Negro leaders appeared to be appalled. Those who ran berserk were representatives of nothing but their own thrill-seeking emotional excitability.
>
> The hope of all men aspiring to freedom is in the law and the courts. The Sheraton-Palace demonstrators turned their backs on the institutions that make men free.

The response to the San Francisco sit-in was to use the legal system to prosecute the very people who were seeking racial justice. The response to Ossian and Gladys Sweet's attempt to protect their home was to use the criminal system to prosecute everyone in their house for conspiracy to commit murder. Three days after Mayor Smith's inflammatory letter the preliminary examination began. Dr. Sweet's family lawyer was a leading black trial attorney named Julian Perry. He was a partner in a well-respected firm of black lawyers, including Cecil Rowlette. Perry and Rowlette, along with another black lawyer named Charles Mahoney, defended the Sweets and their friends. After the three-day hearing the defendants were "held to answer" for felony trial and no bail was allowed except for Gladys Sweet, who was released on a five-thousand-dollar bond three weeks later.

Perry, Rowlette, and Mahoney were capable attorneys who were ready to represent the defendants. However, the NAACP wanted to focus national publicity on the trial because violent attacks had been increasing nationwide on the few middle-class blacks who were attempting to move into all-white neighborhoods. The NAACP persuaded Dr. Sweet to allow them to contact Clarence Darrow. A meeting was arranged among two attorneys for the NAACP, the well-known black poet James Weldon Jones, a renowned white civil liberties lawyer named Arthur Garfield Hays, and Darrow. They met in Hays's home in New York, and Darrow agreed to join the defense as chief counsel. Darrow and Hays conducted almost all of the courtroom examinations. Rowlette, Perry, and Mahoney channeled their frustrations into their work, and ultimately all the attorneys meshed into an effective defense team. (It is a disturbing commentary on the subtle effects of racism on white Americans that when noted liberal author Irving Stone wrote the definitive biography of Darrow, *Clarence Darrow for the Defense,* he never mentions the African American lawyers who were cocounsel in the Sweet trials. This is another sad example of the invisibility of the contributions of black people in the history of America as written by white people.) [5]

The trial was to be held before Judge Frank Murphy. The defense team had been considering filing a motion for a change of venue, but Darrow was so impressed with Murphy's sense of justice that they decided to go ahead with the trial in Detroit. Judge Murphy later became mayor of Detroit, then governor of Michigan, and eventually had a distinguished career as a Justice of the U.S. Supreme Court.

The trial began less than two months after the incident. Tensions between the black and white communities were at a fevered pitch. Although blacks comprised almost 10 percent of Detroit's population, the jury consisted of twelve white men. Many blacks came to the courthouse but could not gain admittance. The defense team went to the judge and insisted that the black community had a right to attend the trial. After this complaint, black people were allowed in but had to sit in the back of the courtroom. As the trial progressed, more and more blacks attended until the entire large back portion of the courtroom was filled with black spectators.

Throughout the proceedings, Judge Murphy made sure the defendants received a fair trial. He allowed the defense lawyers wide latitude in their cross-examination of the police and other witnesses who denied that there had been a large crowd and that white people had started the violence. Darrow and his associates argued that a man's home is his castle and that the Sweets had acted in self-defense. Also, because all eleven people in the house had been charged, it was hard for the jury to assign criminal responsibility to each one. Indeed, at the time of the shooting, Gladys Sweet had been in the kitchen cooking a ham.

The two most effective pieces of testimony were the cross-examination of the state's witnesses and the testimony of Dr. Sweet. In cross-examination Darrow was able to get a few of the people who had been on the scene to admit that there was a large, unruly crowd. This testimony dovetailed with Dr. Sweet's description of racial violence. Sweet was properly allowed to testify to his state of mind on the night that the shots were fired. But when he began to testify to events in the distant past, prosecutor Robert Toms jumped up and objected: "Is everything this man saw as a child justification for a crime twenty-five years later?" Darrow responded:

> This is the question of the psychology of a race, of how everything known to a race affects its actions. What we learn as children we remember—it gets fastened in the mind. I would not claim that the people outside the Sweet home were bad. But they would do to Negroes something they would not do to whites. It's their race psychology. Because this defendant's actions were predicated on the psychology of his past, I ask that this testimony be admitted.

Judge Murphy accepted Darrow's argument and ruled that the recollection of incidents in the past was relevant. Dr. Sweet continued his testimony, explaining why he perceived the crowd as an imminent danger. He talked of personally seeing white mobs chasing blacks through the streets of Washington, D.C. He told of the four Johnson brothers—one a doctor like himself, one a dentist like his brother—who had been dragged from a train in Arkansas and lynched. He knew of Dr. A. C. Jackson, an eminent surgeon, who was murdered by the police when he gave himself up after trying to protect his home from a mob in Tulsa. Dr. Sweet became emotional when he described what had recently happened to Dr. Turner in Detroit. He recounted how Dr. Turner and his wife had bought a house on Spokane Avenue and moved in under police guard. But a mob of whites broke in, smashing everything in the house and stoning the couple as they ran from their home. When Ossian Sweet was asked about his state of mind as he viewed the people surrounding his house the night of September 8, he answered:

> When I opened the door and saw the mob I realized I was facing the same mob that had hounded my people through its entire history. In my mind I was pretty confident of what I was up against. I had my back against the wall. I was filled with a peculiar fear, the fear of one who knows the history of my race. I knew what mobs had done to my people before.

At the end of seven weeks the case went to the jury. The jury deliberated for three days. It was reported that the yelling in the jury room could be heard through the hallways, and that furniture in the jury room had been smashed during arguments among the twelve men. They were unable to come to a unanimous verdict, so Judge Murphy declared a mistrial and discharged the jurors. The judge then accepted the defendants' motion for bail. At last, the ten black men were temporarily free to return to their homes and jobs. Dr. Sweet was finally out of jail but could not return to his new house because of death threats. The police maintained guard over the house and were able to put out a fire that was set to destroy the Sweet's home.

The defense filed a motion arguing that in future trials each defendant should be tried separately. This motion was granted, and the prosecution chose Henry Sweet, the twenty-year-old younger brother, to be the first one tried. Darrow defended him, joined this time by one of Michigan's finest trial attorneys, Thomas Chawke, and also by Julian Perry, who had done excellent work in the first case. The proceedings began five months after the initial trial. Henry's trial was held in Detroit's Recorder's Court, with Judge Murphy presiding. It took a full week to impanel a jury. One hundred sixty-five prospective jurors were called; only one was black, and he was dismissed. Once again, Henry Sweet's fate would be decided not by his peers but by twelve white men.

The prosecution's case was the same as in the first trial, with an additional emphasis on Henry's actions. The Wayne County prosecuting attorney argued that a small group of neighbors had come to Dr. Sweet's residence out of curiosity, and that these neighbors did not initiate the violence. He entered into evidence Henry Sweet's "confession" that he had shot at the crowd. He called Henry a "coward" who had killed Leon Breiner by shooting him in the back as Breiner sat in a chair on his porch smoking his pipe. In his closing argument, the prosecutor took the same tack as the prosecutors in the William Freeman and Steven Robinson trials, arguing that there was no race question involved—it was just a typical murder case. When Darrow rose to give his summation, he immediately attacked this notion of colorblindness.

> My friend Mr. Moll says . . . race and color have nothing to do with this
> case. This is a murder case. We don't want any prejudice; we don't want the

other side to have any. Race and color have nothing to do with this case. This is a case of murder.

I insist that there is nothing but prejudice in this case; that if it was reversed and eleven white men had shot and killed a black while protecting their home and their lives against a mob of blacks, nobody would have dreamed of having them indicted. I know what I am talking about, and so do you. They would have been given medals instead.

Darrow had the luxury of having no time limit on his closing argument. The custom was to allow lawyers wide latitude in their closings. The oral tradition was more respected then than it is today. Television, remote controls, movies, and videos have created a population that finds it difficult to sit through an hour speech, much less an attorney's seven-hour lecture on history, philosophy, and the fate of mankind.

Darrow was a superb speaker, able to move people with his words. He spoke to the white jurors in ways they had never before heard. These men were unaware of the black experience; to them, colored people were objects. They were considered inferior, not worthy of serious attention. Their emotional rage was invisible to white eyes. Therefore, Darrow knew that when he talked of black history, he would find receptive, curious ears. He also felt, as he always did, that he could challenge jurors to rise above their class and race prejudices and to understand the shared human condition.

Part of Darrow's argument sounds as though he jumped ahead sixty years and read Charles Lawrence's treatise on unconscious racism, as he explains how it is that the jurors themselves could hold prejudices of which they were not aware.

The black and the white both will live together and play together, but as soon as the baby is born we begin giving him ideas. We begin planting seeds in his mind. We begin telling him he must do this and he must not do that. We tell him about race and social equality and the thousands of things that men talk about until he grows up. It has been trained into us, and you, gentlemen, bring that feeling into the jury box. . . . Was Mr. Moll right when he said that color has nothing to do with the case? There is nothing else in this case but the feeling of prejudice which has been carefully *nourished* by the white man until he doesn't know that he has it himself.

Darrow repeatedly returned to his theme of society's racism and the jurors' racial prejudice. He told the jurors that he believed they could look deep into their hearts and recognize their own prejudices. He spoke to their empathy, saying that "there is no difference between the love of a black man for his offspring and the love of a white." He believed, and urged the jury to believe, that human experience allows us to "find each other and understand each other." Having warned them to guard against their prejudice and to find common ground with persons of another race, he specifically told them he was confident that they could see past their prejudices and do justice.

The defense team's strategy was to give meaning to the word "justice" by helping the jury see that a black family had the constitutional right to defend its home against any onslaught:

> It has been the law of every English-speaking country so long as we have had law. Every man's home is his castle, which even the king may not enter. Every man has a right to kill, to defend himself or his family, or other, either in the defense of the home or in the defense of themselves. . . . There isn't a man in Detroit who doesn't know that the defendant did his duty, and that this case is an attempt to send him and his companions to prison because they defended their constitutional rights.

After Darrow discussed the themes of racial prejudice and the constitutional right to protect one's home, he explained the rule of self-defense: "A man has the right to shoot in self-defense, and in defense of his home; not when these vital things are in danger, but when he thinks they are." Darrow correctly raised the issue of Henry Sweet's state of mind. What facts had Henry known? What emotions had he felt that led him to reasonably and honestly believe that he and his family were in imminent danger? In answer to these questions, Darrow asked the jurors to put themselves in the Sweet house on that fatal night: "Put yourselves in their place. Make yourselves colored for a little while. It won't hurt, you can wash it off. They can't, but you can; just make yourself black for a little while; long enough, gentleman, to judge them."

Darrow then argued that Henry was well aware of the history of his race. Darrow talked movingly of that history, calling it a "story that would melt hearts of stone." He talked of slavery, of lynching, of murders, and of riots against blacks in Washington, St. Louis, Chicago, and Detroit. Many of these examples had been elicited through Dr. Sweet's testimony. But other examples, particularly the historical events that brought Africans to America by force and caused them to suffer as slaves, had not been a subject of actual testimony. Darrow was allowed to refer to these instances of racial oppression even though the defense had not presented expert witnesses to testify to these facts. The law allows a lawyer in closing argument to refer to facts of common knowledge. This rule used to be given a broad interpretation. Today, judges have constricted the rule in their ongoing quest to shorten the length of trials and to keep political, economic, and social conditions out of the courtroom. Darrow faced no such restrictions.

The prosecution argued that Henry had not shot in self-defense because he had pulled the trigger too quickly; that it was unreasonable to believe there had been an imminent danger. To counter this argument, Darrow tried to place the jurors in the mind of Henry Sweet. During the trial, the defense had humanized Henry Sweet by bringing in the president of the college in Ohio that Henry attended in order to testify to his good character. They also had his teachers and a Methodist bishop testify to his ability and moral character. Having personalized the young black man to the white jurors, Darrow stressed the loving relationship between Dr. Sweet and his younger brother.

> Dr. Sweet was his elder brother. He had helped Henry through school. He loved him. He had taken him into his home. Henry had lived with him and his wife; he had fondled his baby. The doctor had promised Henry money to go through school. The doctor had bought a home. He feared danger. He moved in with his wife and he asked this boy to go with him. And this boy went to help defend his brother and his brother's wife and his child and his home. Do you think more of him or less of him for that? I never saw twelve men in my life—and I have looked at a good many faces of a good many juries—I never saw twelve men in my life, that if you could get them to understand a human case, were not true and right. Should this boy have gone along and helped his brother? Or should he have stayed away? What would you have done?

The issues of racial prejudice and the defense of one's home against mob violence created a stage for Darrow. Darrow stepped onto that historical stage and addressed the social issues.

> There are bigger issues in this case than [whether the fatal bullet came from Henry Sweet's gun]. The right to defend your home, the right to defend your person, is as sacred a right as any human being could fight for, and as sacred a cause as any jury could sustain.
>
> The issue not only involves the defendants in this case, but it involves every man who wants to live, every man who wants freedom to work and to breathe; it is an issue worth fighting for, and worth dying for, it is an issue worth the attention of this jury, who have a chance that is given to few juries to pass upon a real case that will mean something in the history of a race.

Ossian Sweet and his family did not fit the stereotype of violent, lower-class colored people. One a doctor, one a dentist, young Henry a year away from completing college—Darrow described them as intellectually and morally superior to the white neighbors who mobbed their house. Prosecutor Toms was also aware of this fact. He later confided that he considered the colored people involved to be "far superior" to the white witnesses, "intellectually, in appearance, in culture and in sympathy-eliciting quality."

One might wonder how Darrow would have defended an unemployed, uneducated black man who had killed a white man. (Indeed, some of Darrow's rhetoric foreshadowed the movie *Guess Who's Coming to Dinner,* in which Hollywood thought it was courageously tackling the issue of racial intermarriage. Of course, in the movie, the black man who was to marry the white woman was a highly educated doctor, played by the handsome, charming, erudite Sidney Poitier. Who wouldn't want Sidney as an in-law? By choosing a "super-negro," Hollywood ducked the harder issue of white society's failure to accept African Americans *as they are,* with their failings as well as their strengths. Afraid of offending white viewers, the producers would not allow Poitier and his white fiancée to kiss.) Yet Darrow did not fall into the trap of describing Dr. Sweet and Henry as better than the thousands of uneducated, unskilled black laborers. But he was cognizant of Dr. Sweet's professional standing and referred to it often. It was as if he was posing a question to the jury: Who wouldn't be proud to live next door to Dr. Ossian Sweet, a man who fought his way out of poverty, who had worked alongside Marie Curie, who spent time educating himself in Europe, who had achieved the dream of becoming a doctor, and asked only that he and his family be allowed to live peacefully at the corner of Garland and Charlevoix?

Darrow had stood in front of the jurors all day long. He had lectured them about race, he had challenged their prejudices, and in his final comments he asked them to speak out for justice.

> Gentlemen, what do you think is your duty in this case? I have watched day after day, these black, tense faces that have crowded this court. These black faces that now are looking to you twelve whites, feeling that the hopes and fears of a race are in your keeping.
>
> This case is about to end, gentlemen. To them, it is life. Not one of their color sits on this jury. Their fate is in the hands of twelve whites. Their eyes are fixed on you, their hearts go out to you, and their hopes hang on your verdict. This is all, I ask you, on behalf of this defendant, on behalf of these helpless ones who turn to you, and more that that—on behalf of this great state, and this great city which must face this problem, and face it fairly—I ask you, in the name of progress and of the human race, to return a verdict of Not Guilty in this case!

Judge Murphy instructed the jury that if the accused honestly believed that he and his family were in actual and imminent danger under the circumstances at the time, he was acting in self-defense. Therefore, he instructed them,

> You are to consider what were the circumstances which confronted the accused at the time; their situation, race and color, the actions and attitude of those who were outside the Sweet home. All have a bearing on whether or not the sum total of the surrounding circumstances as they appeared to them at the time were such as to induce in a reasonable man the honest belief of danger.

The jury deliberated less than a day and brought in a verdict of not guilty. The Michigan state's attorney dismissed all charges against the other ten defendants. A year later, the two prosecutors told Darrow that they believed justice had been done in the courtroom. But outside the courtroom justice was not so easily recognized. Within a year after the second trial, both Gladys Sweet and her two-year-old daughter died of tuberculosis. Julian Perry and his family bought a house in South Marlborough, near Grosse Pointe Park, but the house was attacked by white neighbors and they had to flee.

Both prosecutors became judges. Charles Mahoney became a commissioner of labor in Michigan and in 1954 was a delegate to the United Nations. Henry Sweet returned to college and graduated. The two trials had a profound impact on him; he went back to college and became a lawyer.

Ossian Sweet paid dearly for his courage. After a while he was able to move back into the house on Garland Street, where he lived for twenty years. But without his wife and child he retreated into himself. We do not know whether he blamed himself for the jailing and prosecution of his wife, brothers, and friends. We do not know what the lasting impact was of having seen the hate-filled eyes of his neighbors and having heard the screams of "nigger" and the sounds of shattering glass. But we do know that at the age of sixty-four Dr. Ossian Sweet went to his office one day and put a bullet into his brain.

Darrow's lifework consisted of forcing the criminal law system to acknowledge the influence of class and race. He consistently forced judges and juries to consider the effects of environment on criminal behavior. He put the government and its institutions on trial. In the Sweet trials he and his cocounsels attacked the façade of racial harmony erected by the mayor and city officials. They helped an all-white jury understand that black and white people share the same feelings of love of family and longing for a better life. They integrated the reality of race relations with the rules of law. That is the essense of the black rage defense. Their efforts resulted in a legal victory for the Sweets and the education of thousands of people in Detroit and throughout our country.

We black folk, our history and our present being, are a mirror of all the manifold experiences of America. What we want, what we represent, what we endure is what America is. If we black folk perish, America will perish.
—Richard Wright, *Twelve Million Black Voices*

Chapter 9

A Survey of Black Rage Cases

It is difficult to survey black rage cases because most of them have not been reported in the news or in legal literature. As the modern version of this defense was being shaped in the 1970s, the political perspective of the establishment press resulted in little interest in cases that did not involve famous lawyers or sensational events. The pre-Watergate media was not interested in young lawyers exposing societal racism in criminal trials. Even in today's atmosphere, unless the case is considered "newsworthy" little is reported other than the facts of the crime and the ultimate disposition.

The legal process itself serves to hide the frequency of black rage defenses. An overwhelming percentage of all cases are disposed of without trial through the process of plea bargaining between district attorney and defense counsel. It is during this critical stage that social framework evidence can be presented to persuade the prosecutor to reduce charges or recommend a reduced sentence. But these negotiations take place in private and their contents remain unknown to both the legal community and the general public.

If a black rage defense is successful at trial, the prosecution is forbidden from appealing by the double-jeopardy protection of the Constitution. And since there is no appellate opinion, the defense will rarely find its way into the legal research computer banks.

Since most black rage cases go unnoticed by the public and the legal community, it is incumbent on lawyers handling such cases to link up with groups of people attempting to change the legal culture. Legal organizations such as the National Conference of Black Lawyers, the National Lawyers Guild, and California Attorneys for Criminal Justice have promoted creative legal strategies through seminars and literature. In this manner the black rage defense is continuing to make inroads into the traditional legal system.

Fortunately, there are black rage cases for which the closing arguments, partial transcripts, and record of the surrounding circumstances are available. Analyzing a few of these cases will help us flesh out this defense, expose its strengths and weaknesses, and show its potential use for other races and ethnic groups.

Black rage defenses are state-of-mind defenses. They are not only applicable in self-defense and insanity cases, but also may be used to negate the specific mental state required for a first-degree murder or attempted murder charge. In a riot situation where a defendant injures someone and is charged with attempted murder, a traditional defense is to argue that the defendant did not have the "specific intent to kill." In these situations attorneys have presented evidence of racial tension leading up to the riot in order to show that their clients were caught up in the violence, and that although they attacked people they did not intend to kill anyone. Therefore, they argue, the defendants may be guilty of assault but not attempted murder. The epitome of this type of case took place during the 1992 riot that rocked Los Angeles after the Rodney King verdicts. It involved the prosecution of a young African American man named Damian Williams for smashing a brick into the head of white truck driver Reginald Denny, an incident videotaped by a local news helicopter and shown on television in every city in America. The South-Central Los Angeles riots were black rage in action. Williams was consumed by that anger and his defense team took on the task of making that rage understandable to a jury.

The fires of 1992 find their kindling in the economic hopelessness and political resignation that is daily reality for residents in South-Central. They were fueled by institutional racism and continual acts of police misconduct. In 1990 alone, the City of Los Angeles paid victims of police abuse over a million dollars. Those who did not believe the police were capable of systematic unconstitutional behavior were shocked on March 3, 1991, to see a videotape of policemen repeatedly clubbing and kicking Rodney King. Two weeks later, a fifteen-year-old African American girl, Latasha Harlins, was shot to death by a middle-aged Korean American woman grocer, Soon Ja Du, after a dispute in a South Los Angeles grocery store. In November 1991 Soon Ja Du, convicted of manslaughter, was given probation, community service, and a five thousand dollar fine. California State Senator Diane Watson responded to the extremely lenient sentence by saying, "This might be the time bomb that explodes." Two weeks later, Los Angeles police officers fatally shot a twenty-eight-year-old black man, Henry Peco, causing a standoff with more than a hundred residents of the Imperial Court housing project in Watts. Two months later, the trial of the four policemen charged with assaulting King began, after the case was moved from Los Angeles to the primarily white, conservative venue of Simi Valley.

On April 29, 1992, a jury devoid of African Americans returned a verdict of not guilty on all charges except one count of excessive force against officer Lawrence Powell. The verdict was announced on live television. More than two thousand people gathered for a peaceful rally at the First African Methodist Episcopal Church in South-Central. But other residents took to the streets. There was a small confrontation between police and angry people at the intersection of Florence and Normandie in South-Central. The police left and a mob furious at the not guilty verdicts poured into the area. White, Asian, and Latino motorists were pulled from their cars and beaten. Reginald Denny was driving his large truck through the intersection. Bricks were thrown into his windows. As he came to a stop he was pulled from the truck and beaten. A television helicopter videotaped the scene. Twenty-nine-year-old Henry Watson was seen with his foot on Denny's neck as he lay on the ground. Nineteen-year-old Damian

Williams was videotaped as he smashed a brick against Denny's head and strutted away in celebration. Denny managed to crawl back into his truck, where sympathetic blacks climbed into the cab of the vehicle to help him. One person held him in her arms while another man drove the truck to a hospital, saving Denny's life.

The riots swept through Los Angeles and nearby areas. Fifty-eight people were reported killed. There were more than two thousand injuries, more than seven thousand fires, $3 billion worth of damage, and 12,111 arrests. Though at least as many Latinos as blacks were arrested, the events were perceived nationally as a black riot. Many, if not most, of the participants were burning and looting out of economic envy and class rage, but there is no question that the injustice of the not guilty verdicts was the catalyst.

Williams and Watson were charged with the beatings of Denny and seven other motorists. Included in the charges were attempted murder and aggravated mayhem, both of which carry life imprisonment. A defense committee called "Free the LA Four" was formed for them and two other defendants. Williams was fortunate to obtain the services of an outstanding lawyer, Edi M. O. Faal. Faal was born in Gambia, West Africa, and trained at Middle Temple Inn of Court in London, where he became a barrister. A dignified-looking man in his late thirties, he was highly regarded among his peers for both his legal ability and his political acumen. His primary strategy was to show that any criminal acts Williams committed were a result of the unthinking emotion generated by the riot.

In early 1993 the four police officers who beat King were tried in federal court for violating his civil rights. Two were acquitted, but Officer Powell and Sergeant Stacey Koon were convicted. Facing a maximum of ten years and a $250,000 fine, they each received a thirty-month sentence. Two weeks later, Williams and Watson went to trial in front of a racially mixed jury consisting of four blacks, four Latinos, three whites, and one Asian.

Faal, with the aid of Wilma Shanks and David Lynn, attempted a two-pronged strategy that can be described as "he didn't do it, but if he did, he didn't do what the prosecutor is charging him with." Once in a while, a jury will accept this defense when they recognize that the defendant has committed a crime, but that the district attorney is guilty of overcharging. In Williams's case, Faal argued that Williams was mistakenly identified as the perpetrator. However, even if the jury believed that his client was the perpetrator, he argued that they should still find him not guilty of the two most serious crimes because he did not specifically intend to kill or permanently disfigure Denny.

Faal delivered a six-hour closing argument over two days. He had to go over all the evidence regarding each of the people Williams had been charged with assaulting. The *Los Angeles Times* described his closing as one that combined "sarcasm, eloquence, indignation and wit." After putting forth the weak defense of mistaken identification, Faal began a persuasive discussion of the riot and how the collective frenzy of the group was responsible for his client's acts. His legal point was quite clear: in order to convict Williams of attempted murder and aggravated mayhem, the jury had to find premeditation and specific intent. Faal had presented as an expert witness a local sociologist named Armando Morales. Morales testified to the phenomenon of mob psychology, in which individuals are caught up in the "mass hysteria and mass convulsions" of the crowd. People act without reflection, without rationally considering what they are doing; they act impulsively, unpredictably. Faal tied Morales's testimony to the riot and put it all in the social context of a community's frustrated and indignant reaction to the not guilty verdicts of the four police officers.

> We know that on April 29th, 1992, many people in many communities; Black, White, Hispanic, experienced tremendous disappointment from the verdicts that came down from Simi Valley. I'm talking about the acquittal of the police officers that were accused of beating Rodney King.
>
> People near Florence and Normandie congregated to grieve together or to express their disappointments together. The police came, there was a slight confrontation, the police left. A mob developed. The mob, true to its name which is a mob, got into a frenzy. People started acting in manners that they would not act otherwise and that whole situation became the 1992 riots, the L.A. Riots.
>
> People caught up in that frenzy were acting out their frustration, their anger, their disappointment. They were so consumed with emotions that they could not have rationally been entertaining the type of reflective thought which gives rise to specific intent to kill or to disfigure.

The defense was in the favorable situation of being able to contrast the injustice of the Simi Valley verdicts on assault charges against the police with the more serious charges of attempted murder and mayhem against their clients. Earl Broady, counsel for codefendant Watson, specifically told the jury that the defendants were in court because four L.A. policemen had been found not guilty of beating Rodney King. This was strongly contested by prosecutor Janet Moore:

> I say Mr. Faal and Mr. Broady are dead wrong. We are in court because of what these two men chose to do on April 29, 1992. They have no one else to blame but themselves.
>
> They are here because they acted in a violent and unconscionable way. They are not here because we are holding them responsible for the entire Los Angeles riot.

Faal was sophisticated in his concluding words. Instead of referring specifically to the Simi Valley verdict he talked about "justice," and he urged the racially mixed jury to rely on their personal experiences in coming to a fair result. His underlying theme was that the riot was caused by an injustice, and that by their verdict they could balance the scales of justice.

> Ladies and gentlemen, before I conclude the closing argument that I am giving on behalf Mr. Damian Monroe Williams I have to remind you of a few things; number one, that justice does not exist in a vacuum. It's not a concept that you say justice and just put it in isolation.
>
> Justice exists in the real world. The court has given you the law to evaluate and the law to apply, and you are to evaluate the facts of this case. And in evaluating the facts and coming to your determination as to what facts have been proven and what facts have not been proven, you are not relying on the law alone, you are relying on your common sense. You are relying on your personal experiences and you are relying on your sense of fairness and justice in evaluating the facts of this case.

At the end of Faal's closing argument, supporters in the courtroom stood and applauded, some even wept. As Faal left the courtroom, he was embraced. People appreciated that throughout the long trial he had consciously articulated the frustration and rage of the African American community.

The jury deliberated for more than two weeks. They acquitted Williams of attempted murder and aggravated mayhem, the two charges that carried life imprisonment. They also acquitted him of all the other felonies except one—simple mayhem. He was also convicted of four misdemeanor assaults. Williams was sentenced to eight years in prison. As of 1995, he was in Pelican Bay—California's notorious high-tech, maximum security prison where conditions are so bad that a federal judge held that it had violated the cruel and unusual punishment prohibitions of the Constitution.

Reginald Denny seemed to understand the social context of the crimes against him. He said, "Things could have been a lot worse. I mean the next step for me would have been death. But I've been given a chance, and so I'm gonna extend that courtesy towards some guys who obviously were a little bit confused." [1]

One woman, Cynthia Henry, who lived near the now infamous intersection, spoke for many people when she said, "I'm happy with the verdicts. I know that what they did was wrong, but it was in the heat of passion. I was watching what happened [in the King trial] on TV, and it hurt me to see that. But I could understand because I was angry too." [2]

In Williams's trial racial and class politics surrounded the facts and informed the defense's strategy. In many potential black rage cases, the relevance of race is not so immediately apparent. Two cases, a 1977 bank robbery and a 1988 murder, offer examples of lawyers attempting to uncover the racial issues in their cases. The different types of crimes involved in the two cases and the contrasting tactics of the lawyers provide insight into the use of black rage defenses. The first case is the *United States v. Robert Witherspoon*.[3] Witherspoon was a thirty-seven-year-old African American who had no criminal record. In fact, less than two years before his arrest he had received a commendation from the police department for preventing an armed robbery. In April 1977, an unshaven and disheveled Witherspoon walked into Gibraltar Savings and Loan in San Francisco. He went up to the branch manager, pulled out a gray .22 caliber derringer, and said, "I want thirty or forty thousand dollars." As they went to the bank vault, Witherspoon surprised the security guard and disarmed him. The manager gave Witherspoon two metal cans from the vault. Without looking inside the cans, Witherspoon exited out the side door and got into a white-and-red Lincoln. The manager easily got the license plate and phoned the FBI. Witherspoon drove aimlessly around San Francisco for an hour, until his car was stopped and ten armed federal agents arrested him. The two metal cans contained nine dollars.

Witherspoon hired attorney Doron Weinberg. After gaining his client's trust, Weinberg probed deeper into the reasons for this strange robbery. Robert Witherspoon's life unfolded in those interviews. He was the oldest of seven children of two hard-working parents who held out the American dream to their children. His father had worked his way up to director of the post office in San Francisco's largest African American neighborhood. His mother also worked at the post office until suffering a nervous breakdown. There was pressure on Robert to be a doctor, but he chose to become a businessman. He opened a record store, and by working sixteen to eighteen hours a day he was able to open a second store. He created jobs for two of his brothers and two of his cousins. His record stores financed two liquor stores and a gift shop. He was a model businessman in his community and a source of immense pride for his family. Then, in 1975, his main store burned down. For reasons Robert interpreted as racist, he had been underinsured. The insurance company only offered him sixteen thousand dollars for more than one hundred thousand dollars worth of inventory. Even after they settled on an amount, the company delayed payments. Banks would not loan him money for reasons that raised suspicions of racially discriminatory redlining. Unable to obtain adequate financing, his entire economic structure began to collapse. He developed a drinking problem and had to be hospitalized for a nervous condition. Still, he bounced back and maintained operation of the liquor store. By undercutting other stores he was able to rebuild the business. But the Alcoholic Beverage Control agency revoked his license under the Fair Trade Liquor Law, which required minimum prices—even though most white-owned liquor stores engaging in the same practices seemed to be having no problems with the government. Ironically, the Fair Trade Liquor Law was ruled unconstitutional soon after Robert robbed the Savings and Loan, too late to resuscitate his business.

As Weinberg listened to Robert's history and saw his sincere feelings of shame, dishonor, and depression, he recognized that the essence of the case was sympathetic. But how could he best put that story into a legal framework? Weinberg was aware of the black rage defense and saw its applicability to Witherspoon's case. He took a simple, direct approach, similar to the strategy in the Robinson bank robbery trial. He did not use any sociologist or political scientist to make a case for racism's impact, relying instead on the authenticity of the story told by the defendant and his lay witnesses. He called only one expert to the stand, psychologist Daniel Goldstine, who diagnosed Robert as acting out of a transient situational disturbance. Goldstine, an intelligent, experienced psychologist, could communicate psychiatric theory in understandable terms, and his unpretentious manner was well received by the jury.

Weinberg's theory of the case was that Witherspoon was not a criminal, so there had to be another explanation for why he had committed a criminal act. The answer was that he had broken under stress, exacerbated by positive racial expectations in a negative racial reality. The bank robbery was Witherspoon's unconscious plea for help.

Weinberg began his summation by explaining the philosophy behind the law of insanity and relating it to his client. He then moved on to the facts and began to weave in the racial issues. One does not have to give a jury a lengthy lecture about racism. Witherspoon's trial, like most criminal trials, took less than a week. Closing argument was therefore appropriately short, forty-five minutes to an hour. During that time Weinberg spent only five or ten minutes on race. He reiterated the testimony showing that Witherspoon had suffered from discriminatory treatment. And he tied the resulting financial failures to their devastating effect on Witherspoon's psyche and pride, after his attempts as a black man to take part in the American dream.

> By the end of 1976, and by the beginning of 1977, he had nothing. He was a disappointment to his family, a failure. And it was a humiliation of the kind that makes it difficult for him. I mean, it is difficult for him to present all of this to you, you are strangers. But it is unbearable for him to present it to his family, so much so he couldn't even bear to have them in court with him.
>
> That kind of humiliation is what you have to understand is the underlying basis; plus, plus this second aspect. And that is not just that he was a striving businessman, not just that he was a successful businessman for whom there is this collapse; but that he is a Black man. And I think that single fact is very important.
>
> Dr. Goldstine was very sensitive when he talked about it. Dr. Cook ignored it completely.

A good lawyer is not afraid of taking risks. When you present an imaginative strategy like the black rage defense, you should not be afraid of trying tactics upon which the established bar might frown. Weinberg was willing to try something out of the ordinary. He decided to speak directly to the women on the jury in an attempt to bridge the gulf between race and gender.

> Of course, not all of you on the jury are black. But some of you, particularly the women among you who have chosen professions, I think will understand particularly. Although I think all of you will understand, what it means for someone from an essentially disadvantaged group, from a group that is not expected to be successful, from a group for which it is difficult in the extreme to be successful, to step out there, try to do it, to do it, to succeed, to be a big person, to be self-sufficient and self-reliant and to be recognized as that, and to then have that collapse, to then have that collapse in part precisely because you are a black person.

Weinberg finished his argument by returning to his opening theme. He moved closer to the jury box, made eye contact with the jurors, and was able to express his belief in his client's innocence.

> This man is intelligent and capable. He is not a psychopath. He has no anti-social personality traits. He is not your common criminal.
>
> What do you think he was doing there? What do you think he was doing there? Do you think he pulled off a purposeful bank robbery? Do you think he would have done it that way if it was purposeful? Of course not.
>
> But you must conclude—whether you conclude that or not—you have got to conclude that the government has absolutely failed in making its proof beyond a reasonable doubt that he was sane. Absolutely failed without question, and therefore you have to acquit Robert.
>
> You have to give him a chance to continue to put his life back together again.
>
> Thank you.

Presiding over the trial was Chief Judge Robert Peckham, a liberal man with a kind heart. Peckham was moved by Witherspoon's plight and treated both the defendant and Dr. Goldstine with respect when they testified. When the judge instructed the jury, he repeatedly emphasized that the prosecution had the burden of proving guilt beyond a reasonable doubt. In retrospect, Weinberg felt that the judge's favorable attitude helped influence the jurors toward an acquittal. Indeed, the jury found Robert Witherspoon not guilty.

The Witherspoon case highlights a problem defendants now face in federal court. Since the federal rule of insanity has been changed to the M'Naghten right-wrong test, it is much harder to win a psychiatric defense. In Witherspoon's case, the psychologist had specifically testified that the defendant did know the difference between right and wrong but because of the transient situational disturbance (TSD) could not control his behavior. Similarly, Steven Robinson, despite suffering from a TSD, knew the difference between right and wrong. Therefore, even though the judges and juries in both cases believed that these defendants were not criminals, that they suffered racial discrimination and deserved a second chance, under the present federal law they would not have been allowed to present this defense. Today, many men and women who deserve that second chance are precluded by an archaic and restrictive law foisted on the courts by a politically opportunistic Congress.

The Witherspoon trial received no media attention. In contrast, the Lonnie Gilchrist, Jr., trial in 1989 was on the front page of the *Boston Globe* and was described in the *American Bar Journal* as a "black rage" defense. It was also the basis for an episode on the popular television show *Law and Order* that negatively portrayed the black rage defense. Gilchrist's case differed significantly from Witherspoon's, and those differences spotlight the varied tactics used under the rubric of black rage.[4]

Lonnie Gilchrist, Jr., a forty-one-year-old African American, was employed as a stockbroker at Merrill Lynch in Boston. The day after he was fired by his boss, a white man named George Cook, he returned to work seeming normal and rational. After completing a large bond transaction, talking to another stockbroker about suing Merrill Lynch, and taking care of personal business, he entered Cook's office and shot him five times. Cook, bleeding from his wounds, managed to run out of the office, where in full view of many employees Gilchrist pistol-whipped him in the head and continued kicking him as he lay on the ground. Steven Lively, an African American coemployee and former football star, tackled Gilchrist and restrained him in a bear hug.[5] Cook died on the way to the hospital. Gilchrist was arrested. Nine hours after the shooting, while in police custody, he told a psychiatrist that Cook "was trying to destroy me, to suffocate me. He had his foot on my neck. I had to get him off. He was trying to suck my blood; Mr. Cook was screwing me for the last time. I wanted to hurt him. . . . He took away my manhood."

Gilchrist was defended by Norman Zalkind, an experienced criminal lawyer who had done volunteer civil rights work with the Lawyers Constitutional Defense Committee in Mississippi in 1964, and in the ensuing years had built a well-respected law firm in Boston. In the Gilchrist case, his cocounsels were Robert Johnson, Jr., and Harvard law professor Charles Ogletree, who had a distinguished career as a public defender, private practitioner, and law professor.

The defense was insanity under Massachussetts law, which was the same as the federal rule during the Witherspoon case. The defense's diagnosis was that Gilchrist was suffering from a long-term paranoid personality disorder and committed the homicide during a brief reactive psychosis. As jury selection began the defense persuaded Judge John Irwin, Jr., to question each juror carefully and individually as to race prejudice. During the voir dire one prospective juror finally admitted that there had been talk at his job among the white employees that since the defendant was black, "he would get away with it." The juror said that he could not overcome his own racial prejudice and was excused. Ultimately, a jury of nine whites and three blacks was seated. Of the twelve jurors, nine were women.

As in all well-prepared insanity cases, the childhood and life history of the defendant was presented. Lonnie Gilchrist, Jr., grew up in the projects in the South End section of Boston. He was the oldest of seven, all of whom succeeded educationally. Zalkind described them as a "proud family, a family that's going to get themselves out of the disadvantages of poverty, of the projects."

Gilchrist's father was an alcoholic who beat his wife and the children. When Gilchrist was a teenager he took a baseball bat and, with the help of his brother, stopped his father from beating their mother. But the years had left scars and created a feeling of powerlessness that haunted him his whole life. Nevertheless, he did have numerous successes while growing up. He had a high IQ and was a good student and athlete at Brighton High School, where he had friends of all races. He graduated from the University of Massachusetts and earned a postgraduate degree from the prestigious Wharton School of Business. But for all his intelligence and education, he did not succeed in his career. After losing several jobs, he moved back into his little room at his mother's house in the projects. According to his friends and family and the psychiatrists who evaluated him, he was preoccupied with racism and blamed it for his work failures.

After he was hired at Merrill Lynch his pattern of failure continued, leading to his firing and to his homicidal detonation.

Gilchrist, like Witherspoon, had no criminal history. His lawyer, like Witherspoon's, told the jury that since Gilchrist was not a criminal, not an antisocial person, there had to be another explanation for his crime. The reason was mental illness. But unlike the Witherspoon, Robinson, and Johnson cases, the lawyers chose not to put the defendant on the stand. There are many cases in which it is better not to have the defendant testify. However, in an insanity defense this traditional tactical choice usually results in the trial becoming, as one law professor commented, "a debate among psychiatric witnesses." In Gilchrist's trial, the majority of the nine days of testimony was taken up by the defense's psychiatric experts. Altogether, five medical experts gave their opinions on Gilchrist's state of mind—three for the defense, two for the prosecution. The consequences of this tactic are visible in the closing arguments. The prosecutor, Ronald Moynihan, relentlessly attacked the entire concept of relying on experts.

> And you as jurors have the right to consider the expert opinions, if you want to, or to not consider their opinions at all. You may decide individually and collectively whether or not you want to use their opinions to assist you in your analysis. Judge Irwin will instruct you at the end that you don't even have to do that at all. You can try this case and deliberate this case on the evidence—the evidence, the facts, and what the lay witnesses tell you; because you don't have to be a psychiatrist, with all of the fancy degrees, to determine whether or not a person is psychotic.

The defense usually wants to be in the position of telling the jurors to use their common sense and rely on their experiences. But here it was the prosecutor who was able to use such an argument effectively and also to play to the jurors' sense of their own importance.

> You don't need all the degrees from Harvard and all the wonderful establishments that have been referred to here. . . . The psychiatrists aren't any smarter than you, and they don't have any more common sense that you. And they don't have any more common life experiences than you do, individually and collectively.
>
> And that's why each and every one of you were hand-picked for this case.

> You went through a very lengthy jury process. People were eliminated; you
> people were chosen, because of your common sense and because of your
> backgrounds; and because you're qualified and you're capable to be jurors
> in this case, based upon your own native intelligences.

In one of the best prosecution closing arguments I've ever read, Moynihan was able to poke hole after hole in the psychiatric testimony. Because
the defense relied on that testimony as the heart of its case, it was badly
damaged.

The defense also was weakened because it contained a serious contradiction. Racism was supposed to have been a contributing cause of the
homicide, but Gilchrist was not shown to have been a victim of racial
discrimination. He had gone to the best schools and had achieved a privileged economic position. His lawyer told the jury numerous times that
Gilchrist's failures were not caused by racial discrimination, but rather by
his own weaknesses. Defense counsel explained that his client's mental
illness caused him to blame white people for his own shortcomings.

> This is a very intelligent man. And he's starting to have problems; and
> he's blaming it on racism. He's obsessed with this racism. . . . Twenty
> years—the same conversation in the street—the target, the Man. You heard
> Steve Gilchrist talk about it. The Man. The Man. The Man. He's having
> problems at the Shawmut Bank; and he blames it on the Man.
> But, he's ill, ladies and gentlemen; and his illness is getting worse.

Zalkind discussed an incident at a company called Digital in which
Gilchrist stood up in a meeting and challenged people to fight him because
he felt he was being treated unfairly. But once again there was no proven
race prejudice. "Somebody with a paranoid illness, they can't see themselves. . . . Everything is racism. He claims everything at Digital is racism.
There was no evidence of racism at Digital."

When Zalkind discussed the shooting of Cook, he frankly admitted that
Cook was not a racist and that Gilchrist was "obsessing" about racism
because he was a "sick human being, who has serious problems."

Outside the courtroom, lawyers and commentators discussed the case
as if racism were the major theme, although inside the courtroom it was
not. In media interviews, two well-respected psychiatrists, Price Cobbs
and Alvin Poussaint, attempted to put the case in a broader perspective.

They pointed out that living in a racist society forces African Americans to question the motives behind the actions of all white people. Such constant cautiousness and pragmatic mistrust leads some people to develop a true mental illness marked by paranoia. This is a profound insight into the consequences of generalized racism, but this point was not made in the defense's closing argument. There was no attempt to show how living in racist America had caused Gilchrist to become obsessed with racism and ultimately to explode at what he perceived as an attack on his black manhood. Instead, his attorney seemed to argue the opposite to the jury—that Gilchrist's focus on race was not a result of his environment, but merely a product of his individual psyche: "He starts to dwell on blackness. Now we have some black jurors sitting before us. We have white jurors. And obviously there's prejudice in life. Nobody can deny that. But this wasn't the beginnings of prejudice. This was the beginnings of his paranoid illness."

The problem with this defense is that it feeds into the stereotypes held by many white people that blacks charge racism whenever they fail. It also resonates with many black people who are critical of other blacks who cry racism just as the boy in the children's story cried wolf. They feel that when the real wolf comes, when it is a case of real racism, no one will believe them because of people like Gilchrist.

After closing arguments the judge instructed the jurors that if they found that Gilchrist was not insane but was sufficiently mentally impaired, they could return a verdict of second-degree murder or manslaughter.

The jurors deliberated for five days and then told the court they were deadlocked. The judge sent them back to deliberate with an instruction that strongly encouraged them to come to a verdict. Four hours later they returned with a verdict of guilty of first-degree murder. Two of the white jurors wept as the verdict was read. An African American juror told the *Boston Globe* that she had no sympathy for Gilchrist "because he committed a crime. . . . I myself have felt angry about being discriminated against, but I don't take it that far." Her comment belies the mistaken perception, strengthened by the verdict in the O.J. Simpson criminal trial, that all African American jurors will acquit black defendants because of their race. Gilchrist was sentenced to life imprisonment without parole.

Gilchrist's trial demonstrates the difference between a black rage case and a black rage *defense.* There are thousands of cases in which African

Americans commit crimes because of blind rage resulting, in part, from attempting to cope with a racist environment. But very few of them result in a black rage defense—a strategy rooted in the concrete racism suffered by the particular defendant. To succeed, a black rage defense must show a persuasive link between racial injustice and the criminal act. The defense team in Gilchrist's case must have determined that the link was missing. Therefore, they raised a conventional insanity defense. Given the facts of Gilchrist's case, one cannot fault their choice. But we should recognize that notwithstanding some of the media's description, the trial was not an example of a black rage defense. It was, as Zalkind clearly articulated in his closing argument, a case of a man whose mental illness took the form of racial paranoia. James Johnson also suffered from paranoia with strong racial aspects, but his experiences on a Mississippi plantation and in a Detroit auto plant provided the link between racial oppression and his mental illness. Therefore, his lawyers were able to present a successful defense. As the Gilchrist defense team understood, racial anger, by itself, is not a basis for a black rage defense.

Anger plays such an important role in black rage cases that the lawyers must be sensitive to how the client's feelings impact on the trial. A defendant is sometimes experiencing so much hostility that he or she will not open up to a lawyer unless the lawyer first reaches out. Often, unresolved anger bursts loose in the courtroom in ways that hurt the defendant. An instructive example of how a lawyer handling a black rage or black rage–type defense should communicate with the client can be found in the two trials of Inez García. Although García was not African American, we should remember that the black rage defense is both a specific defense for black men and women and a generic defense in which social reality is thrust into the courtroom.

Inez García's case began in 1974, the same year that Joan Little had become a national symbol of women fighting back against sexual violence and racial oppression. Little, a twenty-year-old African American, was acquitted of killing a white jailer who had sexually assaulted her in the Beaufort County Jail in North Carolina.[6] The same year Little was defending herself, García was sexually assaulted in an alley in Soledad, California. The twenty-nine-year-old woman was dragged out of her apartment by two men. While one man weighing three hundred pounds hemmed her into a closed space the other raped her. Several minutes later the two men phoned her apartment and told her that if she resisted next time, they would "do worse to her." Scared for her life, she took her .22 caliber rifle and left the house. Half an hour later she came across her two assailants. She saw a knife in the hand of one of them, Jiménez, and immediately shot and killed him. The police did not believe she had been raped, and at trial the district attorney argued that the killing was in retribution for the previous beating of a friend of hers. García's lawyer persuaded her to use a psychiatric defense instead of self-defense. García had shot Jiménez from approximately fifteen feet away and had shot him six times, facts that made a self-defense argument difficult. García, who had a history of some emotional problems, accepted the mental defense with her attorney's firm commitment to make the rape central to the case. However, the judge did everything possible to keep the issue of rape out of the trial. During opening statements, when defense counsel began to discuss the police's reluctance to investigate rape charges, the judge interrupted.

> **Judge:** "Counsel, I cannot permit this. We are trying a woman for murder. There is no man on trial for rape, and the attitude of the police for rape and murder has nothing to do with the guilt or innocence of this woman."
> **García:** "But, your honor, that is the reason I killed this man."
> **Judge:** "We are not trying a cause, we are trying a woman, Mrs. García, and I am not going to make this courtroom a forum for a cause."

As the trial proceeded, García became more and more infuriated at the judge's rulings and comments. When the judge refused to allow the defense doctor to testify about the emotional trauma of rape because she had not conducted any "experiments" on rape, García exploded, leaping up from her seat and rushing towards the judge's bench. "Why don't you just find me guilty?" she yelled. "I killed the fucking guy because he raped me! That's why I did it." As the bailiff pulled her out of the courtroom the jury could hear her shouting, "Keep your hands off me, you pig!"

García's attorney admitted he was as stunned as the jurors by the outburst. This was because he failed to understand the incredible anger García still felt about being raped. Furthermore, he was portraying her as a demure, shy, innocent woman. His own clouded lens kept him from seeing the strong, volcanic woman sitting next to him in the defendant's chair.

Later in the trial, García's rage again erupted. She was enduring a brutal cross-examination with no objection from her lawyer.

Q: "Why didn't you tell the police about the rape?"

A: "Because you just don't—I was ashamed to talk about it, that's all."

Q: "Besides your face, were you hit anywhere else?"

A: "I don't know. I was too nervous, and I was scared. All I knew is that I didn't want to get killed."

Q: "After you say Luis ripped your blouse, you then said you just took your clothes off yourself?"

A: "Yes, I did. I gave in. I took them off."

Q: "What was the first thing you took off, do you remember? Were you wearing a brassiere?"

A: "No, I don't wear a brassiere."

Q: "Did you take your panties off, too?"

A: "Yes, I did."

Q: "Then what happen after that?"

A: "You want me to tell you what happened after that?"

Q: "Yes."

A: "He fucked me! What else do you want me to tell you?"

Q: "What was Miguel doing while Luis, you say, was having sexual intercourse with you?"

A: "He was watching me having sex with this creep, and he was enjoying watching the other creep have sex with me!"

Q: "What did you do after you called your family?"

A: "I took my gun, I loaded it, and went out after them. If I would have had to walk to Jiménez Camp I would have. Another thing I want to say, I am not sorry that I did it. The only thing I am sorry about is that I missed Luis."

Why had her experienced lawyer not objected to the demeaning cross-examination? I spoke to him that evening and learned that he felt the examination was so ugly that it was swaying the jurors to García's side. He was ready for her to begin crying, which he thought would have cemented the sympathy of the jury. But his stereotypical views of women had kept him from understanding Inez García's rage, and her shame and humiliation had left her unable to share those feelings with him.

After her statements in court, there was no chance for an acquittal. The jury of seven women and five men convicted García of second-degree murder.

Inez García spent two years in prison before her conviction was reversed on appeal because of an improper jury instruction on how to measure reasonable doubt. In her retrial she was represented by radical feminist attorney Susan B. Jordan with the help of Ann Jennings and Linda Castro. Jordan was one of the first women criminal lawyers to come out of the feminist movement of the sixties. When she practiced with the People's Law Office, a leftist legal collective in Chicago, she was one of the only young women lawyers in the tough criminal courts, and she endured sexual harassment and unwanted advances from judges, other lawyers, and even the bailiffs. By the time she took García's case her ordeal had produced a lawyer with a fearless spirit and extraordinary technical skills. She was representing a woman who had never let herself cry about the rape, who had spent two years in prison, and who had unresolved anger about what she had suffered. These factors made García a difficult client who would threaten to fire her attorneys and then ask them to come back. Jordan hung in through the displaced fury. When García didn't want to take the stand because of the humiliation of her first experience, Jordan patiently explained the need for her to testify and promised to protect her dignity.

García's case had become a cause célèbre. A play based on the transcripts of the first trial had been produced, a defense committee was active, and García had spoken on behalf of rape victims. At the retrial, Jordan was able to do extensive voir dire regarding rape. After the trial, she wrote, "We addressed the prevailing myth that rape victims 'ask for it' head on. Despite García's sexy appearance, no woman should be subjected to sex against her will, and once raped, a victim is still entitled to respect, at the police station and in the courtroom."[7] Jordan was also able to educate the jurors that rape is a crime of violence, not of sex. The prevailing view in the public's mind was that rape was a sex crime. In fact, California statutes did not even categorize rape as a "violent crime."

In the first trial, the tactic was to hide García's anger for fear that it would reinforce the prosecution's theory of a premeditated murder. The result was that the unresolved anger broke loose in detrimental ways. In the retrial, García's anger was put forth as a reasonable and normal reaction to her rape. Because her legal team had a better appreciation of her rage, García was able to cope with the trial pressures and was a persuasive witness on the stand. The strategy of *self-defense* made sense to the jurors who understood García's reasonable fear as she was confronted by the two men who had raped her and had threatened her with more harm. The jury of ten men and two women found her not guilty.

Rage, whether it is felt on the streets of America's ghettos or the thirty-sixth floor of America's financial centers, will not go away. Fury resulting from discriminatory business practices, or from being sexually assaulted, remains a volatile part of our society. When people's wrath lands them in criminal court, it is the responsibility of the good advocate to understand both the social and the personal dimensions of such anger. Only then can the counselor gain the client's trust. Only then can the lawyer develop a strategy that exposes racism or sexism, protects the defendant's dignity, and creates an opportunity to win.

When I hear shooting my job is to get my two-year-old sister and hide in the bathtub.

—A six-year-old girl in urban America

Chapter 10

Urban War Zones

Doris first became a mother at fifteen, and then again at sixteen. She delivered her third child, Felicia, into the world at eighteen, in Milwaukee, Wisconsin.[1] For the first years of her life Felicia Morgan lived with Doris and her father. Her parents had a volatile relationship and often would bring guns to the dinner table to protect themselves from each other. They beat Felicia with leather belts, extension cords, and switches. Her father left for Mississippi when Felicia was seven, and she went to live with her grandparents. At eleven she returned to her mother's home, where the violence continued. One night her mother put a knife to Felicia's throat and threatened to kill her. Felicia escaped to the basement, where she broke the light with her hand so her mother could not see her. Recalling the event years later, she said, "I cut my hand and peed on myself. I didn't want her to kill me." In spite of this, Felicia, like so many abused children, remained loyal to her mother. She said, "My mama ain't no bad person. Whatever happened to me, I still love my mama."

Later that year her mother's boyfriend sexually abused Felicia. When her mother found out, she grabbed her gun and, in front of Felicia, shot at the boyfriend as he ran out of the house.

At fourteen Felicia moved back in with her grandmother. Her home life was more peaceful, but the streets had become more violent. She was jumped by a group of girls in an attempted robbery and beaten with a bat; her ribs were broken and she suffered internal bleeding. She was so scared afterwards that she became afraid to walk in the neighborhood. She began to drink and smoke marijuana heavily.

The same year, the landlord's son entered her home and sexually attacked her. She threw hot grease at him, but he overpowered her, tied her hands to the bed, stuffed a sock in her mouth, and raped her. Soon afterwards, Felicia swallowed some pills from the medicine chest in a failed suicide attempt. She began to hear voices telling her to kill herself. Although the content of the messages would change, she continued to experience auditory and even visual hallucinations.

A year later, her aunt Joyce's boyfriend pulled a gun on her aunt. Felicia stepped into the path of the gun, seemingly oblivious to the danger, and the incident was defused. A few months later, Felicia's cousin Shanna was shot during a street fight and lost the use of her arm. Felicia continued to suffer harassment and violence. At fifteen a group of young men grabbed her, stole her rings at gunpoint, punched her in the eye, and threw her in a large dumpster. Remembering this incident Felicia said, "Sometimes I wish I was dead. I wish I wasn't born so this never would have happened to me."

Felicia described her years dealing with the streets of Milwaukee. "I had too much shit happened to me my whole life. Every motherfucker punkin' me out, jumping me. I got tired of running home every day, tired of running from people jumping on me, somebody trying to fight me, trying to make me kiss a tree, kiss their feet."

In September 1990, sixteen-year-old Felicia lost her favorite uncle, who was just nineteen when he was shot to death. She saw him being taken from the scene in a body bag. Felicia said that she had conversations with her uncle after he died and that he would visit her and they would hug. Two days after her uncle's funeral, her cousin Anthony was killed in a drive-by shooting.

In December, Felicia was robbed of her coat at gunpoint by a group of teenagers. A few weeks later, her sister's boyfriend Tomas was shot. Tomas had been like a father figure, urging her to go back to school after she had dropped out in the ninth grade and counseling her about life in general. He was permanently paralyzed from the shooting. Felicia had dreams that he could walk again. As bad as 1990 had been, the next year would be even worse.

In September 1991, Felicia obtained a clerical job through a youth training program. One evening after buying some clothes, she was approached by a group of girls at the bus stop who attempted to steal her new shoes. Although she fought them off, they got away with her shopping bag of clothes and some of her money. She was so distraught that it took her hours to be able to give a coherent description of the assault. A month later, she was present when a gang shot at some of her friends. Felicia tried to hide, covering her eyes and ears.

On October 18, a man who was visiting her mother's home pulled a gun on her mother. Felicia, as she had done before, stepped in front of the gun. Her mother remembered that Felicia was "hysterical" and seemed "out of touch with reality."

On October 12, Felicia was at a "dope house" with an acquaintance named Dixon. He pulled out a revolver and fired at some bottles, terrifying Felicia.

On October 24, Felicia's boyfriend R.C. gave her a gun to hold for him. The next night, she and a fifteen-year-old friend named Monique were hanging out when R.C. came over and became angry with Felicia, slapping her repeatedly in the face. Then another young man threatened to slap her. Felicia became agitated and furious. She defied him as she said, "I'm gonna stand up for myself. I done run too many fuckin' times in my life. I run and got my ass kicked. I don't care if you are six feet tall, I ain't running from you."

The two boys left, and then Dixon said he would take the girls to a party. Felicia kept saying she wanted to go home, but they pressured her and she eventually went along. It turned out to be a night that Felicia would dream about over and over, and a night that would bring anguish and sorrow to the family of Brenda Adams.

As the three young people were driving along, Dixon saw some girls, one of whom was wearing a gold necklace. Stopping the car, he gave Monique a small caliber gun, told her to get the necklace, and ordered Felicia to watch Monique's back. When Felicia did not get out of the car, he said,

"I thought you were her friend." She then got out of the car. Soon Monique and Felicia came running back with a pair of shoes, saying that three guys who had been nearby had jumped the girls and stolen the necklace.

Less than ten minutes later, they saw three more girls and a boy walking down the street. By now it was after midnight and no one else was around. Felicia and Monique got out of the car and, pointing the gun, stole a necklace, a baseball hat, and the boy's jacket.

A few minutes later, they arrived at the scene of the party. Felicia saw a girl named Brenda Adams outside and said, "I want that trench," pointing to Brenda's leather coat. Dixon handed Felicia a gun and said, "Let Monique do what she got to do and don't let no niggers get into it." There are differing versions of what next took place, but it seems that Felicia and Monique fought with Adams and pulled her coat off. Someone across the street from where the three girls were fighting fired a number of shots from a .38 caliber gun. In the midst of this chaos, Felicia shot Brenda at close range and killed her.

The next day, Felicia surrendered to the police. She told them she heard shots being fired. When she opened her eyes, her arm was pointed at Brenda Adams shoulder area. She grabbed Brenda's necklace, but when she saw the blood she dropped it and ran into the car.

Although Felicia was seventeen she was processed into adult court, where she was charged with five armed robberies, one attempted robbery, and first-degree homicide. She was lucky to have an experienced lawyer named Robin Shellow appointed to represent her. Born in Milwaukee, the thirty-four-year-old Shellow majored in English and psychology at Sarah Lawrence College and obtained a master's degree with honors from Cambridge University. Her thesis, on "Tragedy," would prove prophetic for her defense of Felicia.

Shellow's practice was primarily devoted to representing juveniles charged with crimes. She spent 70 percent of her time defending young people against homicide charges in juvenile and adult court. With her background in psychology and her knowledge of post-traumatic stress disorder (PTSD), it was natural that Shellow would raise an insanity defense in Felicia Morgan's case.

In Wisconsin, such a trial is divided into two phases. In phase one, the guilt or innocence of the defendant is argued. In phase two, the issue of insanity is decided. Shellow argued that Felicia was suffering from a mental illness, which negated the intent necessary for first-degree murder. However, the trial judge refused to allow such a defense in the first phase, a decision that was subsequently upheld by the Court of Appeals, over a vigorous dissent.[2]

In phase two, Shellow produced three psychologists to support her defense. First was Charles Ewing, author of *When Children Kill: The Dynamics of Juvenile Homicide.* In his report he described Felicia as "a short, light-skinned Black girl who looks her stated age but relates in a rather immature and childish fashion, more in keeping with a younger 13 or 14 than an 18 year old. Her hair was braided and she was neat and clean in her appearance." Ewing testified that Felicia thought Brenda Adams was the same girl who had robbed her a month earlier at the bus stop. She heard a voice in her head telling her to "get her back, she helped take something from you, so take something back." (Despite clear evidence that Brenda was not the girl who had robbed her, Felicia adamantly clung to the belief that she was the same girl.)

Felicia said that when she heard the gunshots from across the street, she began to sway back and forth and felt like she was going to pass out. Her eyes became heavy, and she felt like she was in a trance. She did not remember shooting anyone. But she understood that witnesses had said she killed Brenda, and she had accepted it as true. While she lay in her jail cell she had dreams that Brenda was still alive, that they were friends, and that they talked "girl-talk together at school."

Ewing concluded that Felicia was suffering from "chronic symptoms of post-traumatic stress disorder secondary to a lifetime of physical, psychological, and sexual abuse" and suffered a "brief reactive psychosis triggered by the violence surrounding her that night." In Wisconsin, the legal test of insanity is whether the defendant (1) had a mental disease at the time of the crime; and (2) as a result of that disease lacked the substantial capacity either to appreciate the wrongfulness of her conduct or to conform her conduct to the law. Ewing concluded that she fit the definition of legal insanity on the night of October 26, 1991.

Also testifying for the defense was Dewey Cornell, a clinical and forensic psychologist. He agreed with Ewing's diagnosis and added that Felicia also had a borderline personality disorder. Cornell concluded that Felicia's abnormal mental condition did impair her ability to control her behavior, but he felt that there was not enough information to conclude "unequivocally" that she lacked a "substantial" capacity.

Shellow attempted to call James Garbarino to the stand. Garbarino is an internationally recognized expert in post-traumatic stress. He has won numerous awards, has published extensively, and had gone to Kuwait and Iraq at the request of UNICEF to study the effects of the war on children. He had recently published a book entitled *No Place to Be a Child: Growing Up in a War Zone.* The judge, from the start of the trial, had been hostile to the environmentally based psychiatric defense. Consequently, he called a hearing out of the presence of the jury to determine whether he would allow Garbarino to testify. At the hearing, Garbarino explained how people in a war zone focus solely on survival, and that this can negate their capacity to make moral decisions about right and wrong.

PTSD was first associated with single horrible events such as a train or plane crash, but it is now understood that the trauma can result from chronic and cumulative exposure to stress, such as spending a protracted period of time in a war zone.[3] Garbarino likened Felicia's life history to living in a combat situation. He then made the critical point that most people experiencing severe trauma have the support of others, which allows them to recover. But someone like Felicia had neither a societal nor a family support structure, and therefore did not have the resilience and coping mechanisms necessary for recovery.

Judge Michael Guolee became antagonistic during this testimony. Garbarino commented on the judge's hostile tone, and eventually the judge made a mild apology for raising his voice at him. The judge stated that to allow a defense based on environmental hardships would open the "floodgates" and "thousands of children, thousands of defendants would come to court saying that they have this Post-Traumatic Stress Disorder and therefore we should have a different standard for them in regards to their responsibility." He ruled that Garbarino's testimony was "irrelevant" and, because two other psychologists had testified to PTSD, also "cumulative." He refused to allow Garbarino to testify in front of the jury—a ruling that eventually would be criticized by the Court of Appeals, which specifically stated that the testimony was relevant. Appellate Judge Schudson wrote in the opinion that "the grotesque reality is that rapacious, murderous violence to children in their houses and on their streets causes Post-Traumatic Stress Disorder that, in turn, can cause trance-like traumatic flashbacks comparable to those experienced by Vietnam veterans." He concluded that Garbarino's "scholarship exposes the devastation of children throughout the world, pierces the conscience of those who are able to shed denial, and motivates all who will listen, learn, and fight for the protection of children." However, the Court of Appeals, as appellate courts so often do, upheld the verdict anyway, ruling that the failure to allow Garbarino to testify was "harmless error."[4]

Felicia wanted to take the stand on her own behalf. She did, and her testimony was both helpful and harmful. The young woman was emotionally out of control, and therefore she said things that weakened the case. She often sounded like an angry, streetwise child. On the other hand, Shellow was correct in understanding that the jurors and the judge had to have the opportunity to see Felicia as a human being. At the end of her testimony, it was clear that she was a confused young girl and not the monster depicted by the prosecution.

Under Wisconsin law, the prosecution has two advantages in an insanity trial. First, the defense, not the state, has the burden of proving insanity to a "reasonable certainty." Second, a verdict need not be unanimous—a decision of 10–2 is sufficient. In Felicia's case, these advantages resulted in a verdict of guilty, by a vote of 10–2.

Felicia's sentencing is an example of how a black rage defense based on environmental hardship can have a positive impact on the participants. Because such a defense exposes the societal factors that contribute to the criminal act, the stereotype of the defendant as a selfish, heartless, useless person is undermined. As the defendant's life is examined, the judge, the jury, even the victims are able to understand what drove the defendant to the brink of despair and pushed her over the precipice into destruction. In Felicia's case, the combination of parental abuse and the daily consequences of living in a neighborhood virtually written off by the government had an impact on everyone involved. At the sentencing hearing, Brenda Adams's sister and father made statements. Their words were filled with anger and pain, but also with compassion. Brenda's sister Yolanda expressed the view of many people when she said that poverty is not an excuse for crime.

To prepare myself for this occasion last night I stayed awake watching tapes of the proceedings and clips from the news, and for the first time I saw my sister taken out in a body bag. And I asked God why. Poverty is not an excuse to maim, mangle or murder anybody. I don't care who you are, what you come from or how your life was. I didn't have a good time growing up, either, and my environment was far from being nurturing sometimes. But I chose a different route. Felicia, I've had a hard, hard time trying to come to grips with this. Hating you will not bring my sister back. You receiving life will not bring my sister back, but the only restitution is for you to be rehabilitated, reformed.

Due to the nature of the defense, Brenda's sister was able to see and to say that there were two victims—her sister and Felicia. And understanding Felicia's life, she was able to forgive her and to ask the judge not to impose a life sentence.

After Brenda's sister finished, her father addressed the court:

I don't forgive and forget. I am a very hateful person. But I will forgive you. . . .

I want to see if she can do something for herself. If she can get a college education in 10 or 15 years, I want the Court to set aside the first-degree intentional homicide sentence and give her a second chance at life.

The district attorney did not accept the environmental defense, legally or philosophically. She described the crime as the result of "peer-related antisocial behavior." Characterizing the crimes as a shopping spree, she urged the court to sentence Felicia to life with a parole eligibility date of forty years, *and* an additional twenty years to run consecutively, for a total of sixty years.

Robin Shellow took the podium. Her presentation was a lesson in lawyering, as she tied the sympathetic factors of the case into a concise presentation of the law that allows a judge to mitigate the sentence. After analyzing the sentencing guidelines, Shellow reached out and addressed the pain in the courtroom.

I ask you to take into consideration the fact that we are not here weighing pain today. There is enough pain in this courtroom to last a thousand lifetimes. There is the pain so eloquently articulated by Brenda Adams's family. There is the pain that has been talked about that Felicia has undergone, and this isn't about weighing pain. If we were weighing pain, we would have to have scales that were far bigger than this room.

Shellow asked the court for the minimum sentence, which would allow a parole date after thirteen years, and then concluded her effective presentation:

> I hope that this Court realizes that my client was the victim of things that no one should have to be a victim of.
>
> We have had many philosophical disagreements. We put those all aside, and I come to this Court asking for the same thing that every single defense lawyer in the building asks for—compassion and mercy, sense of justice. I ask that this Court follow the recommendation of the family that has been most aggrieved, Brenda Adams's family, who has shown this Court so much dignity.

Before the judge pronounced sentence, Felicia Morgan was given the right of elocution—the right to speak before being sentenced. She said only a few words and chose to direct them to Brenda Adams's father.

> I will finish my education, and I want you to know that a day ain't going to go by that I don't think about the situation I am in or that your daughter is gone. If I could change back the hands of time I would take her place, but I can't. I know I will never take the place of your daughter.

Judge Guolee had spent many days considering the case and its philosophical implications. He had taken his duty seriously and knew that he held the life of a young girl, almost a child, in his hands. After giving a lengthy and informed dissertation on the history of punishment, he expressed his concern that the defense of environmental hardship "deflected" responsibility away from the defendant.

The judge's statement goes to the core of the criticism of the black rage defense. In a murder case, this gut feeling that the defendant is not accepting responsibility for the awful crime is often the reason jurors will convict, even though, as in Felicia's case, they become sympathetic to the defendant.

Though the judge had expressed his disagreement with the defense, it seems to have influenced his understanding of Felicia. Along with the lay psychiatric testimony, it served to offset the "hardened criminal" portrayal by the prosecution. Obviously moved by the plea of Brenda Adams's family, the judge rejected the state's recommendation and fashioned a life sentence that would allow early parole after thirteen years.

A significant benefit of a black rage defense is that it allows the defendant a perspective from which she can look at the factors that shaped her and then commit to changing the direction of her life. Since she has been in prison, Felicia has completed four years of high school and is changing the "negativity into positivity." Another benefit of the environmental hardship defense is that it can result in an understanding and bonding between the defendant and the lawyer. Every Saturday, like clockwork, Felicia telephones her lawyer and friend Robin Shellow.

Shellow continues to represent young people. In 1996 Wisconsin passed a law providing that in first-degree homicide cases there would be mandatory adult court jurisdiction for any defendant ten years of age or older. This shortsighted, counterproductive law will result in Shellow representing more children in adult courts. During Felicia's sentencing, Shellow told the court, "on behalf of Felicia Morgan I hope that I have fought a long and hard battle." She certainly did. Shellow represents the best in American defense lawyers—those who merge aggressive advocacy with creativity and compassion.[5]

George Williams, the father of the girl who was killed, has embraced life and redemption instead of death and hate. He recently testified against the death penalty at Wisconsin legislative hearings.

As lawyers struggle with the consequences of urban war zones, they look for legal strategies to defend their clients. Psychological defenses, although very difficult to win, are at the top of the list. In an enlightening and practice-oriented article entitled "Not Guilty by Reason of Victimization," Susan Rutberg encourages lawyers to use environmental background as part of their defense strategy.

> As criminal defense lawyers we are privy to our clients' psycho-socio histories in a way that others in the system are not. We have a responsibility to educate judges and juries about the relationship of traumatic events to the formation of specific intent, and to the significance of PTSD as a factor in mitigation at sentencing.[6]

Rutberg correctly states that PTSD is used almost exclusively in homicide cases. Rutberg, who was an outstanding public defender, challenges lawyers to use the PTSD defense when representing first-time offenders in crimes other than murder, before "a client's mental state has degenerated to the point where they face the most serious crime."

In addition to PTSD, Rutberg discusses other mental-state defenses. It is important to recognize that not all, perhaps not even most, criminal acts that grow out of the rage, despair, and violence of urban America fit within the definition of PTSD. This psychological classification first developed out of union advocacy on behalf of railroad workers traumatized by train wrecks. It gained legal acceptance in the form of the Vietnam Vet Syndrome.[7] Lawyers saw the analogy between combat conditions in Vietnam and conditions in high-violence areas in America and began to use the PTSD analysis developed in the Vietnam Vet Syndrome cases to defend nonveterans.

Clinical and forensic psychologist Daniel Goldstine of the Berkeley Therapy Institute cautions against lawyers' hastily assuming that a client's act is a consequence of PTSD. He agrees that there are many different psychological disorders resulting from the poverty, chronic joblessness, and daily gunfire found in America's ghettos. But he argues that there has not been enough research and analysis into the nature of the mental illness created by these awful conditions. He suggests that a syndrome other than PTSD may more accurately explain the behavior of young people who have to hide under beds and in bathtubs to avoid gunshots.

A San Francisco rapper named Charley Hurbert expresses the life our urban youth face in the last years of the twentieth century:

> We're all broken bits
> Piece it together, some will never fit
> Living on the Jagged Edge
> You start to resemble it[8]

The boys and girls, young men and women who cannot fit, who become the jagged edge, need our help.

I'm gonna go kill me a Chinaman.
—Unemployed white man,
California 1995

Chapter 11

White Rage—Hate Crimes

One of the primary criticisms of the black rage defense is that it opens the door to a white rage defense. In his book *The Abuse Excuse,* Alan Dershowitz presents this critique: "If the black rage defense were to succeed, we would see white skinheads invoking 'white rage' in defense of white-against-black racist killings. Rage is simply not a valid excuse for violence against members of a different race." Many skinheads and racist whites have been prosecuted for violence against blacks, Asians, and other racial or religious minorities. I am not aware of any of them arguing that they should be acquitted because of their hatred of other races or religions. However, there is a famous case in which white rage was a determining factor and which allows us to explore the viability of a white rage defense.

The case took place in Hawaii in 1932 and involved U.S. Navy lieutenant Thomas Massie, who was accused of murdering Joseph Kahahawai. Ironically, Massie was defended by Clarence Darrow, who was criticized by Hawaiians as taking the side of racial prejudice. Darrow had retired two years after the Sweet trials. After four years of relative inactivity, however, he felt the urge to take another trial. He was also worried about his family's financial future because the Great Depression had wiped out his savings.

When he was asked to defend Massie he reluctantly agreed, and he and his wife set off for Honolulu.

Lieutenant Thomas Massie was born and raised in Kentucky. At the time of this case he was twenty-seven years old and lived in Honolulu with his twenty-two-year-old wife, Thalia Fortescue. Thalia came from a socially prominent family in Washington, D.C. The Fortescues were proud their daughter had married a graduate of the Naval Academy at Annapolis. Thomas was in the submarine service and after his marriage was sent to the large naval base at Pearl Harbor. He and Thalia had lived in Honolulu for two years before the fateful events that brought the seventy-five-year-old Darrow to Hawaii.

Those events began one evening when the lieutenant and his wife attended a party at the Ala Wai Inn. After a public quarrel with her husband, Thalia left the inn around midnight and began walking home. She walked past an area where Navy men rented bungalows, which they used for consorting with prostitutes. Thalia later testified in court that four or five Oriental men grabbed her and threw her into their car. She said she was taken to Ala Moana Drive, where she was raped and her jaw was broken. She was found walking on the road by motorists, who drove her home. She was then taken to a hospital for an examination and treatment. Five Asian men were arrested, four of whom she identified.

The trial took place in a racial cauldron. The Asian community raised money for the defense of the Hawaiian, Chinese, and Japanese defendants. Hundreds of people lined up to be admitted to the court proceedings. The jury was unable to reach a verdict, a mistrial was declared, and the men were released on bail.

The hung jury was split mainly along racial lines, as was the public. Hawaiians and the diverse Asian community felt that the four young men, called the "Ala Moana defendants," were innocent. The *haole* (white) community was certain the men were guilty. Police had to disperse crowds of sailors and soldiers who roamed angrily through Honolulu. Just a week after the mistrial one of the defendants, Shomatsu Ida, was kidnapped by several carloads of whites while standing on the street near his home. He was whipped across his face and shoulders and left on the beach semiconscious. He managed to get to a police substation, where official photographs were taken showing the welts on his body. Meanwhile, there were insistent rumors that Thalia Massie had been unfaithful and that, in fact, her husband had broken her jaw the night of the alleged rape. These rumors made their way into the newspapers and contributed to the boiling racial conflict.

In 1932, Hawaii was controlled by the "Big Five," five companies, owned by white people, that dominated the economy. American Factors, Alexander and Baldwin, Castle and Cook, C. Brewer and Company, and T. H. Davies and Company owned the sugar plantations, the sugar refineries, and the shipping lines and controlled all the major stores and banks. The U.S. Navy was another powerful and conservative force. The Navy was very stratified, with all white officers, a great many of them from the southern states. The Navy's ideology was the military equivalent of Manifest Destiny—its policymakers believed in the white domination of Asia. Pearl Harbor, the largest naval base outside the United States, was the focal point for naval operations in the Pacific.

Hawaii gave the appearance of a melting pot, but the social and economic order was dominated by whites. The society was very stratified, with a white upper class, referred to as the "elite *haoles*," at the top. Housing on the islands was segregated. Racial discrimination was a way of life for the Big Five and the United States Navy. Social mores replicated those on the mainland. Although white men were free to sleep with Hawaiian, Filipino, Chinese, and Japanese women, it was impermissible for white women to have sexual relations with any person of color. The strong presence of southern naval officers fortified the notions of white superiority and the so-called protection of white womanhood from the "colored natives."

Lieutenant Massie, a southerner by birth and conditioning, could not stand the innuendos and rumors that he had broken Thalia's jaw when she returned that night because he had not believed her story of rape. Massie, his mother-in-law (who had flown to the island), and two other sailors kidnapped one of the defendants, a Hawaiian named Joseph Kahahawai. Kahahawai was well known on the island, having been a professional boxer. They took him to Mrs. Fortescue's cottage and threatened to beat him. Massie called him a "black son of a bitch." Finally, Kahahawai is alleged to have said, "Yeah, we done it." Lieutenant Massie would later testify that when he heard those words his mind went blank and he shot Kahahawai, killing him.

In fact, Massie did not kill Kahahawai. Many years later, Deacon Jones, one of the sailors accused of the murder, admitted to writer Peter Van Slingerland that he was the one who had shot Kahahawai:

Q. What was Kahahawai's response?

A. He was scared. He was scared almost white. Let's put it this way: supposing you and me are sitting here and we got a nigger sitting right there and I got a gun. He's going to be scared, isn't he? Unless he's a God damn fool, and this guy was no fool.

Q. Now, you had no personal reason for animosity toward Kahahawai?

A. Well, I don't hate anybody. Hate is another expression of fear and I didn't fear this black bastard, although I had no use for him. To me, it was a challenge.

Q. You say Massie was questioning him. Then what happened?

A. Massie asked him a question and Kahahawai lunged at him. I say, "lunged." Somebody else might say he just leaned forward.

Q. And then?

A. I shot him.

Q. *You* shot him?

A. You're God damn right I did. I shot him right underneath the left nipple and to the side. When the slug hit him he just went over backwards on the chaise longue. The bullet didn't go through him. It stayed in his body. That was the climax, right there.

Q. Did you know what you were doing?

A. When I shot that son-of-a-bitch, I knew what I was doing.[1]

There was a massive funeral for Kahahawai. An older Hawaiian, David Kama, whose brother had been shot by a soldier years earlier, gave the eulogy. He expressed the anger of Hawaiians.

> Poor Kahahawai! These haoles murdered you in cold blood. They did the same thing to my brother. They shoot and kill us Hawaiians. We do not shoot haoles, but they shoot us! Never mind—the truth will come out! Poor boy, God will keep you. We will do the rest.[2]

Among the political establishment and the media there was hardly any public criticism of what Hawaiians were calling a "lynching." However, the *Hawaii Hochi,* a Japanese-English newspaper, expressed the views of the Asian majority when it published the following editorial:

Admiral Pettingill told the world Hawaii was not a safe place for wives of Naval officers, because one woman was outraged. . . . The Hawaiians are asking a question that perhaps Admiral Pettingill or Admiral Stirling can answer. They are asking whether Hawaii, their own homeland, is now safe for Hawaiians!

Massie, his mother-in-law, Deacon Jones, and the other sailor who had participated in the kidnapping were charged with murder. Under the law of felony murder, anyone who participates in a felony is guilty of a murder resulting from that felony. That is why all four were charged with murder, even though the mother-in-law and other sailor may not have been in the room when the shooting took place. Darrow and George Leisure, a Wall Street lawyer who was cocounsel, had to choose from three possible defenses. First, if they knew Jones had shot Kahahawai, and it is doubtful that they had such knowledge, they could have used a white rage defense. According to Dershowitz's notion that such a defense is feasible, Darrow could have argued that Jones was crazed with racial hatred for any person who was not white. Second, the defense could have argued that Lieutenant Massie had been driven crazy by the thought of an Asian having sex with his wife, and that a lifetime of racial conditioning caused him to lose control and shoot Kahahawai. Third, the defense could rely on the "unwritten law" that a man is justified in killing the person who rapes his wife. Darrow chose the third alternative.

This unwritten law was more than an expression of justifiable revenge. Among the southern naval officers it was considered a "code of honor." When a married woman was raped, it was considered a stain upon the entire family. It was an insult to the husband. In the male-dominated Navy world, where a wife was seen as an appendage of her husband, rape was a humiliation of the husband.

Thalia Massie was made into a symbol: the loyal, faithful wife of a bereaved, justifiably angry husband. She was held up as the symbol of "decent white women." This imagery was repeated over and over, not only on the islands but also in mainland America. The Hearst-owned *New York American* falsely stated that there had been forty rapes of white women in Hawaii, a charge also made by the commandant at Pearl Harbor. The *American* ran an article entitled "Martial Law Needed to Make Hawaii Safe

Place for Decent Women." The racism of the article saturated its pages: "The situation in Hawaii is deplorable. It is an unsafe place for white women outside the small cities and towns. The roads go through jungles and in these remote places bands of degenerate natives lie in wait for white women driving by."

Two books on the Ala Moana and Massie trials, *Rape in Paradise* by well-known journalist Theon Wright and *Something Terrible Has Happened* by Peter Van Slingerland, afford an exhaustive study of the official investigations and the trials. *Rape in Paradise* also provides an excellent discussion of the race and class oppression of native Hawaiians. But both books were published in 1966 and neither of them is informed by the insights provided by the feminist movement. Neither author understood the burdens a woman faced when bringing an allegation of rape into the criminal law system. Nor did the authors understand how the Massie murder trial was an expression of a male-dominated view of the world. We do not know whether Thalia Massie, twenty-two years old in 1932, accepted that view of the world. But we can conclude that she suffered a great deal.

The story of Thomas Massie and his code of honor was articulated by Darrow during the trial. But the story of Thalia Massie has never truly been communicated. She was subjected to innuendo and rumor during the trials, and afterwards had to endure doubt and disbelief. The governor's official investigation, which was completed by the Pinkerton Agency after the trials, concluded that Thalia Massie was not kidnapped or raped by the Ala Moana defendants. One theory was that she had mistakenly identified the defendants. A less charitable theory was that she intentionally misidentified the four young men in order to hide something.

Less than two years after her husband's trial she was divorced, stating that "Tommy insisted we get a divorce. It was the terrible publicity of the trial." A month after the divorce she slashed her wrists. In her later years she continued to have problems, and in 1962 she died from "an accidental overdose of barbiturates" at her apartment in West Palm Beach, near her socialite mother's home.

The actual trial was hard on the aging Darrow's health, and he became ill, necessitating a brief continuance. But his intellectual vigor and persuasive advocacy were still apparent to all. Legally, the defense was temporary insanity. Two psychiatrists testified that Lieutenant Massie acted in "a walking daze, in which a person may move about, but is not aware of what is happening" and that his act was "an uncontrollable impulse." Emotionally, the defense was the "unwritten law." This appeal found some sympathetic ears in the all-male jury. The jury, consisting of seven whites all born on the mainland, three Chinese, one Portuguese, and only one Hawaiian, rejected the murder charge but brought in a verdict of manslaughter, with a recommendation of leniency. The judge sentenced the defendants to ten years in prison but allowed them to stay free on bail while their lawyers prepared to file legal motions.

The trial and verdict were reported by newspapers across the mainland. The American political establishment was outraged that there had been any verdict of guilt at all. Senator Lewis of Illinois called for President Herbert Hoover to investigate the injustice, and Congressman Thatcher of Kentucky circulated a petition in the House of Representatives calling upon the governor of Hawaii to pardon the four defendants. The House Territories Committee voted for a widespread investigation of the government of Hawaii. Politicians in Hawaii buckled under the pressure. The attorney general of Hawaii visited Darrow at his hotel and urged him to bring his clients to the governor's office. When they met with Governor Judd, he commuted the ten-year sentence to one hour.

Darrow was asked to stay in Hawaii and, for a fee, help prosecute the remaining three young men charged with raping Thalia Massie. But he refused, saying he had never prosecuted anyone and was not going to start now. He then helped persuade Thalia Massie to forgo the strain of another trial, to put the whole incident behind her and return to the states. She did so, and charges were dismissed against the three men.

Looking back at the trial, we must ask why Darrow did not choose to use a white rage defense. The answer is clear: Darrow understood that such a strategy was doomed to failure. A defense based on Lieutenant Massie's or sailor Jones's racial hatred would not elicit sympathy. Unlike a black rage defense, it would not expose how society oppressed the defendants. Instead, such a defense would show how the defendants themselves benefited from racial discrimination. The white rage defense also would have exposed the defendants' ideas of racial superiority, highlighting their bigotry, their arrogance, and their disdain for Hawaii's people of color.

Darrow went to considerable lengths to keep any mention of race out of the trial. In his autobiography, he states that he considered picking the jury the most important part of the case, and he is quite frank in admitting that he tried to get white men on the jury and to disqualify nonwhites. In total contrast to his defense in the Sweet trials, in the Massie case Darrow did not allow any "question of race" to be discussed in the trial because he felt "it would have been fatal to our side to let anything of that sort creep in." He adopted such a strategy because he knew that a white rage defense rooted in race hatred was a losing proposition, as it would be in Dershowitz's hypothetical case of a white skinhead charged with assaulting or murdering a person of color. Dershowitz's hypothetical case is not a serious and realistic criticism of the black rage defense. No successful black rage defense has been based on race hatred. Rather, the defense is used to explain how racial and economic oppression cause a person to commit a crime.

The fact that Darrow's defense of Lieutenant Massie and cohorts put him on the wrong side of the most racially charged trial in the history of Hawaii raises important questions regarding lawyers' responsibility to their clients and to society. The values one is defending and the messages one is sending to the public are critical to a lawyer embarking upon a white rage or black rage defense. Examining Darrow's actions can shed some light on these issues and help advocates think through their political responsibilities when making a choice to defend someone.

How did Clarence Darrow, a man who dedicated his life to fighting injustice, end up in the final case of his career implicitly supporting racial prejudice? Darrow was once described by the great African American scholar and activist W. E. B. Du Bois as "one of the few white folk with whom I felt quite free to discuss matters of race and class." Why was he blind to the negative role he played in the Massie case? The answer lies in the culture of American law. Lawyers are taught that their first and utmost responsibility is to their client. This principle of American law has a positive and negative side. On the positive side, it allows lawyers to represent people whom the state would crush. We have only to look at other nations to see how political dissidents and alleged criminals are arrested, imprisoned, even executed without any semblance of due process. In a nation where lawyers are not allowed to represent their clients forcefully, the state inevitably destroys the life of the innocent as well as the guilty.

American defense lawyers are part of a tradition that respects individuals and is suspicious of state power. When a public defender in an empty courtroom in a small county stands up to a dictatorial judge or an overreaching prosecutor, she is part of a historical struggle against the growth of the police state. Legal culture encourages lawyers to defend their clients vigorously and passionately whether they be political pariahs, destitute immigrants, or crazed criminals. It can be an emotionally difficult job, but it is essential to a democracy.

The negative side of the emphasis on advocacy and winning is that it can produce lawyers who go beyond the bounds of morality to win their cases. It also creates lawyers who, like leeches sucking blood, draw sustenance from confrontation. Instead of looking for ways to mediate conflict, they jump into battle blindly pushing for the win, often leaving emotionally scarred bodies strewn behind them, including those of their own clients. Lawyers often refer to their victories and losses as their "track record," as if the lives of their clients were part of some sort of athletic game in which the attorneys were shooting for an all-star position.

A key feature of our legal culture is that lawyers can be on either side of an argument. Lawyers are taught that it is acceptable to represent women suing a corporation for discrimination in hiring one day, and then turn around the next day and defend a corporation against discrimination claims. In law school, during moot court exercises minority students will often be assigned to defend alleged discriminatory practices. The rationale given is that it will sharpen their advocacy skills, but the political message is that a lawyer has a duty to represent any side of a case. When I told one of my law professors that when I became a lawyer I would not defend a Nazi, the following exchange took place:

> **Professor:** "You are not playing the game."
> **Student:** "It's not a game to me."
> **Professor:** "Then maybe you should not be allowed to play."

This kind of teaching and indoctrination produces lawyers who feel free to disregard the social consequences of their actions.

Darrow's weakness in the Massie case was characteristic of this legal culture as he failed to examine his actions in the harsh light of the racial and political realities of the islands. In his autobiography he discussed the historical exploitation of the Hawaiians, but he kept his eyes closed to the influences of that history on the Massie case.

Darrow had totally committed himself to his client's view of the case. In order to do that, he had to accept the white Navy lieutenant's view of Hawaii. His blind commitment to Massie influenced his trial strategy in a manner that many would consider racist. Darrow understood that race prejudice was part of the case. He said, "It had to be admitted that the race question was a disturbing factor in the case." But he tried to shed himself of any responsibility for supporting prejudice by his exclamations that he, personally, had no racial bias and did not have any "race feeling" growing out of the case.

Darrow wrote that Joseph Kahahawai's funeral was the largest ever held on the islands, except those for a prince or princess. He had jumped into a case that symbolized race relations in Hawaii. By defending an outraged white man who admittedly killed a brown man whom he believed had raped "his" white woman, Darrow became part of a long, ugly, historical tradition of white supremacy. U.S. history is replete with examples of brutal beatings, castration, and lynching of men and boys of color who just talked to, much less had sex with, white women. By relying on the "unwritten law," by hiding the racial aspects of the case, and by keeping Hawaiians off the jury, Darrow was part of a process that supported racial oppression.

Except for the Massie case, Darrow's professional life is an example of a lawyer who did not give up or seriously compromise his political principles when defending a client. Attorneys face issues of racial, class, and gender stereotyping in many cases. They should not hide behind a shield emblazoned with the slogan "Do Anything to Win." Lawyers can hold dear the tradition of staunch advocacy but not accept the notion that it is supportable to represent anyone in any way that results in victory.[3]

A fairly recent California white rage case sheds additional light on the unfeasibility of a defense based on race hatred. The town of Novato, less than an hour north of San Francisco, is often described as a quiet, affluent, bedroom community. Its tranquility was shattered on November 8, 1995. On that day, Robert Page, an unemployed twenty-five-year-old white man, woke up and decided he was going to kill a Chinese man. At approximately noon he entered the parking lot of a supermarket, where he saw twenty-three-year-old Eddy Wu. Page ran at Wu, grabbed him from behind, and stabbed him twice in the back with a long knife. Wu ran into the supermarket for safety, but Page ran after him and stabbed him two more times, puncturing his lung. Fortunately, Wu survived. Store employees followed Page for four blocks as he walked away wielding the ten-inch bloody knife. They waved down an unarmed community service officer, who ordered Page to lie down on the street. Page complied and soon patrol cars arrived and arrested him. Page told the police he was a white supremacist, and that he did it "to defend our country." In the statement he gave the police, he wrote the following: "It all started this morning. I didn't have anything when I woke up. No friends were around. It seemed that no one wanted to be around me. So I figured . . . I'm gonna go kill me a Chinaman."

A week before the attack, Page had walked off his job as a meat carver at a local Hof Brau, muttering that he did not get any respect. His mother told the police that a few days before the stabbing she had moved out of the home they were sharing because he had been "acting strangely" and had threatened her. She was afraid he might hurt her or his own two-year-old son.

A few months after the arrest, Page pled guilty to attempted murder that was racially motivated. He was sentenced to eleven years in prison. Page had committed what is termed a "hate crime." More than half the states have passed laws making acts of violence against property or persons *because of race or religion* a separate crime. For example, in California if one commits a murder for reasons of race, color, religion, or national origin, the punishment is death.

The California penal code makes it a crime to interfere with a person's constitutional rights or damage his or her property because of the person's race, color, religion, ancestry, national origin, gender, disability, or sexual orientation. There are also enhancement code sections, under which additional years in prison are added to the time a defendant receives if the crime is proven to be a hate crime. According to FBI data, in 1994 blacks and Jews were the main targets of hate crimes. In that year alone, 2,100 hate crimes against blacks and 908 against Jews were reported and hate crimes against Asians rose by 35 percent. (The sharp increase in crimes against Asians may be the result of recent political campaigns that have put forth strong antiimmigrant proposals and rhetoric.) When analyzing hate crime statutes, it is important to note that prosecutions are not limited to whites; blacks and Latinos have also been charged under these penal codes in California.

The fact that these statutes exist means that a defense based on race hatred would run into serious obstacles. First, if the defendant admits that his motivation was racial, he would be setting himself up for additional charges and a more severe sentence if convicted. Second, a hate crime charge allows the prosecutor to take the offensive. A district attorney can properly put the philosophy and ideas of the defendant on trial. Evidence toward proving the defendant's bigotry and race hatred motive is admissible. When the prosecutor charges the defendant with a hate crime, he changes the atmosphere of the courtroom. A white rage defense that develops environmental reasons for the crime will most likely be viewed as an attempt to justify racial hatred.

Some critics of the black rage defense argue that white rage defenses of hate crimes have been successful. They refer to the jury acquittals of white men who shot civil rights activists in the South in the sixties. They point to Sheriff Lawrence Rainey and some of his associates, who were found not guilty of charges relating to the murder of black and Jewish civil rights workers James Chaney, Michael Schwerner, and Andrew Goodman during Mississippi Freedom Summer in 1964. They also call attention to Byron de la Beckwith, who assassinated NAACP leader Medgar Evers in Mississippi in 1963. Beckwith was tried twice during the sixties for murder. Both trials resulted in hung juries. Finally in 1995, with the help of new evidence and an integrated jury, he was convicted.

State of Georgia v. Bruener, a less publicized case than Rainey's and Beckwith's, is more typical of the kind of cases commentators use to criticize the black rage defense. In 1968, a deputy sheriff in Thomasville, Georgia, arrested a small, young black man for a parking violation. At the jail the deputy attacked the young man from behind, splitting open his skull. He then took the man's twenty dollars for the parking fine and sent him home bleeding from the head saying "that will teach you to say 'yes, sir' and 'no, sir.'"

Because of their newly won voting rights, the black community had some leverage in Thomasville. The liberal white solicitor general agreed to prosecute the deputy for assault and battery but did not want to be in the public position of handling the case himself. So he asked legendary civil rights lawyer C. B. King to come from his private practice in Albany,

Georgia, and prosecute the case. King, an African American, was the only attorney in all of southwest Georgia who would handle civil rights cases. Blacks and whites alike attested to his courage and eloquence. Every summer, law students from around the country would come to Albany to volunteer in his office. Among King's alumni are U.S. solicitor general Drew Days III, former U.S. congresswoman Elizabeth Holtzman, critical race scholar Charles Lawrence, Dennis Roberts, the first white law student from the North to go to the South to do civil rights work, and many others who became committed, progressive attorneys.

King and three of his law student interns entered the Thomasville courtroom and were greeted by the unusual sight of black people sitting in the spectator section. The jury pool was all white, and twelve men were seated to be jurors. King presented an overwhelming case against Deputy Sheriff Bruener. In spite of the evidence, however, the jury deliberated just ten minutes and delivered a verdict of not guilty.

Rainey, Beckwith, and Bruener are all examples of the miscarriage of justice because of white supremacy. But the critics are incorrect when they use these types of cases as examples of white rage defenses. The defendants did not admit their participation in the crimes and then argue white rage as their defense. Sheriff Rainey and the others relied on the traditional "I didn't do it" defense and hoped that the all-white juries would disregard the facts and protect the white defendants. The subtext of the defense was an appeal to racism, but that is not comparable to the black rage defense, nor to the hypothetical white rage cases described by Dershowitz and other critics. In a black rage case, the defendant admits the act and argues that the social context must be taken into legal consideration. Steven Robinson admitted the bank robbery; James Johnson admitted the homicides; Henry Sweet admitted shooting into the crowd. Rainey and Beckwith, on the other hand, attempted to hide the truth. The black rage defense is so powerful precisely because the accused admits his actions. Whereas Rainey hid the racial and social factors that led him to kill the three young men, the black rage defense seeks to explore, with the jury, the entire social context of a crime. For these reasons, the defenses of Rainey and Beckwith cannot be equated with the black rage defense, and they do not offer the basis for a valid critique.

Let us move from Mississippi to Southern California, and from the sixties to the nineties. The acquittals of the police officers who brutally beat Rodney King can be analogized to the cases in Mississippi. The Los Angeles police officers did not argue that they were expressing their anger at African Americans, that they were acting out of racial frustration and hate. They argued the opposite—that they were not racists. Their defense was that the vicious beating was a use of reasonable police force in an attempt to subdue a criminal (not a "black" criminal) who was violently resisting a legal arrest. If they had followed Dershowitz's hypothetical and argued that white rage was the reason for their actions, even an all-white Simi Valley jury would have convicted them. Looking at the cases of Massie, Page, Rainey, Beckwith, Bruener, and the California police officers, we can see the implausibility of a race hatred defense. Such a defense brings out the worst about the defendant. It brings out all the twisted, vicious parts of the person. A strategy that is based on white supremacy does not reveal the pain of being oppressed because white supremacy is the historical doctrine of the oppressor. To the extent that such a defense informs us that racism warps the racist himself, it may have some social value, but it would still be offensive to a jury. As long as the defendant holds onto his racial hatred, there is no potential for the defense to enlarge the human spirit. There is no potential to evoke a jury's empathy. It is a repugnant defense. Deacon Jones, who shot Joseph Kahahawai in cold blood, could not have been acquitted using a white rage defense, nor could Robert Page be acquitted of stabbing Eddy Wu in the back. An all-white Mississippi jury would not have acquitted Beckwith if he had admitted gunning down Medgar Evers. Even in Sheriff Rainey's trial, Deputy Sheriff Cecil Price and six of the coconspirators were convicted by an all-white Mississippi jury and given prison sentences ranging from three to ten years.

The black rage defense is brought by a person who is a victim of white supremacy. The black rage defense has been successful because it shows the jury the social wreckage caused by racism. It brings to light the heartache, agony, and righteous anger felt by the oppressed. Black rage is not a defense based on a philosophy of racial superiority. We should not abandon it because of the empty threat that white supremacists will use a white rage defense.

A criminal is not different from
yourself. Indeed, if you turn the
searchlight inward and look into
your soul, you will find that the
difference is only one of degree.
—Mohandas Gandhi

Chapter 12

White Rage—Do Prisons Cause Crime?

Alan Dershowitz's criticism of the black rage defense is not convincing.
However, there is another criticism that does have some validity. In law
school it is called the "slippery slope." This criticism speaks to the fear
that once the legal system permits a black rage defense, we will slide head-
long down a slippery slope and find ourselves allowing Latinos, Asians,
Native Americans, and poor whites to use a comparable defense. This
critique is supportable. The answer to it is that a person of any race should
be allowed to try to persuade a jury that severe environmental factors
contributed to a criminal act. This is what David Bazelon and Richard
Delgado have argued—that the causal relationship between environment
and crime should be recognized in various forms of legal defense. The
black rage–type defense is no more limited to African Americans than are
civil rights. Rather than worry about sliding down a slippery slope into
disaster, we should embrace the possibilities created by the expansion of
the black rage defense.[1]

A case I tried in 1974 reveals the use of a white rage defense not based
on race hatred. A few months earlier I had lost a black rage case. It had
been a retrial on a charge of bank robbery, after a previous hung jury. I

was sitting in the law collective office reading a letter from the twenty-four-year-old convicted bank robber. He wrote that the black rage defense had opened his eyes to his destructive behavior. Sitting through the two trials and listening to our presentation of his life had given him insight into the unresolved problems of his youth. He now felt he could understand why he had robbed the bank. Instead of lying on his prison cot blaming society, he wanted to work on improving his life. From deep in his heart he thanked the psychologist who had helped him understand his life. I have always felt that a collateral benefit of the black rage defense is the perspective it provides the defendants on their lives. Alan's letter supported that belief of mine and eased the pain of losing his case and watching the judge sentence this decent young man to five years in prison.

A few hours after reading Alan's letter, I received a call from the federal public defenders. I had been appointed to represent a white ex-convict charged with robbing six banks and savings and loan offices. I drove over to San Francisco County Jail and met John Zimmerman.[2] He was thirty-two years old, of German and Italian extraction. He had a cracked front tooth and long hair, stringy and dirty from days in jail. He had spent almost all of the last fourteen years in various prisons. It was my first contact with a long-term convict, and his first experience with a sixties generation lawyer. Sitting in the claustrophobic interview room, we began to interact and after half an hour each of us had let his guard down. He admitted he had committed the robberies, and volunteered that he had also done one in southern California. John's story was engrossing, and I began to consider an environmental defense. His focus was on "just getting it over with." His parole was sure to be revoked, and he would be put back in San Quentin Prison on his original state court sentence of five to life for drug-related robberies. "I'll plead guilty if they'll give me ten years," he said. I responded that I wanted to do some research on his case because I had a psychiatric defense in mind. "Go ahead if you want, but I'm not holding my breath," he replied. "When will you see me again?" I told him I'd see him in court in a few days and explain my ideas.

During the next two months I visited John as often as my schedule permitted. I read the discovery materials I had received from the prosecution, talked to John's drug rehabilitation counselor, spoke to his girlfriend and father in southern California, consulted with a psychologist friend who was an expert in drug abuse, obtained John's artwork, and read his poetry. I began to understand John's life as a poor white person ("white trash" to some people) who was shaped and misshaped by his environment. His poem about San Quentin reinforced my idea that his years in prison had substantially contributed to his abnormal mental state.

> "Quentin" The prison by the bay:
> A relic of man's past
> A monument to man's disgrace
> Of man's neglected task.
> An old and dreary, filthy place,
> Where men walk under guns.
> Where pain and hate corrupt their minds,
> and dampness rots their lungs.
> "Quentin" you're a stinking place,
> as foul as a sewage drain
> and those of you who keep its gate,
> Will never be clean of shame.

At our first meeting, John described how he felt during the robberies. He said that he had developed two personalities in prison. One was Abderrahman, a man of peace. The other was Aleman (Spanish for "German"), who was the strong, tough barbarian that would protect him against the violence of prison. When he committed the bank robberies he felt himself shifting to Aleman, and he experienced the robberies as an outsider, as though he were watching someone else. He described it as an out-of-body experience, like he was watching a television show of a robbery. I felt he was telling me the truth and the psychologist agreed, diagnosing John as a schizotypal personality. I was ready to go to trial, but John just wanted to plead guilty. The U.S. attorney handling the case agreed to recommend a ten-year sentence to run concurrent with John's state sentence. The judge, a recent Reagan appointee to the federal bench, had a reputation as an extremely conservative man who gave harsh sentences. In chambers the prosecutor laid out the terms of the deal, but the judge said, "Hell no!" The prosecutor asked me if my client would accept a fifteen-year sentence. I said, "Yes." But the judge would not be moved. "I am going to make an example of him. He gets the maximum of twenty-five years." I implored the judge to reconsider; the client would not plead guilty if all he would be getting in return was the maximum sentence. He would have nothing to lose by going to trial. The judge was adamant, and in order to pressure John to plead guilty he set the trial to begin in just three days. As we left chambers the prosecutor was furious. He could not believe that he had to prepare a trial in only three days when the defendant had been ready to accept a fifteen-year sentence. Fortunately, I had already prepared for trial in case plea negotiation failed. But even with a headstart on the prosecutor, my weekend would consist of fourteen-hour days of hectic, intense, and challenging work.

We selected a jury on Monday and began trial the next morning. John had given me a portrait of him drawn by a fellow inmate. It was stunning. John looked like Jesus, with long hair and a large teardrop falling from his eye. There were seven cobras coming out of his head. The borders were filled with ancient symbols such as the Star of David and the yin-yang circle. There was an alphabet John had created. And on the bottom were the following words:

WANTED DEAD
For Bank Robbery and Treason
ABDERRAHMAN, Warrior Priest of the
Seventh Tribe of Man is Guilty of
LOVE, COMPASSION and BELIEF in
UNIVERSAL BROTHERHOOD. To Be
Considered Armed and Dangerous,
Armed and Dangerous, Armed and Dangerous.

I had the drawing blown up to poster size. When the U.S. attorney finished his opening, I immediately walked over to the jury box to grab their attention and break the momentum the prosecutor had achieved. I began my opening. "Sometimes in order to understand a crime you must understand the man charged with that crime. In this case that man is John Zimmerman, who is Aleman the Gladiator and Abderrahman, Warrior Priest in the Seventh Tribe of Man."

The judge was staring at me coldly. I reminded myself of that old English barrister Rumpole's advice, "Fearlessness is the number one essential of an advocate," and I walked over to the easel and uncovered the poster. "This picture was designed by the defendant and drawn by a cellmate. Its relevance will be explained to you later during the presentation of testimony. For now, let me briefly discuss the evidence which will show how a small, sensitive, asthmatic twelve-year-old named John Zimmerman became Abderrahman, priest and witch in the Seventh Tribe of Man."

I moved away from the easel and stood a few feet from the jury box, leaving the dramatic poster behind me for the jurors to look at. After telling the story of John's life, I highlighted the psychological testimony and its legal relevance. As I concluded, I attempted to create an atmosphere of serious reflection and to pique the curiosity of the jurors.

> At the end of the trial we hope that we have given you an insight into prison life, an insight into the plague of drug abuse sweeping our country, and an insight into John Zimmerman. For if you understand this man [I now stood directly behind John so that the jurors would have to look at him], then I believe you will find that the government has not proved beyond a reasonable doubt that he could control his conduct at the time he robbed those banks, and therefore he will be entitled, under the law, to a verdict of not guilty.

The prosecutor's case was clear-cut. He showed photos from the surveillance cameras and brought witnesses to establish that John robbed all six financial institutions. The government psychiatrist testified that John did not suffer from any psychotic condition and was able to control his actions at the time of the crimes.

The next day we began to present our evidence. As John saw that, unlike all the previous authority figures in his life, I recognized the positive parts of his personality, he opened up and embraced our trial strategy.

John Zimmerman could have been described as a pitiful, weak heroin addict who had been a petty criminal since the age of fifteen and had finally flipped out. Or he could be described as a frightened, talented, sensitive person who was unable to cope with the violence of his environment. I chose the latter.

John grew up in a rough, white working-class neighborhood in which gangs predominated. He was a small, skinny kid with asthma. His German father, a short, tough man, and his Sicilian mother provided for him but could not protect him from his environment. His father insisted that John, his only son, take karate lessons so that he would not be a "chicken."

On the borders of his neighborhood was a Mexican gang, "Los Pachucos," and a black gang, "Little Watts." Some of his schoolmates were in a gang called the "Dogpatch." At thirteen, for protection, he joined one of the "rat-packs" called the "Quakers." He took part in gang wars, always terrified he would be badly hurt, but unable to find a way out of the gang. He smoked pot and at fifteen began to use heroin to tranquilize his fears. At seventeen he was put in a reformatory for petty thefts.

At nineteen he was released from the Preston School of Industry and began to use heroin regularly. Soon afterwards he was arrested for being a heroin addict and sent to an adult jail. The courts ruled that it was not a crime just to be a drug addict; they required that an arrest be made based on possession or sale of a drug. Therefore, John was released. He was out for eighteen months, during which time he developed a heavy drug habit, using a quarter of an ounce of pure heroin each day. He was arrested in Texas for smuggling one-half ounce of heroin and was sent to a federal prison for five years. There, the Aryan Brotherhood, a white supremacist prison gang, tried to recruit him, but he refused to join.

He was transferred to McNeil Island. On the way there, they stopped at the San Diego County Jail, where he had his first out-of-body experience. John was in pain and prayed for help. He heard a voice in his head that said he could stop the pain and have knowledge and happiness if he would serve "Him."

Arriving at McNeil Island, he was put in a cell with a charismatic convict known as "Wizard." John helped him organize the Seventh Tribe of Man, named after an ancient group of magicians that they believed had disappeared from the face of earth. They practiced communal LSD trips and then would have group therapy under the Wizard's leadership. They smuggled methedrine (speed) and LSD (acid) into the prison. John used acid two to three times a week, often taking six times the normal dose. There were ten inmates in the cell. Someone stole some paint and they drew a zodiac on their cell floor and painted religious symbols on the bars. John read books, meditated, studied Eastern religions, painted, became a vegetarian, and vowed never to physically injure another person or animal, not even the big black bugs that crawled through his cell.

John was released in 1968. In his mid-twenties, with no skills for employment or social success, he began using heroin again. Within a few months he was hooked. He began to steal to support his habit of one hundred dollars a day. He was caught and charged with robbing two finance companies and a donut shop. He told his public defender that he felt strange doing the robberies, like he was "watching two movies at once," one of the robbery and the other of him watching the crime being committed by someone else. The lawyer did not request that a psychological interview be done, and John pleaded guilty. He was given five years to life under California's then-existing indeterminate sentencing law.

In prison, John's nonviolent behavior and innate intelligence came to the attention of the authorities. He was sent to the California Rehabilitation Center (a prison), where he became a resident drug counselor. Because of his criticisms of the authorities and his testimony before a grand jury investigation into prison conditions the Warden excluded him from the program, and he was sent behind the walls of the forbidding and dangerous San Quentin Prison. At San Quentin he was again recruited by the Aryan Brotherhood. Because he was German, it was expected that he would join their prison gang. But John refused. He associated with different races, at one time having as his closest friend a black inmate. He communicated with prison revolutionary and author George Jackson about how drug use inside California's prisons was being allowed in order to keep inmates away from the intense political organizing then taking place. John was in San Quentin when George Jackson was shot to death by a guard after inmates had taken over the Adjustment Center, a maximum security building within San Quentin where Jackson, Black Panther Johnny Spain, the Soledad Brothers, and other politically active prisoners were isolated and locked in their cells twenty-three hours a day. After Jackson was killed, tensions at the prison grew and John was unable to keep up his friendships with black inmates. He became a pariah, left alone by all sides and looked upon with suspicion by the prison officials.

At the trial, John testified about how guards manipulate the racism among prisoners in order to set one group against another and thereby keep control by the age-old practice of divide and conquer.

One day, fearing for his life, alone and in pain, he called out for "Aleman." Aleman the Gladiator, Aleman the Barbarian, was a power that protected John. It (or he) had receded during John's time at McNeil Island. But in the desperate isolation of San Quentin he called upon Aleman to help him. On the stand, John described his meeting with his strange protector: "I asked for Aleman and all his ancestors of the past to help me bear the load. I signed a treaty with him to allow him to protect me from harm whenever he felt I was, or we were, in danger."

After that vision John found that he was able to cope with San Quentin's brutality. A friendly guard encouraged him in his poetry and would secretly mail John's poems to his friends. John took as his identity the peaceful Abderrahman and had a symbol of the warrior-priest tattooed over his heart. But Aleman was always hovering nearby, ready to defend John against insults, beatings, or rape.

Upon release from San Quentin on parole, John went to a drug rehabilitation center. He went regularly for a few months before the center was closed due to lack of federal funds. The man who ran the center also testified and corroborated John's progress in rehabilitation. The director told the jury how the center was forced to close its doors, and how John and the others suddenly were left with no place to go and no one they trusted.

John had fallen in love with a young woman who was living in poverty with her seven siblings. He tried to take care of her, but he had no experience other than reformatory, jail, and prison. John and his girlfriend got a van and drove up the coast to the San Francisco Bay Area. Haunted by LSD flashbacks and cast adrift by the closing of the drug rehabilitation center, he started robbing banks, using the money to take care of his girlfriend and buy heroin. He testified that before and during the robberies "Aleman the Barbarian," who had protected him in prison, took control of his being, and that he felt he was watching his body go into the banks, talk to the tellers, and walk out with the money.

After a series of bank robberies, John and his girlfriend drove along the picturesque Pacific Coast Highway. He parked the van and they went to sleep. It was late at night when suddenly John heard pounding on the side of the van. He opened the door and through the bright headlights lighting up his van, he saw eight men in uniforms pointing shotguns at him. Someone shouted, "Police, come out with your hands up!" John said to his terrified girlfriend, "God, it's finally over."

I had finished direct examination of John. As I took my seat I felt he had been able to tell his story and to communicate his character. The

prosecutor rose to begin cross-examination. He was in a somewhat difficult position. He had no evidence to contradict John's description of his
life in prison, nor could he rebut the facts about the drug center closing.
All he could do was hammer away at John's claim that "Aleman took
control of his body and did the robberies." The prosecutor went through
each of the six robberies, one by one, focusing on John's rational acts, such
as writing a demand note or asking the teller for money. He considered the
insanity claim ludicrous and treated John with sarcasm and disdain. The
highlight of the cross-examination took place when the U.S. attorney attacked John head-on.

> Q. "Mr. Zimmerman, why don't you change into Aleman right now and fly
>   out of the courtroom to freedom?"
> A. "I would if I could. But I'm not *that* crazy."

Most of the jurors laughed at the response. They were laughing *with*
John and at that instant I knew they saw him as a man, not as a lying,
dangerous convict.

The psychologist we presented was named James Daley. He was in his
early thirties and had never testified in court. He was an expert in drug
abuse, having had extensive clinical experience with heroin addicts and
LSD users. Daley was excellent on the stand. He described, in terms a
layman could understand, how LSD affects the brain. He explained how
long-term use and large doses of LSD can cause flashbacks and bouts of
extreme anxiety for years afterwards. The most telling points he made
were that heroin acts as a "super-tranquilizer" and that John had used it
to relieve the terrible anxiety and fear he felt. His diagnosis was that John
was a schizotypal personality, and that as a result of that mental disease
he lacked the substantial capacity to conform his conduct to law at the
times of the bank robberies.

A lawyer should always humanize a client. One way I could do this was
to enter some of John's paintings and poems into evidence. The legal basis
of this tactic was that the psychologist had examined them and relied on
them, as well as the life history and psychiatric reports, in forming his
opinion as to insanity. Although this was a correct legal position, many
judges would not have allowed them into evidence because of their desire
to help the prosecutor obtain a conviction. However, this judge, even

though he was proprosecution, allowed me to show the jurors three paint-ings and to recite two poems. He did this because he felt our defense was ridiculous, and that the jury was sure to convict regardless of any evidence I produced or arguments I made.

The paintings were quite good. The psychologist testified that based on his experience with LSD users, he believed John had done the paintings while on LSD. This was important because we had proved that the paint-ings had been done in prison, which gave credence to John's testimony that he had access to LSD while inside prison.

I read two poems to the jury. One was entitled "The A-Bomb Genera-tion," which expressed his love of people and his deep-seated fear of death and the severe anxieties from which he suffered. The other poem was about drug addiction, in which he described the psychology of the addict. This poem was particularly important to our strategy because John did not describe himself as a victim or a helpless person with an "illness." Rather, he took full responsibility for his addiction, and the poem con-veyed his contempt and self-loathing when he used drugs.

It is useful in a trial to inject some drama. Unlike trials on television, most cases have long periods of boredom. The rules of evidence often result in an antiseptic presentation of testimony. Lawyers are not allowed to turn to the jury and explain why a piece of evidence that has just been admitted is important. Witnesses do not necessarily testify in logical order, and the one or two statements they make that are crucial to the overall theory of the case can go unnoticed. Around three o'clock in the after-noon, in a warm courtroom, a lawyer will look at the jury and one person will have his eyes closed while others will be watching the sparse audience, looking at their wristwatches, or counting the lights on the ceiling. To break the monotony, lawyers sometimes become inappropriately theatri-cal. Overemotional, exaggerated actions by a lawyer do not ring true with a jury. In John Zimmerman's case, the display of the paintings and recita-tion of the poems allowed me to grasp their attention without theatrics. The paintings and poems made the trial more interesting and genuinely dramatic. This was different from the evidence they had seen in other criminal trials. It individualized the case. It helped them to see John as a unique person, not just one of a thousand ex-cons having trouble ad-justing to society.

The night before the closing arguments I began my usual routine. I helped put my kids to bed, put on the taped music, sat at the dining room table, and finished constructing my argument. I listened to Bob Dylan's song "Chimes of Freedom." It expressed perfectly the emotional essence of the defense:

> Tolling for the aching whose wounds can not be nursed.
> For the countless confused, accused, misused, strung out ones and worse.
> And for every hung up person in the whole wide universe.
> And we gazed upon the Chimes of Freedom flashing.

I wished I could intersperse music with my rational arguments. Art expresses truth better than logical discourse.

I began to draw the landscape of John's life. His teenage years had been difficult but not abnormally harsh. His parents had loved and provided for him. The gang fights terrified John, but the neighborhood had not yet degenerated into the urban war zones of the nineties. When he entered the penal system he was a nonviolent drug addict. After spending half his life in prison he had become a crazed bank robber. I wanted the jury to make a moral choice. Was society's disregard of John Zimmerman so substantial that it had lost the right to further criminalize and punish him? Although I would not use those words in my closing argument, it was the subtext of the defense.

As usual, I finished writing about midnight. I stood up and practiced delivering the closing out loud. It was one hour long. I practiced it twice, so I would not have to look at my writing tablet more than a few times when I was speaking to the jury. I was satisfied with my presentation. I was filled with a deep contentment. As I laid down to sleep, I felt I had touched another man's soul and looked forward to passing on that understanding to twelve people who had never known the terrible pain of years in prison.

The next morning's closing argument was an emotional experience for both John and me. I hoped the logic and reason of my argument had been as effective as the emotion. A juror may bond emotionally with your presentation, but without reasonable arguments she will not be able to persuade other jurors.

After two days of deliberation the bailiff informed us the jury had reached its verdict. We were called back into the large, imposing federal courtroom. We all sat in nerve-racking silence: John, myself, John's father and girlfriend, the prosecutor, and the FBI case-agent. The jury walked in and took their seats. They avoided my eyes, but that meant nothing. Jurors rarely give away their verdict. The bailiff took the verdict from the foreperson and handed it to the judge. The judge read it silently to himself. Was that a grimace I saw fleetingly cross his face? The judge handed the verdict form back to the bailiff and directed the defendant to stand. I stood up next to John. The bailiff began reading the verdict—not guilty on all six counts. John broke into a wide smile. A few of the jurors smiled at us. The judge turned to the jury, attempting to control the anger in his voice. "I have been a state court and federal court judge for over ten years. I believe in the jury system, but in this case you have been sold a bill of goods!" He abruptly stood up and strode from the courtroom. There was total silence. Then an older juror began to cry as she put her hand up to her forehead and said, "I knew I shouldn't have voted not guilty." But it was too late to change her vote. Because of the judge's rigidity and vindictive philosophy, John had avoided a guilty plea and a fifteen-year sentence. His life story had been told and the acquittal was a measure of compassion and respect for his humanity. Standing next to me, in the county jail orange jumpsuit, he was a man, not a convict.

The U.S. attorney in southern California indicted John Zimmerman for the one bank robbery he committed in his jurisdiction. A public defender in Los Angeles named Tom Pollack consulted with John and me. He used a similar environmental insanity defense and did an outstanding job. Once again John was acquitted.

A few months later I received a letter from John. He was back in prison. His state parole had been revoked, as we had expected. The letter reinforced some of the reasons I continue to represent people who commit crimes.

> There is Life, there is Love, there is Beauty, there is Peace! You are a Beautiful, Bad and deserving Warrior. . . . I love you, My Brother, I will always remember you! There is no darkness where there is a little light.

We need not recoil from a white rage defense. As the gap between rich and poor continues to grow wider, and as prisons are embraced as the political solution to crime, more and more white people are going to find themselves casualties of a dysfunctional social system. An environmental defense focuses attention on the harsh economic inequality of capitalism. It will allow judges and juries to factor society's responsibility into the equation of the individual and the crime.

If you don't understand a person's
culture, how can you sit there and
judge a person?
—A juror in the Croy
murder trial

Chapter 13

The Cultural Defense and the Trials
of Patrick Hooty Croy

In recent years the media has shown increasing interest in defendants who
use a "cultural defense" to excuse, justify, or mitigate their criminal conduct. What is a cultural defense? Simply stated, it is the use of social
customs and beliefs to explain the behavior of a defendant. It is sometimes
called social framework or social context evidence. It is very similar to the
black rage defense in its use of social, economic, and psychological evidence, but there are significant differences. The black rage defense is an
explanation of how American racism impacts on African Americans. It has
a powerful political message because it exposes the oppressive structure of
American economic and social life. On the other hand, some cultural
defenses offer an explanation of how a foreign culture affects a person,
usually an immigrant, who currently resides in America, comparing that
culture's mores and legal standards with those of the United States. To a
less frequent but significant extent, this defense is also used by America's
indigenous peoples and by those who are immersed in the country's non-
dominant cultures.

Just as the black rage defense has been used since the 1800s, the cultural defense is not new to American courts. For example, in 1888 Native American defendants were allowed to put their customs into evidence to show the absence of malice in their killing of a tribal doctor after having been instructed to do so by the tribal council. In the 1920s Italian immigrants used cultural evidence to defend themselves against statutory rape charges when they abducted for marriage Italian American women under the age of consent whose parents had not agreed to the marriages.

Like the black rage defense, use of the cultural defense increased in the 1970s and 1980s, for a number of reasons. First, the development of the battered woman syndrome, used to explain the actions of women who have defended themselves against physically assaultive men, has educated the legal community about the appropriateness of and need for social context evidence. The significant increase in minority and women lawyers, law professors, and judges has also opened the legal system to claims of racial, gender, and cultural bias. The result of this consciousness-raising is that the courts are more amenable to the introduction of social framework evidence.

Another reason for the rapid growth of the cultural defense is the influx of Asian immigrants who come from countries with cultural norms and beliefs dissimilar to America's. Many of the cases discussed in the anthropological and legal literature involve people from Vietnam, Laos, and Cambodia. Much of this immigration is a consequence of the United States' interference in and destruction of those countries during what the Vietnamese call "the American war." A number of cases reported by the media and analyzed in the literature involve the Hmong people. The Hmong were tribal mountain people who were specifically recruited by the CIA and the U.S. military to fight against the Vietnamese National Liberation Front. After America lost the war, thousands of the Hmong who became at risk in their country had to relocate to this country, where at times the two different cultures have clashed. Although most of the attention has been on cases involving Asians, the cultural defense has also been used in cases involving Salvadorans, Nigerians, Puerto Ricans, Cubans, Mixtecs, Jamaicans, Ethiopians, Arabs, Alaska Natives, and Native Americans.

There is a good deal of misinterpretation of culture defenses, both inside and outside the legal system. A clear light piercing this veil of confusion is a brilliant law review article entitled "Cultural Evidence and Male Violence: Are Feminist and Multiculturalist Reformers on a Collision Course in Criminal Courts?"[1] by Holly Maguigan, professor of the criminal law clinic at New York University Law School. Maguigan was a public defender and then a criminal lawyer in private practice in Philadelphia, and she brings that real-life litigation experience and insight to her article.

Maguigan explains that the cultural defense is not an independent, "freestanding" defense. Some judges and many commentators have made the mistake of thinking that both black rage and cultural defenses are separate from conventionally recognized defenses. Working from that incorrect assumption, they posit horror stories of the law being abused by separate standards of conduct based solely on race or culture. In fact, both defenses must be part of a recognized rule, such as insanity, self-defense, mistake of fact, or diminished capacity. The cultural evidence must be relevant to the defendant's state of mind when committing the crime. An example of a case in which a cultural defense was used as a persuasive part of a conventional legal rule involved a young man named Kong Moua. Moua was one of approximately thirty thousand Hmong people relocated to the San Joaquin Valley of California. In 1985 Moua was a student at Fresno City College. He abducted a Hmong woman whom he believed was to be his bride, took her to his cousin's house and, in spite of her protests, had sexual relations with her. The woman reported the incident to the police, and the surprised Moua was charged with kidnap and rape. During plea negotiations between the district attorney and defense counsel, the explanation given by Moua was that he was fulfilling the custom of *zij poj niam*, the traditional Hmong marriage ritual. According to the cultural norms among the Hmong in their former homeland, the mountains of Laos, a man abducts his intended bride after informing her parents. Before the marriage a courtship takes place, including the exchange of small gifts and chaperoned dates. On the chosen day, the man captures the woman, takes her to a family home, and consummates the union. The woman protests to show her virtuousness. The man, to display the strength necessary to be her husband, persists in face of the protests. Moua said he believed that his bride-to-be's protests represented the customary resistance, and that he did not intend to have sexual intercourse with her against her will.

If there was an independent cultural defense, a judge would instruct a jury that if they agreed that Moua honestly believed the woman was voluntarily engaging in the ritual of *zij poj naim,* they should find him not guilty. But since no freestanding cultural defense exists, Moua's attorney argued the conventional defense of mistake of fact. That is, Moua, because of his cultural beliefs, mistook the woman's protest to be part of the ritual and assumed she was actually consenting. The district attorney was convinced of Moua's sincerity but was unwilling to drop the charges because of the need to show the Hmong community that in America they must abide by American laws and customs. However, he reduced the charges to a misdemeanor of false imprisonment. Moua pled guilty. Before the sentencing, the judge educated himself as to the ritual of marriage-by-capture and consulted the elders of the victim's and the defendant's families. He sentenced Moua to ninety days in jail and one thousand dollars restitution. During the sentencing, the judge made it clear that his decision was not based on a cultural defense per se, but that the cultural beliefs of Moua and the Hmong community had influenced his lenient sentence.

Some commentators have criticized the disposition in Kong Moua's case as an example of the legal system treating crimes of violence against women less seriously than other crimes. Maguigan agrees with this criticism. But she does not agree that abolition of the cultural defense is the answer. She shows that cultural evidence often works in favor of women defendants.

The murder trial of Kathryn Charliaga is a good example of the positive aspects of social framework evidence, both in educating the public to women's oppression and in winning a favorable disposition for women defendants. Kathryn Charliaga is an Alaska Native (the phrase used by Alaska's indigenous peoples to describe themselves). At the time of her case, she was a thirty-five-year-old preschool teacher living in the small Aleut community of Larsen Bay. She began dating Simeon Charliaga when she was just fifteen years old, and they were married when she was nineteen. After the wedding her husband began to beat her. For Kathryn it brought back memories of her father beating her mother and hitting and sexually abusing Kathryn when she was a small child. During the sixteen years of their marriage, Kathryn's husband had choked her, chased her with a knife and with a gun, and beaten her in public.

On New Year's Eve in 1990, Kathyrn and Simeon were at home. They drank some brandy and began to quarrel. He locked the door and blocked it with a freezer chest so she couldn't run out of the house as she had done many times before. Kathryn testified at her trial that his eyes had the look of "a devil." Faced with his fury and his known potential for violence, she grabbed a knife and stabbed him repeatedly. Kathryn was indicted for second-degree murder and two lesser counts of homicide. She pled not guilty and went to trial arguing self-defense.

The legal problem Kathryn and most women face when they use a weapon to defend themselves against husbands or boyfriends is that the man is often unarmed. The law of self-defense requires that a person be in imminent danger of serious injury or death. It also requires that a "reasonable person" would have perceived the threat as imminent and would have reacted in the same way as the defendant. In order to help the jury understand a defendant's reaction, prior threats by the victim against the defendant are admissible. In battered women defenses, it is proper to admit "context" evidence. By explaining the prior instances of violence, and how the man tended to behave as he built up to the actual attack, the defense enables a jury to understand why it is reasonable for a previously battered woman to perceive that her life is in danger when the man is "just" yelling at her and has not yet physically attacked her.

The law of self-defense mandates that the force used be proportionate to the threat. One is allowed to use a weapon against an unarmed aggressor, but one's reasons must be very persuasive. Most juries convict women who have killed an unarmed man. Therefore, lawyers have used the battered woman syndrome to supplement conventional self-defense arguments. This allows the jurors to see how a woman may reasonably believe that she will be badly injured or killed and must use a weapon to defend herself against the man's usually superior physical strength and fighting experience. The battered woman syndrome also enlightens the jury as to why women do not leave their battering husbands, thereby negating the common feeling that the woman is at fault because she had the alternative of ending the relationship.

In Kathryn Charliaga's case, public defender Michael Karnavas called as a cultural expert Rena Merculieff, executive director of the Native Nonprofit Health Corporation. Merculieff testified that in Aleut villages a woman's role is one of subservience: "It's as if they [the men] own their wife and have a right to do whatever they want to them." One result of this philosophy is that battering is a common occurrence. Help is very difficult to find. In small, isolated villages, intervention is highly unusual and escape virtually impossible. People "expect a woman to do whatever the husband tells her."

The cultural evidence was persuasive in negating the jurors' feelings that Kathyrn could have received help or gotten away from her husband in the years preceding the killing. The jury of seven men and five women deliberated for two days and reached a verdict of not guilty on all counts.

As more cases involving cultural defenses reach the appellate courts, we can expect more decisions favoring the admissibility of such evidence. This should also, by inference, allow evidence of African American culture as well.[2] Any lawyer planning to use a cultural defense should read the California Court of Appeals decision in *People v. Wu*.[3] Helen Wu, a native Chinese woman, strangled her eight-year-old son and then unsuccessfully tried to commit suicide after she found out that her Chinese American husband was unfaithful and had been treating their child badly. The defense argued that the humiliation and shame felt by Helen Wu and her belief that she would be reunited with her child after death were strongly influenced by her cultural background. In an attempt to strengthen his contention that Wu was guilty of manslaughter and not murder, the defense lawyer offered a jury instruction that read as follows: "You have received evidence of defendant's cultural background and the relationship of her culture to her mental state. You may, but are not required to, consider that evidence in determining the presence or absence of the essential mental states of the crimes defined in these instructions." The judge refused to give this instruction to the jury, stating that he did not want to put the "stamp of approval on [the defendant's] actions in the United States, which would have been acceptable in China." The Court of Appeals reversed the trial judge, explaining in detail how the cultural evidence was legally *relevant* to the charges. The court pointed out that in a murder case one's mental state is an issue. The cultural evidence was relevant to motive, intent, and what kind of mental state Helen was in leading up to and during the homicide. It was also admissible to prove that she acted in the heat of passion, which, if accepted by the jury, would reduce first- or second-degree murder to voluntary manslaughter. The Court of Appeals concluded that "upon retrial defendant is entitled to have the jury instructed that it may consider evidence of defendant's cultural background in determining the existence or nonexistence of the relevant mental states."

At the first trial Helen Wu had been convicted of second-degree murder. At the retrial she was convicted of the lesser charge of manslaughter. She received a sentence of eleven years in prison. The decision in *People v. Wu* is an affirmation of the use of cultural evidence and persuasive precedent, which can also be used by judges and lawyers in black rage cases.

Some cultural defenses have the same potential as the black rage defense to educate us about racism. A profound example of the constructive use of cultural evidence is the high-profile case of Patrick Hooty Croy. His case is a journey that begins with the Native American people of northern California in the 1800s, erupts in bloodshed in Siskiyou County in 1978, continues on Death Row at San Quentin Prison, and ends in a San Francisco courtroom in 1990. We start the journey in a small town named Yreka.

Yreka, California, is nestled in the Shasta Valley, 320 miles north of San Francisco. It is situated near the Oregon border and the beautiful Klamath River, where the U.S. government and Native Americans have fought for years over salmon fishing. Yreka prides itself in being "a city that exemplifies all that is grand about a 'small' town, U.S.A."[4] The town was born in 1851 when gold was discovered in Black Gulch. Six weeks after the discovery, two thousand miners arrived and the life of the Tolowa, Yurok, Karuk, and Shasta Indians was forever changed. Reading the pamphlets and brochures from the Yreka Chamber of Commerce, you would hardly know of the history or the present-day existence of Siskiyou County's original peoples. There are only two references to Indians. The first is one line stating that the name "Yreka" is a Shasta Indian word for Mt. Shasta. The second reference is a description of "Indian Peggy" as one of the town's "famous personalities" who "is considered the savior of Yreka for warning the whites of an impending Indian attack in the '50's." It is not surprising that the Chamber of Commerce literature would leave out the fact that between 1850 and 1870 80 percent of the Native Americans in the county were killed. It is also no surprise that Indians in Siskiyou County still feel the same discrimination and prejudice their ancestors suffered.

Patrick Hooty Croy was born in Yreka in 1955. His parents were Native American, descendants of the Karuk and Shasta tribes that had lived there for centuries. His life was typical of an Indian boy in that county. He felt out of place in school, was harassed by the police, and was turned down for good jobs. He vividly recalled the police barging into his family's house and taking "poached" deer out of their freezer. He remembered seeing relatives coming out of the local jail with bruises from police beatings. Although he did fine in school, very little was expected of Indian kids, and he dropped out by the tenth grade. He got into minor troubles and was sent to the California Youth Authority for six months. He returned to Yreka, worked various jobs such as logging, and participated in the local Native American community. But essentially he was an alien in his own homeland.

There is an old saying: "If you want to understand someone, walk a mile in their shoes." Let us step into Hooty's shoes, go back in time to July 16, 1978, and begin to walk his path. On that Sunday evening, twenty-two-year-old Hooty decided to go to a party at the Pine Garden Apartments in Yreka. It was a typical party—there was some drinking and some marijuana. After a while Hooty went to sleep in one of the apartments. A small fight broke out between two people in the parking lot. The police were called by some white neighbors because of the loud noise, but soon things quieted down and the police left. Hooty woke up, and he, his sister Norma Jean, and his cousins Jasper, Darrell, and Carol talked about going deer hunting; deer meat was one way Indian people in northern California supplemented their diet. Hooty went to his girlfriend's house and picked up his .22 caliber rifle. On their way out of town the group stopped at the Sports and Spirits liquor store in downtown Yreka. There, a scene was played out that occurs almost daily somewhere in America.

The white store clerk and Hooty's sister and cousin got into a verbal altercation. The clerk shoved Norma Jean, and she picked up a can opener and brandished it toward the clerk. Jumping to the conclusion that they were going to rob him, the clerk ran out of the store. Hooty was standing by the car and the clerk ran up to him and said, "I think they are going to rob me." Hooty tried to calm him down. "They are not going to rob you," he said. Then he went into the store to get his sister and cousin. But by now the historical burden of dysfunctional race relations had taken hold.

A police car was driving by and the officer saw the clerk yelling that the store had been robbed. He was pointing at Hooty's car and shouting "get them!" One thing Hooty and his sister knew was that the police would never believe their side of the story. Hooty rapidly drove the car away, trying to get to the safety of their grandmother's cabin in the hills outside of town. Two police cars began a chase that would end in blood.

During the five-mile chase, Darrell leaned out the car window and fired one shot in a failed attempt to hit the police car's tire. After arriving at Rocky Gulch, Hooty and Norma Jean started running up a hill into the woods. Darrell grabbed the rifle and followed them. The police arrived and began shooting. Seventeen-year-old Jasper and eighteen-year-old Carol had not run into the hills; they surrendered and were handcuffed to some bushes. The police called for help, and soon there were twelve to fourteen cars with law enforcement personnel: California Highway Patrol, deputy sheriffs, and off-duty police. One of those off-duty policemen was Jesse "Bo" Hittson. He had won a stock car race earlier that evening and had gone to a barbecue where he had a few drinks. Hearing the police radio call, he rushed to the scene and jumped out of his vehicle, forgetting his bulletproof vest on the seat. He had his .357 magnum loaded with hollow-tipped bullets, which explode inside the body.

Hooty, Darrell, and Norma Jean were pinned down by the gunfire. Headlights and searchlights from the police cars were pointed at them as they crouched behind the same trees that had failed to offer adequate protection to their ancestors. Bullets from M-16s, AR-15s, shotguns, and revolvers were smashing into the trees. They had one small-caliber rifle. Darrell and Hooty passed the hunting rifle between them and fired five to ten shots. A few bullets hit the police cars; one policeman got shot in the hand. The police had no command center; there was no supervision. They just kept firing into the woods. Between 75 and 150 shots were fired at the three Indians. Darrell stood up, trying to surrender, and was shot in the groin. Norma Jean tried to run and was shot in the back.

Darrell yelled out, "I'm wounded and Norma Jean is dying!" The police yelled back, "We'll give you a half-hour to surrender!" There was no more shooting. Hooty, now with the rifle, started making his way back to his grandmother's cabin to see if she and his elderly aunt were still alive. At the same time, Hittson and another officer began moving toward the cabin, although other police were yelling at them "get away, stay down."

Hooty made it to the cabin and started to climb in through the window. At that instant, Bo Hittson came running around the side of the cabin. Hittson opened fire at Hooty's back. One bullet smashed into Hooty's buttocks and traveled into the spinal area. The other hollow-tip bullet exploded in the back of his arm, tearing a hole through it. Hooty whirled around and fired one bullet. It hit the officer directly in the heart, killing him.

The other policeman arrived at the scene, but all he saw was Hittson falling backwards. Hooty managed to crawl behind a building, where he lay in his own blood. Hearing the gunfire, other police ran up to the area and began firing at Hooty's position. He tried to yell out, "I'm wounded, I'm wounded!" The police fired another barrage, but by some miracle he was not hit. A few minutes later they dragged him out, and Hooty, either in shock or unconscious, was taken by ambulance to a hospital. Norma Jean was arrested with Darrell and was given medical treatment.

Four days after the shootings, a funeral service was held for Jesse Hittson. Over a thousand people attended, including approximately three hundred uniformed law enforcement officers from all over northern California. Flags were flown at half-mast, and city offices were closed from ten in the morning until two in the afternoon.

Hooty and the four other Indians were charged with conspiracy to commit murder, first-degree murder, four counts of attempted murder, four counts of assault with a deadly weapon, and robbery. Under an aiding and abetting theory and a conspiracy theory, all five could be tried for actions the others took. Hooty, Norma Jean, and their cousin Jasper were to be tried in one group. Darrell and Carol were to be tried in another proceeding.

Six weeks after the incident, Hooty still had to be brought to court in a wheelchair due to the gunshot wounds. The defense lawyers had hired a sociologist from a nearby college to survey the community for potential bias. He testified that more than 25 percent of those questioned believed that the defendants were guilty. He also concluded that the "drunk Indian stereotype is still quite strong in the county." Based on his testimony and the pretrial publicity, the case was transferred to nearby Placer County.

Other than the public defender no lawyers from Yreka would defend

Hooty, so a lawyer from another county was appointed. He was a former prosecutor who had a caseload mainly of civil cases and had never defended an Indian. He and Hooty had little or no communication. Hooty was sure the white man's court would offer him no justice. Fatalistically, he accepted what history had taught him—Indians are killed. He assumed he would be executed by the State of California.

At Hooty's trial two very damaging, but untrue, pieces of evidence were presented. First, white neighbors from the Pine Garden Apartments testified that they heard some Indians say, "Let's get a gun and shoot some sheriff." Legally, this testimony is considered hearsay because it is one person reporting on what another person said and therefore is susceptible to misinterpretation or outright falsehood. But it was allowed into evidence because there is an exception to the hearsay rule called a "declaration against penal interest." This means that a statement overheard by another person can be testified to if it admits to a criminal act or intention. Although the words were not said by Hooty, they were admitted as evidence against him because a conspiracy to murder was charged. In a conspiracy case, the words of one conspirator can be used against a coconspirator even if the coconspirator was not present at the time the statement was made.

The second erroneous piece of evidence was the testimony of a police officer who was present at the hospital. He testified that when the doctor asked Hooty what happened, Hooty replied, "I got shot robbing the liquor store." This hearsay statement was also allowed into evidence under the exception rule. Of course, Hooty did not rob the store, nor was he shot at the store, but that would make no difference to the jury.

The lawyers did not view this trial as a political case. Hooty's attorney did not attempt to expose the racism or misconduct of the police, nor did he want to explore the social conditions that Native Americans lived under in Siskiyou County. Hooty was not advised that a powerful self-defense argument was possible. Instead, his lawyer presented a weak "diminished capacity" defense.

Hooty, resigned to what he believed was his historical fate, offered no real defense. When he took the stand, he said he had been drinking and did not remember what happened. Why did he testify in that manner? Probably to help Darrell, who was the one who actually brought the rifle from the car. Probably because he knew he was going to receive the death penalty and there was nothing he could do to stop it.

Hooty and Norma Jean were convicted of every charge except two attempted murders. Jasper was convicted of second-degree murder and sentenced to seven years. Hooty's cousin Darrell was convicted of second-degree murder and sentenced to six years and six months. His cousin Carol was also convicted of second-degree murder and sent to a California Youth Authority prison for four years. Norma Jean was sentenced to life imprisonment. Hooty was sentenced to death.

Norma Jean appealed her conviction, but the California Court of Appeals ruled against her and her lawyer did not proceed any further in her behalf. Meanwhile, Hooty had been shipped to death row at San Quentin Prison. The prison was built on Punta de San Quentin, which was named after an Indian warrior who had led the Lacatvit Indians to their final defeat at the hands of the Mexicans. Fortunately for Hooty, the law provided that if a convicted person received the death penalty, there was an automatic appeal directly to the California Supreme Court. In 1985, the year of his appeal, the California Supreme Court, led by Chief Justice Rose Bird, gave meticulous care to each death penalty case and reversed a number of death verdicts, including Croy's. In his case the conviction was reversed on the grounds that the trial judge's instructions to the jury regarding the law of aiding and abetting were incorrect and prejudicial to Hooty's right to a fair trial. In 1986, Chief Justice Bird, Justice Cruz Reynoso, and Justice Joseph Grodin were recalled in an election rife with law-and-order rhetoric reminiscent of Reverend A. B. Winfield's vitriolic preaching against judges sympathetic to defendants 150 years earlier during William Freeman's case. Since that recall election the California Supreme Court has had one of the lowest rates of reversing death penalty verdicts in the country. Before the reversal of his conviction, Hooty had spent seven years on death row. Now the County of Siskiyou decided to put him on trial again. Norma Jean, meanwhile, was still serving her life sentence.[5]

The retrial would be a completely different political, legal, and human experience for Patrick Hooty Croy. Members of his family had been able to obtain the services of well-known attorney Tony Serra. Serra had grown up in San Francisco and attended Stanford, where he was on the football, baseball, and boxing teams while majoring in epistemology. In 1971, he had run for mayor of San Francisco on the Platypus party platform. His programs included terminating the draft, decriminalizing victimless crimes, returning police policies to the citizens, self-determination for communities, city-sponsored art activities, and other ideas that represented the politically aware segment of the flowering counterculture. He lost the election, but his charismatic personality, creative ideas, and colorful trials made him one of the most recognizable, and one of the best, criminal lawyers in America. In 1976 he went to trial as a defendant himself for refusing to pay income taxes as a protest against U.S. military aggression in Vietnam. He was convicted and spent six months in prison. Perhaps that experience strengthened his empathy for those facing the power of the criminal legal system.

Hooty's case reminded Serra of Chol Soo Lee, who had been given the death penalty for a shooting in Chinatown, based on mistaken identification of Lee by white tourists. Lee's cause had won the support of the Asian community, and eventually his conviction had been reversed. When the state decided to retry Lee, Serra defended him. In a high-profile trial, Lee was found not guilty and went from death row to freedom. Serra hoped he could do the same for Hooty.

Serra headed a defense team of several lawyers, experts on Native American culture, legal workers, and investigators. They immersed themselves in the facts of the case and in the history of Hooty's tribe in California. They understood that to win the trial they would have to get a venue change, and to do so they would have to break the image of colorblindness to which our legal system is wedded. In the hearing on the motion to move the trial to an unbiased venue, eight witnesses, including six Native Americans, testified. Their testimony exposed the historic oppression of Native Americans in Placer and Siskiyou Counties, as well as the racism that still permeated these counties. An interview following the first trial revealed that one juror stated during deliberations that "this is exactly what happens when an Indian gets liquored up or has too much to drink." The judge ruled in favor of the change of venue motion, stating, "The potential for residual bias against the defendant in the context of traditionally preconceived notions [regarding Indian people] raises a risk that prejudice will arise during the presentation of the evidence unrelated to the facts."

After another venue hearing showing anti-Indian feelings in the other northern California rural counties the case was transferred to San Francisco. Though the venue problem had been solved, Hooty still faced not only the robbery charge, but also the charges of assault on police and murdering a policeman. Even in a liberal city like San Francisco, jurors do not look sympathetically on killers.

The defense team realized it needed to explain why Hooty had fled from the scene of the alleged robbery, and why he and Darrell had fired at the police instead of giving up. With regard to fleeing the scene, the law provides that the prosecution can put forth such evidence as "consciousness of guilt"—that is, the defendant's act of running away from the scene of an alleged crime implies that the defendant is guilty of that crime. The judge can then instruct the jurors that they can infer guilt from an act of flight. However, this jury instruction is a two-edged sword that can also be used by the defense to cut away at the prosecution by showing innocent reasons for fleeing. In Hooty's case, this was a means by which the history of Indian–police relations could be placed before the jury. Such evidence would show that Hooty feared the police and did not think they would listen to the Indian side of the story. He fled, not because there had been a robbery, but rather because of his mistrust of the police.

Since the law of self-defense allows for testimony regarding the defendant's state of mind, the defense team hoped to be able to put forth a cultural defense. They made a motion to offer expert testimony on the historical and present relations between whites and Indians in northern California generally and Siskiyou County specifically. This testimony was relevant to Hooty's state of mind, that is, to the reasonableness of his belief that he was in imminent danger of death or serious injury. The defense filed a state-of-the-art brief that tied together the law of self-defense and the law regarding expert testimony with the black rage case of Stephen Robinson, more recent cultural defense cases, and battered women cases.[6] The motion was granted, although the judge limited the number of experts—only five of the nine requested experts would testify.

The defense desired a jury made up of a cross-section of San Franciscans. Although there were no Native Americans on the jury, the jury selection process resulted in a good mix in terms of age, gender, and race. There were five whites, three African Americans, two Latinos, and two Asians. After eleven years in prison, Hooty was getting one last chance to win his freedom.

On November 30, 1989, opening statements began. The district attorney, who had been brought in from Stockton, California, to try the case, presented his opening statement. Then Tony Serra took his place before the jury box. In his late forties, with his cowboy boots and his graying hair tied back into a ponytail, Serra looked a bit like an aging San Francisco hippy. One of the reasons for Serra's success is that he looks different from the straight-arrow, mass-produced lawyer most juries expect to see. His oratorical skills rival any attorney in the country. His forceful and unique personality comes through to a jury, which creates the potential for real communication. Your ideas, your logic, and your sincerity have an impact. Jurors react favorably to skilled verbal advocacy; they react even more positively to authentic human interaction.

Serra understood the overwhelming alienation and impotence a defendant feels in court. The accused sits there for days, sometimes for weeks, without being able to raise his own voice in his defense. You can find expression of this alienation in literature—think of the defendants in Albert Camus's *The Stranger* or Franz Kafka's *The Trial*. Recently a nationally known and respected lawyer, Patrick Hallinan, was prosecuted for conspiring with a former client to import and distribute tons of marijuana. After his acquittal, he wrote an article in which he described how it felt to sit in the defendant's chair: "The hardest part of the six-week trial was sitting quietly at the defense table while I was being vilified by the prosecutor. In my mind I responded to every smear and allegation. . . . No amount of seasoning in the federal criminal courts prepared me for the level of raw and constant anxiety I experienced as a defendant." [7]

Aware that a defendant's voice is silenced, except when he testifies, Serra began his opening statement trying to give expression to Hooty's voice:

> Ladies and gentlemen, a lawyer speaks with many voices in a case like this. And you'll hear I presume throughout the trial the voice of anger, perhaps, voices of sadness. But in opening statement and throughout the course of the trial the main voice that we lawyers speak, from that table, is the voice of Patrick Hooty Croy.

Some cases clearly involve racial issues. Henry Sweet's trial was one of those cases, and therefore Clarence Darrow could hammer home the racial themes. Stephen Robinson's bank robbery was not obviously related to race, and therefore I had to be careful in arguing the racial context to the jury. Hooty's crime, like Henry Sweet's, involved a person of color shoot-ing a white person in self-defense. The racial issues involved in the case jump out at a lawyer, although it is important to note that Hooty's first lawyer either was unaware of or denied the racial reality of the case. Serra did not deny this reality, but rather made it the cornerstone of the defense. Within the first two minutes of his opening statement, he confronted the jurors with the theme of racism:

> This is what the evidence will be. A white police officer shot an Indian twice in the back. This is what the evidence will be. A white police officer shot an Indian twice in the back during a cease fire, a de facto cease fire. That's what the evidence will be. A white police officer shot an Indian twice in the back during a cease fire, while he the officer was under the influence of alcohol. That's why we're here, and that's why, in essence, there are other people who aren't present. Perhaps, who are present symbolically, whose voices will resound during the course of the trial, much more than a trial for an alleged homicide. This will be a trial that will have profound issues regarding racial relations.

The defense team decided to put all five experts on the stand to testify to the history of Native Americans and to the continuing environment of discrimination that Indians face in the northern counties of California. The team felt it was important to use experts who were Native American, in order to break through the stereotype of the uneducated, simple Indian, and to let jurors experience authentic (i.e., not Hollywood) Indians. The public is aware of Crazy Horse and Sitting Bull. Paratroopers in World War II would yell "Geronimo" as they jumped out of their planes. The large reservations of the Lakota and the Navajo have had an impact on the public's consciousness of Indian culture and history in the Dakotas and the Southwest. But most people do not know that there are more Native Americans in California than in any other state. Because the California Indian population consists of many small tribes, and because of the state's failure to take responsibility for the history of genocidal attacks on its indigenous peoples, Indians are almost invisible to the public and to polit-ical institutions. The expert testimony made the life of Indians visible and created a framework for Hooty's contention that mistrust and fear of the police caused him to flee and fail to surrender.

An Indian historian, Jack Norton, testified how California's Indian population in the 1800s was reduced from two hundred thousand to only twenty thousand through massacres of tribes by gold miners, citizen volunteers, and the U.S. Army. He testified to historical incidents that live on in the memory and folklore of the northern California Indians. He told of a time when members of the Shasta tribe were invited to a feast to celebrate a new land allotment, but their food was poisoned and only a few survived. He told of how the coastal Indians in northwestern California were told they were to be relocated to a new reservation on the Klamath River. They boarded ships for the journey down the coast, but they were taken out to sea and dumped overboard. Treachery, betrayal, and murder marked the history of the white man's relations with the original inhabitants of California. This history had not been forgotten by Hooty's tribes, the Shasta and Karuks.

Other Indians, such as Susan Davenport, a former high school teacher who was head of the Tri-County Indian Agency, testified to the discrimination Indian children face in the school districts and in the criminal justice system. Ed Bronson, a non-Indian professor of political science, analyzed the image of Indians in the Yreka newspaper from 1970 to 1978 and explained to the jurors the negative stereotypes of the media coverage.

The jury seemed attentive and responsive to the expert witnesses. The blend of historical oppression and present-day discrimination made the testimony seem alive instead of a dead history lesson about times long ago.

The final piece of the cultural defense was to tie the generalities to Hooty's individual experience. As the Steven Robinson case showed, the life experiences of the defendant can come into evidence through the psychologist and through the defendant, if he takes the stand. In Hooty's case, a Native American psychologist named Art Martinez was allowed to testify even though a psychiatric defense was not being used. Under the self-defense theory, Martinez was able to testify to Hooty's state of mind when the shootout took place. He was able to describe Hooty's experiences and perceptions of racism and how they influenced his behavior. Martinez was perceived as a professional with integrity and dignity, and his testimony helped give the jury a complete picture of Hooty as a human being, not a stereotyped Indian or a rhetorical symbol of Indian oppression.

Hooty then took the stand. He testified about how his father had gone to Washington, D.C., to obtain original copies of the treaty of 1851, which was supposed to have protected the Shasta Indians. Like almost all such treaties, it had been violated by the U.S. government. His father had gone to court to argue that the treaty should be respected and enforced. Hooty remembered that the case had been lost.

One experience Hooty described was particularly moving and relevant. Often the police in Yreka would follow Indian kids. When Hooty was twelve or thirteen years old, the police began to chase him. He hadn't done anything, but he was so afraid he ran into the woods. It was winter, and he ran through the snow and jumped into a river that was frozen. Serra described the experience in closing: "He was there hiding. Think of that, he was a little Indian child hiding and his father is a leader, a wise man, a fighter. He has a right to be proud and be strong, and yet here he is, hiding as a child in the frozen river. He's wet and he's in pain. He hasn't done anything." Hooty was pulled out of the river by the police, who hand-cuffed him and took him to jail. He spent the night in juvenile detention and was released the next day. It turned out that the police had been looking for a different Indian boy.

The most dramatic moment of an otherwise relatively unemotional direct examination was when Croy described what he was thinking as the police were firing at him. "I realized that all the things my grandmother and father had told us were coming true, that they were going to kill us all."

Unlike his first trial, at the retrial Hooty was well prepared to testify. The cross-examination focused on his testimony at the earlier trial, in which he had said he could not remember what happened because he had been drinking. Hooty's explanation of that testimony was that he had not trusted his lawyer and felt he would not get a fair trial. It did not sound like a lie, but rather an understandable reaction of a young Indian man to hostile and dangerous circumstances. This was a theme that Serra would underscore in his closing. Hooty left the stand with his dignity intact. The defense team felt that the jury would be able to empathize with Hooty and understand why he had lied at the first trial.

Serra's closing argument was an example of his oratorical skills. He told parables, referred to philosophy, and discussed history. But he also kept in mind the facts and mixed his rhetorical flourishes with the relevant law. He began by confronting the negative racial stereotyping used by the prosecution.

Similarly, when the prosecutor elicited testimony about the party at the Pine Garden apartments he tried to leave the impression that it was a wild, drunken brawl. The image of the "drunken Indian" had a potent effect in the first trial, influencing the jurors against the defendants. Serra knew he would have to counter that potential influence in the second trial. He met the issue head on and turned it around to Hooty's benefit:

> Has one witness come forward and said to you, "I saw Hooty shoot from the hill?" . . . There's not one shred of evidence that says he shot. And all the Indians say he did not shoot, so the prosecutor has to say, "Don't believe the Indians; don't believe the drunk Indians; don't believe the dirty Indians." That's the bottom line. . . . Do you understand the real hoax, the real fabrication is on the side of the prosecution. If this case stands for anything, it stands for a proposition that everyone has to be treated equal. And that means in court too.

You must reach across racial lines when constructing a black rage or cultural defense. One way of doing this is to speak to shared experiences. The voir dire process in Hooty's case had produced a multiracial jury, more so than in the usual San Francisco trial. Facing this type of jury, Serra felt that some jurors had shared the experience of what he termed "institutional genocide."

> The Indians were all exposed to institutional genocide. It's not just Indians, it's common to all sub-cultures; they're exploited, harassed, discriminated against, acts of brutality, acts of indifference. All sub-cultures have been exposed to that in this country. You mistrust authority. So if the white kids were beating you up, does the Indian call the police? No. The police take the whites' point of view; the police would arrest you. You don't go up to the police. You have to avoid — to run, so Hooty had instilled in him two things, avoid confrontation, and the instinct of flight. You can't win at any level of confrontation. . . . So there was no trust. No trust was engendered in Hooty or any young Indian.

Another means of reaching across racial lines is to let the jury know that people of the defendant's race are hoping that the jurors will overcome their stereotypes and do justice. This is a delicate proposition. You do not want to beat up the jurors for being of a different race or culture. You do not want to offend people by challenging them to prove they are not racist by deciding in your client's favor. Serra walked a tightrope as he referred three different times to the Indian community and how it was looking to the jurors for justice, implying that a not guilty verdict would help heal the wounds of a racist past:

> You heard the history of the Indian people. Their mistrust of authority. The fact that they have never, ever trusted the court system. They have never trusted lawyers; they have never trusted judges. For them, it is an extension of the early settlers, the military, the whites who have always perpetrated a form of genocide of them. They have never cooperated, they distrust, they disdain the judiciary. In this trial it has been reversed. They have come here with open hearts and open hands. They have told you the truth. They have once again placed their faith in white man's law and he, the prosecutor, says they have perpetrated, these Indians have perpetrated a hoax. He said that because he has no evidence!

Most juries take their responsibility seriously. If you invited twelve people to a dinner party and gave them the facts of a typical criminal case they would vote for conviction almost every time. But if you put those same twelve people in a jury box, approximately 10 to 15 percent of the time they will vote for acquittal or come to a divided verdict. One crucial difference between a dinner party and a jury trial is that jurors realize their decision has real consequences for another human being. Most jurors believe in the concept of reasonable doubt, and they will sometimes give a defendant the benefit of the doubt when analyzing the evidence. The democratic tradition in America is founded on the right of the individual against the power and encroachment of the government. In criminal trials, jurors are torn between their fear of crime and their duty to judge each person as an individual. Prosecutors often will speak to the jurors' fears by equating the defendant with the general violence and crime in society. Defense attorneys will focus on the individuality of the defendant and speak to the jurors' desire to give every person a chance before condemning him or her.

A key method of helping the jurors get in touch with their desire to do justice is to remind them of the grave responsibility they carry. Even in a misdemeanor case, the lawyer can convey a feeling of seriousness, of moral weight, of the need to consider the evidence carefully and to respect the rule of reasonable doubt. Once in a great while a case comes along that screams out for righteousness. The Hooty Croy trial was such a case. The facts of self-defense were powerful, and the symbolism of the case was apparent. In this context, Serra was able to tap into the jurors' need to be part of something bigger than themselves:

> We will never forget this case. In a certain way, maybe it will be one of the most meaningful things, the most meaningful decisions, profound decisions, decisions fraught with social and political content—the opportunity to do justice. You might never have another opportunity like this again. It might be one of the more meaningful events that you are going to participate in during your life.

Lawyers often get caught up in their own egos. They have an image of themselves as Spencer Tracy playing Clarence Darrow in *Inherit the Wind,* or Tom Cruise destroying Jack Nicholson during cross-examination in *A Few Good Men.* Caught up in their fantasies, they shout at neutral witnesses as if they were criminal conspirators. They wax eloquent about the American way of justice, when the facts point to a brutal act by an obviously guilty client.

Serra, on the other hand, was in an enviable position. His client actually was innocent and had been mistreated. Hooty had been a victim of a police force that had acted like Custer and the U.S. cavalry. Shot, arrested, and charged, he was then denied effective representation at his murder trial. Sentenced to death, he had been given another chance by a California Supreme Court that in 1985 had at its philosophical core a respect for individual liberty. The reality of the case allowed Serra to end his argument with an emotion and passion that was felt and understood by the jurors.

> Hittson had to be crouched down; and he shoots, bang, bang, bang—at least three times, two of them going into Hooty, and one going up against the wall. . . . Hooty turned and there was this confrontation face to face and there was this shot. And then Hooty collapsed like he said, and he fell and then he started crawling. . . . That is the honest truth of what occurred.

That's a truth that wasn't previously told. That was the truth that wasn't told because Hooty had no faith at that time in the system. So Hooty took the responsibility upon himself. There's no reason now to hide any of the truth. He's told everything exactly the way it was: From the bottom collectively of our team's heart, we urge you to do justice in this case. It is, in closing, reasonable doubt. It is a case that cries out singularly for justice. There have been long delays. Hooty deserves to be set free. This is a wonderful, wonderful case for justice—for you to administer justice. . . . It's your almost sacred duty to find "Not Guilty on these charges." Thank you very much.

The jury deliberated for a full week, and then a second week. An optimistic defense team had expected a quick verdict. Some of the reporters covering the trial began to say that the times were too conservative to allow an acquittal for the killing of a policeman. On May 1, the jury filed back into the courtroom to deliver its verdict. Patrick Hooty Croy was found not guilty on all charges. After years locked away on San Quentin's death row, he was free.

Hooty is now a full-time student at San Francisco State University. He has continued to develop his artistic talents and is studying computer graphics.

After the trial, Karen Jo Koonan of the National Jury Project conducted intensive interviews with several members of the jury. There was no doubt that the cultural defense had created a context for the jurors to react favorably to the defense's presentation of evidence. One juror said that when he heard the charges they sounded "so damming" that he wondered how the defendant could respond. But as the testimony developed he felt that "the main issue was racism."

The interviews showed that the jurors had been influenced by the content of the testimony presented by the cultural defense witnesses. Even more than the content, they were impressed by the expert witnesses themselves. Clearly, the fact that most of these educated and articulate witnesses were Native American added to the impact of their words. The cultural defense succeeded in putting the jurors in Hooty's shoes. They were able to understand that any reasonable person in his situation would have responded in the same way. He would have run from the police even though he had not robbed the store. He would have been afraid to surrender to law enforcement once the shooting had begun. They comprehended the legal rule that if a policeman uses excessive force a person is entitled to respond with force to defend himself. They believed Hooty had acted in self-defense when he shot Hittson.

Hooty's case is an excellent example of taking the offensive when faced with damning evidence. In order to do so effectively, the defense team had to perceive the social conditions under which Hooty lived. They needed to feel those conditions, to grasp Hooty's life experience. The lawyer in the first trial failed to do this because he was blinded by his own prejudices.

The defense team approached the case politically. They consciously uncovered the historical, economic, and social roots of a conflict that led to one dead policeman, one wounded policeman, and three wounded Indians. With this perspective they were able to construct a persuasive cultural defense.

A few words of caution should be noted before lawyers leap into similar cultural defenses. Hooty's acquittal was won in San Francisco, where Indians are not highly visible, are not considered a social problem, and are not threatening to jurors of other ethnic backgrounds. Whether such a defense would have been as persuasive in Albuquerque, New Mexico, or Rapid City, South Dakota, must be left to lawyers, clients, and jury consultants who understand those specific environments.

The United States is a multiracial, multicultural society that is growing more diverse each year. Cultural defenses will be an expanding area of legal activity in both criminal and civil law. Like black rage cases, these cases will send a political message. Lawyers, always intent on winning, should recognize the content of the message they send. This awareness should inform their strategy, the types of experts they call, and how they frame the issues to the public. Sometimes there will be abuses of the cultural defense, but we cannot shy away from this potentially enlightening form of social reality evidence.

Too many people are suffering
Too many people are sad
Too little people got everything while
Too many people got nothing.
Remake the world . . .
Be you black, Be you white.
—Jimmy Cliff, "Remake the World"

Chapter 14

"Remake the World"

What is the future of the black rage defense in America's courtrooms? To answer that question we must first look at the social construction of crime. Second, we need to look at how the cataclysmic economic changes taking place today will affect African Americans. We can then look at two areas where the black rage defense is expanding and suggest situations in which such a defense is most appropriate and useful.

Crime is real. However, the depiction of crime in America is often fictitious. The media's drive for profits results in the overreporting and sensationalizing of murder and assault. Stories are considered newsworthy if they sell newspapers or grab the attention of fidgety remote control–wielding television viewers. The Center for Media and Public Affairs reported that the three network television news shows broadcast four times as many crime stories in 1995 as in 1991, even though FBI statistics show that serious crimes actually decreased during that period.

There is a social construct to crime. The way in which antisocial behavior is characterized, classified, and punished molds the way people think and feel about crime. The savings-and-loan rip-off, fradulent corporate cost overruns, and white-collar crimes cost the taxpayer far more than street crime.[1] Corporate violations of health and safety laws result in thousands of worker injuries and deaths. Corporate crimes against the environment pose a larger threat to the future of society than car theft and robbery. These costly crimes are committed almost completely by white males, yet the social perception of the criminal is that he is a black male.

A telling example of the institutional racism that infects our concept of crime is the controversey around the different punishments for possession of powdered cocaine versus crack cocaine. In federal court possession of five grams of crack draws a *mandatory* five-year minimum while possession of five grams of powdered cocaine has no mandatory minimum and first-time offenders usually receive probation. One has to possess a hundred times more powdered cocaine than crack to be sentenced to five years. This, plus law enforcement's admitted choice to target the crack world over the cocaine world, has resulted in large numbers of poor African American men and women going to federal prison instead of middle-class white men and women.

Sentencing disparity is not limited to the crack–powdered cocaine distinction. In 1995 an official study of all eighty thousand federal convictions over two years showed that African Americans receive sentences that are on average 10 percent longer than those of whites for similar crimes.

Combining state and federal jurisdictions, almost one third (32 percent) of African American men 20–29 years old are incarcerated, on parole, or on probation. This represents an increase of 10 percent over the last five years. Men are not the only ones who are being entangled in the criminal law web. Since 1989, African American women have experienced the greatest increase in involvement with the criminal justice system—a 78 percent jump.

Institutional racism is prevalent in every area of criminal law. A 1996 study in California showed that once arrested, whites have their charges reduced more often than African Americans and Latinos, and that white offenders received community-based rehabilitation placements at twice the rate of African Americans.

In 1995 Paul Butler, a professor at George Washington University Law School, shocked the legal community by advocating that African American jurors in nonviolent cases such as theft and drugs engage in jury nullification by refusing to convict black defendants. Butler was not shooting from the hip; he is a former federal prosecutor and had written a well-documented piece. He argued that a system of white supremacy "creates and sustains the criminal breeding ground, which produces the black criminal." He correctly asserted that rehabilitation is no longer a goal of the criminal law system and concluded that the consequence of the racism in the criminal justice system is that the black community is losing valuable human resources. He suggested that jurors engage in a social cost-benefit analysis and use their power to refuse to be part of the assembly line that sends black men and women to jail.

Although the social construct of crime is based on fiction and tainted by racism, crime itself is real and frightening. In a 1994 *National Law Journal* poll 62 percent of people said they were "truly desperate" about personal safety. That was an almost 100 percent increase since 1989. Thirty-eight percent of African Americans said they have been victims of crimes involving violence or the threat of violence, a substantial increase since 1989. In order to understand the reality of crime, I try to put myself in the jury box. At the inception of a trial jurors are always asked the following question: "Have you or anyone in your family been a victim of a crime?" If I were a juror, this would be my answer: "My sixty-year-old mother was knocked unconscious during a mugging in Hollywood. A few years later her friend was murdered during a street robbery in front of her apartment house in Venice, California. My father had his head split open in Chicago when he helped an older man being harassed by four young men. Years later, as he was walking home he was smashed in the face by a teenager for no discernible reason. He and other passengers were robbed at gunpoint at the subway station. His home was burglarized numerous times. His car was stolen and burned. One of my brothers had a random bullet come through his second-story window. One of my other brothers, while working at a retail store, was thrown to the floor by robbers, who stepped on his neck and held a gun to his head. Another time a gun was pulled on him at the basketball court. A gang of teenagers attacked him, hitting him with chairs and locks, which resulted in thirteen stitches in his head. My stepfather, while in his sixties, was slugged in the face and robbed by two men. My sons have been mugged. Our cars have been stolen and stripped beyond repair. My youngest son has had two friends murdered. My wife was robbed at gunpoint. Another brother had a gun put to the side of his head in a robbery. As he raised his hand in a reflex to push the revolver away he touched its cold steel and froze, knowing he was an instant away from death."[2]

Is crime real? Is the threat of crime terrifying? Of course. But putting more and more people in prison will not change this reality. If California were a country, it would have the world's eighth-largest economy. Prisons are its third leading industry. Investment counselors are actually advising their clients to put money into prison construction as a safe, profitable venture. Nationally, criminal law repression is the growth industry of the nineties.[3] But three-strikes laws and more punitive measures do not change the fact that 95 percent of people in jail will return to the community. Most will return uneducated, brutalized, and filled with rage.

Will crime go away? Given the predicted future of the economy, the only thing that will go away are jobs for what once was a productive, hard-working, semiskilled and unskilled working class. It is noteworthy that the U.S. secretary of labor, a cutting-edge Marxist magazine, and one of the giants of American sociology all concur on much of the economic reality of the 1990s. Robert Reich has likened the conflict between the new technologies and old industrialism to "tectonic plates colliding," destroying the old mass-production system and causing the "economic earth to crack open." *Cy. Rev*, a socialist magazine that analyzes the cybernetic revolution, explains that the new economic changes are being driven by a fundamental shift in how wealth is produced.[4] Information technology is the new means of production. One of *cy. Rev*'s founders, himself a former steelworker, gives a poignant example of the change from physical to intellectual labor. He worked at U.S. Steel in Chicago, eventually moving from unskilled labor at the blast furnace to a five-year program learning to be a machinist. As a machinist in the mass-production economy he would have been ensured a good salary and work almost anywhere in the country. But information technology took what he had learned, imprinted it on a chip, and inserted the chip directly into the lathe. Now the chip runs the machine, and his job was reduced from complex and stimulating work to simply pushing buttons at the beginning of the shift to input that day's production program. One worker could monitor four machines, so three workers lost their jobs. Soon the giant U.S. Steel mill was employing only a fraction of its previous workforce, and a few years it later closed altogether. A study of former steelworkers from this plant showed an increase in divorce, sickness, and failed mortgages and significant feelings of anger and violence.

Reich and *cy. Rev* agree that corporations, driven to compete and maximize profits, are changing workers' relationships to their jobs, creating a new group of people who fall outside the economy. Now that layoffs are permanent, Reich suggests that we should use a new word to describe these workers—"castoffs." These castoffs will have little or no productive role in society.

Many people have warned of the negative impact of the technological revolution on minority communities. As far back as 1970, Sidney Willhelm in *Who Needs the Negro* forecasted that the destruction of the mass-production economy would change the situation of African Americans from "exploitation to uselessness."

Alvin and Heidi Toffler, the "Third Wave" economic theorists admired by both Al Gore and Newt Gingrich, pointed out that just one day before the Rodney King riots began the *Los Angeles Times* published a list of the top one hundred U.S. companies. Missing from the list were the mass-production manufacturers of autos, steel, textiles, tires, and cement that previously had provided stable, decent-paying jobs for a black proletariat. The Tofflers warn against the writing off of entire minority communities such as South-Central Los Angeles.

In the midst of a torrent of statistics on increasing poverty at the low end of the scale and articles analyzing the death of the industrial age,[5] Harvard sociologist William Julius Wilson has written a detailed and profound study of the consequences of these changes, entitled *When Work Disappears* (1996). Wilson's thesis is that a poor but working community is "entirely different" from a poor and unemployed community. In a concrete study of three neighborhoods in Chicago, he shows that long-term joblessness rends the social fabric of the community. Ninety-five percent of these neighborhoods have been and still are African American. In 1950, 70 percent of black males in those neighborhoods were working. In 1990, only 37 percent were working. Williams argues persuasively that this concentration of joblessness robs people of what they need to grow and prosper. The structure provided by getting up and going to a full-time job every day translates into discipline and a sense of responsibility, which form a productive personality. Chronic unemployment causes a chronic illness of spirit. When young men and women have nothing to look forward to, they develop despair, cynicism, and a fatalistic attitude toward their lives.

Williams shows how the decline of the mass-production system has meant the end of work, which in turn has caused a severe disruption of support networks. The church, the family, and civic organizations—all of which played a positive role in counterbalancing poverty and racism—have been damaged by years of persistent unemployment. With the supportive culture of their communities wrecked by forces beyond their control, the citizens of these neighborhoods have been left isolated and hurting. Is it any wonder that crime takes root and thrives amid devastation?

When African Americans such as Butler look at the appalling numbers of their community members in prisons, they see the detrimental consequences of a white supremacy construction of crime. They cry out, "You cannot put every young black man in prison!" When the average white person looks at the same statistics, he believes that they are the natural result of blacks being more criminally inclined than other races. *The black rage defense is a tool to expose the fallacy of such racist thinking.* When shown how racial and economic oppression shape a defendant's actions, other people begin to realize that African Americans are not inherently criminal. The jurors who acquitted Steven Robinson, James Johnson, and Henry Sweet had to confront their own stereotypes and make a connection between societal racism and criminal behavior.

The previous chapters have emphasized psychiatric and self-defense cases. There is another area of law in which the black rage defense is growing and where its capability of overcoming racial stereotyping will be severely tested. This field of criminal law is death penalty mitigation. If a person is convicted of a capital crime, he is entitled to a separate hearing. At that "penalty phase," a minitrial takes place in which the prosecutor introduces "aggravation" evidence. This is evidence that portrays the defendant as an evil person whose crime is not a result of social forces but rather of a "malignant heart." The defense is allowed to introduce "mitigation" evidence. The courts have held that a defense lawyer has a legal responsibility to bring all evidence to the jury's attention that "humanizes" the defendant. This duty grows out of the nature of the sentencing hearing, which is "defense counsel's chance to show the jury that the defendant, despite the crime, is worth saving as a human being."[6] The courts have ruled that evidence of one's cultural backround is admissible. In one case, the Ninth Circuit Court of Appeals determined that it was ineffective aid of counsel to fail to produce evidence of the defendant's Thai culture, "including Thai concepts of remorse and shame which might well have bridged a cultural gap between the jury and the accused."[7] These rulings afford precedent for admitting evidence of black culture and the effects of racial and economic discrimination.

The few lawyers who specialize in death penalty cases are well versed in preparing a social history of their clients.[8] The challenge for all lawyers doing such work is to integrate the fundamentals of the black rage defense into their presentations at both the trial and the appellate levels.

The black rage defense is a strategy used primarily in criminal cases. However, there are times when criminal and civil law intersect. In such situations the basics of the black rage defense may be used in both areas. An example discussed in earlier chapters was the James Johnson cases. The racism practiced by Chrysler Corporation contributed to Johnson's mental illness, providing an insanity defense in the criminal trial and creating a basis for disability in the workers' compensation hearing. This is not an isolated example. There is great potential for black rage–type legal actions, if only lawyers would not be frightened by age-old and narrow interpretations of the rules of evidence. The cases analyzed in this book are part of a legal history that is constantly being shaped by innovative pleadings, new conceptual arguments, and fearless advocacy. What is permissible in court is determined by struggle. In 1996 a case unfolded in Brooklyn that epitomizes the power of such creative legal action.

The Noble Drew Ali Plaza housing project is located in the Brownsville section of Brooklyn. Three hundred seventy-five African American families and eight Hispanic families reside there. The project was owned by three white men (Linden Realty), who hired an all-white group of on-site managers. The project was subsidized by the federal government, and rents were set by the government at fair market rates of $650 per month for a one-bedroom to $950 for a four-bedroom apartment. Each family paid 30 percent of its adjusted gross income, and the rest was paid by the federal subsidy.

During the seven years in which this virtually all-black project was run by an all-white group, conditions deteriorated to the point where living there became an environmental nightmare. Tenant Charlene Burwell and her six children were forced to spend three days with raw sewage, including human excrement, overflowing from the toilets, sinks, and bathtub. Yvette Dozier constantly complained about the rotting bedroom floor, fearing for the safety of her two little children. No repair was made, and one day Dozier actually fell through the floor to the apartment below and herniated a disc. Barbara Kelley had an eleven-year-old daughter who was seriously disabled with cerebral palsy and respiratory illness. They lived on the sixth floor and elevators were always broken. When her daughter Rachel needed emergency medical care, the medical workers could not take her down the stairs on a stretcher. As the terrified girl gasped for air, they had to carry her to the roof, cross over to the adjoining building, carry her down to that building's elevator, and finally rush her to the hospital. During one year Rachel needed emergency medical treatment six times—and each time the elevators were broken. Serena Audain lived with her two children, three and six years old. In just one week she caught eight rats in her apartment as they crawled in through holes in walls and cupboards, which the management had not fixed. Rats roamed unchecked in all the buildings.

All the tenants suffered freezing cold in winter, sewage backup with a persistent nauseating stench invading their homes, water leaks, inadequate security, broken fixtures, and management indifference. As Burwell would state in her affidavit, "If we were criminals and lived in a penitentiary, the way we live would be considered cruel and unusual punishment."

Linden Realty was not the sole cause of this despicable situation. The federal government disregarded its own legal responsibility to ensure "safe, decent, and sanitary" housing to the tenants. The Department of Housing and Urban Development (HUD) paid the owners over $15 million in subsidies during a seven-year period. One of the tenants put her finger on the problem: "Even when we pay white people's rents, they still give us black people's services, which is no services at all."

Brooklyn Legal Services attorney Richard Wagner filed a complicated federal lawsuit against Linden Realty on behalf of the Tenants' Association. Wagner has a reputation as a brilliant legal thinker who has demonstrated an unswerving commitment to racial justice. Within six months the case was won. Title was taken away from the owners, and HUD agreed to do almost $5 million in repairs and renovations, after which ownership would be transferred to the Tenants' Association.

Wagner was not content with this victory. He wanted the previous owners to pay for the damage they had done to the lives of the tenants. Barred from suing for damages by constraints placed on Legal Services by a conservative Congress, Wagner took the case to private attorneys. He described in powerful terms the human consequences resulting from seven years of living in deplorable, dehumanizing conditions.

> Any child, whether white or black, would find life at a Noble Drew Ali Plaza physically miserable. Any child would find it difficult if not impossible to perform well at school. Any child would feel embarrassed and humiliated at the way they are forced to live.
>
> But I submit that NOT any child would blame herself for these conditions. Not any child would associate her environment with "the way black people live," and think of the very concept of decent living conditions as being white and slumlike conditions as being black.
>
> The fatalism, nihilism, loss of self-esteem and individual ambition, and, ultimately, destruction of the future human potential that is experienced by the *black* children is more a function of racism than physical environment. IT IS BLACK RAGE TURNED INWARD AND THE EMOTIONAL, SCHOLASTIC AND ECONOMIC DAMAGE IT DOES TO ITS VICTIMS LASTS A LIFETIME.[9]

Wagner was dismayed by the attitudes of most attorneys he approached. Instead of being excited about developing a strategy to translate black rage into legal damages, they muttered about how future scholastic and economic damage would be difficult to prove. They viewed the situation only through the prism of profit-loss, afraid that the task of pushing the courts forward in recognizing the potential economic and psychological damages caused by racism would be outweighed by the time, energy, and risk of losing that the case entailed. Fortunately, a few lawyers around the country think otherwise. One of them is Mercedes Marquez in Los Angeles. For ten years Marquez has accepted the challenge of proving the harm done to people of color by slumlords and an uncaring government, winning a $600,000 jury award among others, and recently settling a case for $2.5 million.[10] As more tenants organize against life-crippling housing conditions, we need lawyers who will expand the black rage defense to civil actions and educate opposing lawyers, judges, and juries to the destructive effects of present-day racism.

One cannot read about rats biting children at Noble Drew without thinking about Bigger Thomas in Richard Wright's novel *Native Son*. The book opens with Bigger trying to protect his mother, sister, and little brother from a large rat. "A huge black rat squealed and leaped at Bigger's trouser-leg and snagged it in his teeth. . . . Bigger took a shoe and pounded the rat's head, crushing it, cursing hysterically. . . . His mother sank to her knees and buried her face in the quilts and sobbed." Bigger Thomas turned his rage outward, eventually killing two people. As Rick Wagner interacted with his clients, he saw children and teenagers who also turned their fury outward, becoming violent and predatory. He argued that "these children are as much the victims of black rage as those who turn it inward, except that they find ways to share their pain with society in a way that society does not like but for which it refuses to accept any responsibility."

The Noble Drew housing project is an example of existing racism. Unfortunately, as much of the public is unable to understand black poverty and crime as the result of past discrimination, it is therefore incumbent on lawyers defending children who have grown up in slum housing to expose the present-day racism. A black rage defense would show the intersection of greedy private landlords and an indifferent government that fails to enforce the tenants' right to decent, safe housing.[11] Whenever the government prosecutes a young person who has grown up in a place like Noble Drew, the government itself should be put on trial for its willful acceptance of the dehumanizing practices of slumlords. We can and must show how present-day racism warps these defendants just as racism in the 1940s deformed Bigger Thomas.

Since the black rage defense is by definition a discussion of race set in an intensely emotional context, it is necessary for lawyers, legal workers, and defense committees to think through the social and philosophical ramifications of each case.

The different black rage cases analyzed in this book allow us to draw some conclusions about when the defense is appropriate and what elements give it the best chance of winning. The potential for the jury to empathize with the defendant should be an overriding concern, informing all tactical decisions. The strategic questions to be considered are as follows:

1. What is the nature of the crime? A property crime is qualitatively different from a homicide.
2. Who or what is the target of the crime? A robbery of a bank that has refused a loan to a burned-down black church is more understandable than a robbery for personal gain. An attack on a person who has racially humiliated and abused a defendant is quite different from a random assault on a passing motorist.
3. Is there a concrete connection between the crime and the defendant's personal history of racial oppression?
4. Has the defendant suffered serious economic hardship?
5. Does the personal history of the defendant tie into the motivation for the crime in a sympathetic manner?
6. What is the attitude of the defendant? Does she see herself as a victim, blaming everyone else for her problems? Or does she present herself as a proud person struggling in a hostile environment?
7. Are there elements of the defendant's culture, either positive or negative, which can be explained to a judge or jury as contributing causes of the crime?
8. Is the defendant capable of taking the stand and, with proper preparation, making a good impression?

The weight one gives to each element will differ depending on the type of case—self-defense, riot situation, duress, diminished capacity, insanity, or mitigation. The presentation will differ depending on whether one is trying to persuade a jury to acquit, a district attorney to reduce charges, or a judge to lower a sentence. In a civil case there will be other elements to consider. But one must always analyze the interplay between a system of white supremacy and the client's personal history and culture.

Peter Kim, a Korean American student at the University of California at Berkeley and a member of the rap group San Francisco Street Music, has written that "the Black Panthers were more than black." He means that the Panthers' messages of pride and empowerment and their programs of breakfast for children, health care, senior citizen security, and food distribution were relevant to all poor communities regardless of race. Similarly, the black rage defense is not limited to African Americans. The main thrust of the defense is to tie together individual behavior and societal conditions. That is why a black rage–type defense was used successfully in a self-defense case for Native American Patrick Hooty Croy and in an insanity case for white ex-convict John Zimmerman.

The black rage defense refutes the idea that there is a lower class of people who are inherently criminal and can be written off by society. It tries to educate people about the oppressive structures and behaviors in society that produce and increase criminality. It has been said that ignoring race is a privilege that only white people have. This defense forces whites, for a critical moment in time, to give up that privilege and think about the consequences of a system of white supremacy. The black rage defense is not based on race hatred. Rather, it is an antiracist defense, and those who use it should shape their strategies to embrace all people and to teach that society must share the responsibility for crime. This is certainly not a new concept. Indeed, the essence of the black rage defense may have been best stated by the Arabic philospher, artist, and poet Kahlil Gibran more than seventy years ago:

> The righteous is not innocent of the deeds
>   of the wicked,
> And the white-handed is not clean in the
>   doings of the felon.
> Yea, the guilty is often times the victim of the injured,
> And still more often the condemned is the
>   burden bearer for the guiltless and unblamed.
> You cannot separate the just from the unjust
>   and the good from the wicked;
> For they stand together before the face of
>   the sun even as the black thread and the white are woven together.

Notes

Notes to Chapter 1

1. BENJAMIN HALL, THE TRIAL OF WILLIAM FREEMAN iv (1848). This book is a report of the case. It includes testimony, opening statements and closing arguments, the judge's sentencing, the appeals court opinion, the autopsy reports, and an introduction describing the facts surrounding the case. A few libraries have this rare book. Washington University in St. Louis was kind enough to send me their copy through an interlibrary loan. The entire closing argument of defense counsel, William Henry Seward, was also published seperately as ARGUMENT OF WILLIAM H. SEWARD IN DEFENSE OF WILLIAM FREEMAN ON HIS TRIAL FOR MURDER (1846) and is available from some university libraries. Unless otherwise noted, all quotes in this chapter are from Hall's report of the case.
2. From the poem "Justice" by Langston Hughes. See the epigraph to chapter 3.
3. JOHN M. TAYLOR, WILLIAM HENRY SEWARD: LINCOLN'S RIGHT HAND 66 (1991).
4. GLYNDON VAN DEUSEN, WILLIAM HENRY SEWARD 94 (1967).
5. There is no indication in Hall's report of the proceeding or in Seward's closing argument that William Freeman testified in his trial. Van Deusen says that Freeman did testify and that he seemed greatly confused or mentally defective. But Van Deusen makes at least one factual error in describing Freeman's life, and he may have misinterpreted the trial reports. Freeman may have testified at his preliminary hearing, although there is no report of that in Hall's book. Even today, traditional strategy dictates that one does not have a defendant suffering from mental illness take the witness stand. It is a strategy I generally oppose.
6. EARL CONRAD, THE GOVERNOR AND HIS LADY 284 (1960).
7. Even with the help of excellent research librarians, I have been unable to find the Freeman opinion of the New York Supreme Court issued in 1847. However, it is printed in full in Hall's report of the case.

Notes to Chapter 2

1. The names of the defendant and his wife and child have been changed to protect their privacy. The names of all of the other participants are real. All quotes are from my case file and from memory.

2. Transient situational disturbance is no longer categorized as a separate disorder in the American Psychiatric Association's DIAGNOSTIC AND STATISTICAL MANUAL OF MENTAL DISORDERS, 4th ed. It has been folded into the general area of adjustment disorders and in some cases may be described as an acute stress disorder.

3. For a more complex interpretation of black manhood see, for example, the essays by various authors in THELMA GOLDEN, BLACKMALE: REPRESENTATION OF MASCULINITY IN CONTEMPORARY AMERICAN ART (1994).

Notes to Chapter 3

1. Robert Cover, *Violence and the Word*, 95 YALE L.J. 1601 (1986).

2. Peter Gabel and Paul Harris, *Building Power and Breaking Images: Critical Legal Theory and the Practice of Law*, 11 N.Y.U. REV. OF L. & SOC. CHANGE 369, 372 (1983).

3. David Kairys, *Freedom of Speech*, in THE POLITICS OF LAW (1982), edited by David Kairys.

4. *Commonwealth v. Davis*, 162 Mass. 510 (1895).

5. *Davis v. Massachusetts*, 167 U.S. 43 (1897).

6. *Employment Division of Human Resources v. Smith*, 494 U.S. 872, 907 (1990) (Blackmun, J., dissenting); *Teague v. Lane*, 489 U.S. 288, 326 (1989) (Brennan, J., dissenting); *Holland v. Illinois*, 493 U.S. 474, 503 (1990) (Marshall, J., dissenting); *Sandin v. Conner*, 115 Sup. Ct. 2293 (1995) (Breyer, J., dissenting); *Rosenberger v. Rector and Visitors of Univ. of Virginia*, 115 Sup. Ct. 2510 (1995) (Souter, J., dissenting); *Adarand Constructors v. Pena*, 115 Sup. Ct. 2097 (1995) (Stevens, J., dissenting).

7. *Holland v. Illinois*, 493 U.S. 474, 503 (1990) (Marshall, J., dissenting).

8. *See, e.g., Personnel Administrator of Massachusetts v. Feeney*, 442 U.S. 256, 279 and n. 24: " 'Discriminatory purpose' . . . implies more than intent as volition or intent as awareness of consequences. It implies that the decision maker, in this case a state legislature, selected or reaffirmed a particular course of action at least in part 'because of,' not merely 'in spite of,' its adverse effects upon an identifiable group." Although this is a case involving gender discrimination, it accurately states the Court's test in all equal protection cases involving discrimination.

9. 451 U.S. 100 (1981). For an insightful discussion of how residential segregation fortifies the social construction of race, see Martha Mahoney, *Segregation, Whiteness and Transformation,* 143 UNIV. PA. L. REV. 1659 (1995).

10. MARI MATSUDA, CHARLES LAWRENCE III, RICHARD DELGADO, KIMBERLE WILLIAMS CRENSHAW, WORDS THAT WOUND: CRITICAL RACE THEORY, ASSAULTIVE SPEECH AND THE FIRST AMENDMENT 6 (1993).

11. *People v. Taylor,* 5 Cal. App. 4th 1299, 1310 (1992).

12. *See, e.g., People v. Hall,* 4 Cal. 399 (1854). A white man's murder conviction was reversed because the court ruled the testimony of Chinese witnesses was not admissible, citing the law providing that "No Black or Mulatto person, or Indian shall be allowed to give evidence in favor of, or against a white man."

13. Charles Lawrence, *The Id, the Ego, and Equal Protection: Reckoning with Unconscious Racism,* 39 STAN. L. REV. 317, 321–23 (1987).

14. *People v. Ortiz,* 150 NE 708 (1926). *State v. Russell,* 220 P. 552 (1923). Although jurors rarely make racist statements on voir dire, prejudice still infects the criminal trial process. In a 1996 case the California Court of Appeals had to reverse the murder conviction of immigrant Heriberto Marron because jurors made anti-immigrant and anti-Mexican statements during the actual deliberations. In another 1996 decision a court of appeals reversed the murder conviction of a convict who stabbed another inmate because a juror concealed a "clear racial bias and prejudice." The court also criticized the trial judge for his "cursory questioning" of the jurors regarding race. Unfortunately, the opinion, *People v. Davis,* A064550, is unpublished. SAN FRANCISCO DAILY JOURNAL, June 3, 1996, at 1.

15. *United States v. Clemons,* 941 F. 2d 321, 322 (5th Cir. 1991). *Goodman v. Lands End Homeowners Ass'n,* No. 91-2542, 1992 WL 918901 (4th Cir. May 6, 1992). *United States v. Daley,* 974 F. 2d 1215, 1219 (9th Cir. 1992).

16. Jeffrey Brand, *The Supreme Court, Equal Protection,* and *Jury Selection: Denying That Race Still Matters* 1994 WISC. L. REV. 511 (1995).

Notes to Chapter 5

1. *Ives v. South Buffalo Railroad Company,* 201 N.Y. 271, 94 N.E. 431 (1911). In contrast to *Ives,* the California court came to the exact opposite result in holding that the California Workers Compensation Insurance and Safety Act of 1913 was constitutional. *Western Indemnity Company v. Pillsbury,* 170 CA. 686 (1915). By comparing these two judicial opinions we can see an excellent example of how the "Law" is not a fixed objective entity, but rather is shaped by the philosophies of judges and the political and economic forces at work in society.

2. Chrysler appealed the decision. The Workers' Compensation Appeal Board upheld the ruling that Johnson's disability was job related. However, it modified the portion of the decision regarding benefits. The board held that the temporary disability attributable to the *aggravation* of a preexisting condition had ended as of November 14, 1971, and therefore benefits were paid only from July 16, 1970, to November 14, 1971. *James Johnson v. Chrysler Corporation*, 1979 WCABO 1614.

3. DAN GEORGAKAS AND MARVIN SURKIN, DETROIT, I DO MIND DYING 212 (1975).

4. *Id.*, 220.

5. *San Francisco Examiner*, May 1, 1975.

6. *Detroit Free Press*, April 27, 1989, 6A.

7. *Id.*, 7A.

8. *Detroit Free Press*, July 8, 1979, 19A.

9. RACHEL SCOTT, MUSCLE AND BLOOD 137 (1974).

Notes to Chapter 6

1. *United States v. Alexander*, 471 F. 2d 923 (D.C. Circuit 1973).

2. Richard Delgado, *"Rotten Social Background": Should the Criminal Law Recognize a Defense of Severe Environmental Deprivation?* 3 LAW AND INEQ. J. 9 (1985).

3. H. L. A. Hart, *Book Review*, 74 YALE L.J. 1325, 1328 (1965).

4. *Dallas Morning News*, April 21, 1994, 25A.

5. Osby was retried and convicted. In the second trial his lawyers raised a posttraumatic stress disorder defense along with the urban survival syndrome. The judge *severely* restricted those two defenses, and the case was appealed.

6. Judd Sneirson, *Black Rage and the Criminal Law: A Principled Approach to a Polarized Debate*, 143 UNIV. PA. L. REV. 2251 (1995).

7. *Minneapolis Star Tribune*, July 6, 1994, 10A.

Notes to Chapter 7

1. *United States v. Robertson*, 507 F. 2d 1148 (D.C. Cir. 1974).

2. *United States v. Robertson*, 430 F. Supp. 444 (D.C. Dist. 1977).

3. *Vanity Fair*, Jan. 1995, 44–45.

4. *Tampa Tribune*, Dec. 4, 1994, Baylife section, 1.

Notes to Chapter 8

1. All quotes from Clarence Darrow's closing arguments are taken from ATTOR-NEY FOR THE DAMNED (1957), edited by Arthur Weinberg. This book is a compilation of Darrow's lectures and court arguments, with brief descriptive notes by the editor.
2. IRVING STONE, CLARENCE DARROW FOR THE DEFENSE 470 (1941).
3. A well-researched discussion of the Sweet case and the racial context in which it arose is found in DAVID ALLAN LEVINE, INTERNAL COMBUSTION: THE RACES IN DETROIT 1915–1926 (1976).
4. *Id.*, at 165–66. See also KENNETH WEINBERG, A MAN'S HOME, A MAN'S CASTLE (1971).
5. For an excellent history of African American lawyers, focusing primarily on Michigan, see Edward Littlejohn and Donald Hobson, *Black Lawyers, Law Practice and Bar Associations—1844 to 1970: A Michigan History*, 33 WAYNE L. REV. 1625 (1987).

Notes to Chapter 9

1. *Los Angeles Daily News,* Oct. 19, 1993.
2. *Id.*
3. The name of the defendant has been changed to protect his privacy.
4. The appellate decision is *Commonwealth v. Gilchrist,* 413 Mass. 216 (1992).
5. Steven Lively was presented with a commendation for heroism by the Boston City Council. Ironically, five months after the shooting Lively filed a discrimination charge against Merrill Lynch with the Massachusetts Commission Against Discrimination.
6. Little was in jail for theft when a white jailer with a history of abusing women prisoners entered her cell and sexually attacked her, forcing her to perform oral sex. In the ensuing struggle Little managed to stab the jailer and escape. She was indicted for murder and surrendered a week later. A national defense movement was organized. Karen Galloway, a young African American attorney who was cocounsel with well-known anti–capital punishment attorney Jerry Paul, was frequently quoted as saying that Little's case was an example of "the racism and sexism prevalent in North Carolina." The anger of southern African American women, who had suffered hundreds of years of sexual abuse as victims of white supremacy, was expressed by members of the defense committee outside the courtroom. Inside the courtroom the issue of racial prejudice was also raised as the defense argued that a not guilty verdict "will show the

world that women—black women—deserve justice." The prosecutor argued that the jury should not considered race and that "the submission of anything into this case but the facts is anarchy."

This was a case of black rage, but it was not a case of a black rage defense. Since Little had stabbed the jailer *while he was attacking her,* the facts lent themselves to a conventional self-defense strategy. The jury of six blacks and six whites took only an hour and twenty-three minutes to return a verdict of not guilty. Little said that the verdict was "the first step as far as black women are concerned that they have the right to stand up for themselves."

7. *San Francisco Daily Journal,* Feb. 10, 1993.

Notes to Chapter 10

1. The names of some of the people have been changed to protect their privacy. The names of Felicia Morgan and all participants in the trial are accurate.
2. *State v. Morgan,* 195 Wis.2d 388, 536 NW.2d 425 (1995).
3. Post-traumatic stress disorder is defined as the development of symptoms after exposure to "an extreme traumatic stressor" involving the personal experience of death, threatened death, or serious injury. A full discussion of PTSD symptoms and criteria can be found in the American Psychiatric Association's DI-AGNOSTIC AND STATISTICAL MANUAL OF MENTAL DISORDERS, 4th ed.
4. *State v. Morgan;* even though Garbarino should have been allowed to testify in front of the jury, the court held that since two psychologists had testified to PTSD, the trial judge had not "abused his discretion" by ruling that Garbarino's testimony would be cumulative.
5. In her efforts to educate the public as well as the legal community, Shellow has sometimes reached out to the media. One of her cases, involving a fifteen-year-old boy named Garland Hampton, was featured on the front page of *New York Times* (Dec. 12, 1994). Garland was charged with killing another fifteen-year-old in his gang during an argument. Shellow changed what looked like another ordinary gang killing into a story of America's lost and abused teenagers surviving in virtual war zones. She brought Garland's social history into court: his grandmother killed his grandfather; his grandmother threatened Garland with a gun; his mother killed his father in front of him; his mother beat and whipped Garland, threw him down the stairs and threatened to kill him on numerous occasions; his uncle killed two police officers; and his aunt sliced her boyfriend with a razor and tried to kill Garland with rat poison.

When interviewed by the *Times,* Garland said that in his neighborhood there was little time for childhood. "I feel like I've been grown my whole life," he told the reporter. But in fact Garland was still a child and, like so many tough kids, underneath he was scared. "I guess I been scared all my life. For me, living has been the same as running through hell with a gasoline suit on. I don't want people to feel sorry for me, but I really ain't had nothing good happen to me. The ax fell heavy on my head."

Garland Hampton was convicted of murder. In sentencing, Judge White was favorably impacted by the environmental hardship defense and rejected the prosecution's recommendation that the parole date be set in sixty-five years. Stating that she was giving "considerable weight to the background and circumstances of Garland Hampton," she imposed a life sentence with a parole date of twenty years.

6. Susan Rutberg, *Not Guilty by Reason of Victimization*, 20 FORUM, No. 4, 36 (1993). Published by California Attorneys for Criminal Justice, 4929 Wilshire Blvd., Suite 688, Los Angeles, California 90010.

7. One of the best articles about the use of PTSD to defend Vietnam veterans is Peter Erlinder, *Post-Traumatic Stress Disorder, Vietnam Veterans and the Law: A Challenge to Effective Representation* 1 BEHAVIORAL SCIENCES AND THE LAW, No. 3, 25 (1983). A lawyer attempting to use PTSD in any type of criminal defense will be educated and aided by this article.

8. From San Francisco Street Music, *Word of Mouth,* self-published 1995.

Notes to Chapter 11

1. PETER VAN SLINGERLAND, SOMETHING TERRIBLE HAS HAPPENED 318 (1966).

2. THEON WRIGHT, RAPE IN PARADISE 198 (1966). All quotes in this chapter are from the books by Slingerland and Wright, and from CLARENCE DARROW, THE STORY OF MY LIFE (1932), IRVING STONE, CLARENCE DARROW FOR THE DEFENSE (1941).

3. Lawyers have to make political choices. An example of a law firm grappling with the issue of whether or not to represent a person involved in activity that has a negative impact on the community is Ken Cockrel and Justin Ravitz's decision not to defend heroin dealers. In a 1973 newspaper interview entitled "Revolutionary in a Legal Sheepskin," Cockrel said, "We don't represent dealers in heroin and other opium derivatives, although . . . there have been cases where we could have written our own ticket. But how could I go out in the community and speak out against heroin if I came out in a Mark IV that I got by defending dope traffickers."

Cockrel and Ravitz are not the only lawyers who have faced hard choices.

The San Francisco Community Law Collective underwent a similar struggle in deciding whom and whom not to represent. In the early 1970s the Nixon administration began to put law enforcement pressure on the smuggling and sale of marijuana. The result in some cities was that marijuana became difficult to obtain and heroin sales grew rapidly. In San Francisco's Mission District, in which the Community Law Collective was located, heroin flooded the streets. One of the collective's lawyers was asked to defend a heroin dealer involved in large-scale sales, and the firm was offered the highest fee it had ever seen. The collective had been involved in representing community groups who were organizing against drug use. Those groups took the position that persons selling heroin were businessmen sucking the lifeblood of the people and street capitalists whose free-market practices were ripping apart the fiber of the Mission community. The collective's lawyers, legal workers (paralegals), and law students discussed and debated whether they should defend the dope dealer. They believed that everyone deserved a defense, and the firm certainly needed the money. Also, it was a relatively high-profile federal case, which would help build the attorney's reputation as a criminal defense lawyer. Legal worker Otilia Parra persuasively argued that for a law firm that was known in the Mission to be aligned with progressive groups trying to rid the community of drugs to defend a high-level dope dealer would send the wrong message. One of the law students argued vociferously that they should take up the defense. He put forth the position, still prevalent today, that drug dealing was one of the few avenues open to people in ghettos throughout America. Ambitious, organizationally talented young people involved in the drug trade were not unlike successful businessmen in the white establishment world. The only significant difference, he contended, was the lack of legal opportunities for young blacks and Latinos. A legal worker who had a brother addicted to drugs said she understood the economic pressures that drove people to sell drugs, but that there had to be a distinction between those who sold small amounts of drugs to support their habits and those who sold strictly for profit. The addicts were victims of life in the Mission, but the profiteers were exploiting hopelessness and misery. The large dope dealers had to be criticized, shamed, and isolated. She suggested they adopt a policy of representing only addicts who make small sales. After two lengthy debates, the collective agreed by a split vote to adopt this policy and to turn down the large fee it had been offered. The collective's difficult choice had positive consequences. It volunteered its services to a new community antidrug group and allowed a legal worker to spend almost all her time organizing against controversial methadone maintenance programs. The decision also had long-term consequences. None of the lawyers developed skills or built reputations in the area of drug law. Therefore, they rarely were asked to represent people in large marijuana cases, a lucrative field and one in which significant criminal procedure issues in the area of search and seizure and entrapment were litigated. In retrospect, however, they all agreed with the decision because it resulted in their self-education and forced them to take a stand against the death and destruction wrought by the heroin business.

Notes to Chapter 12

1. For the story of one of the most dramatic white rage cases in American history, see FRED GARDNER, THE UNLAWFUL CONCERT (1970). As protest against the war in Vietnam grew, so did dissent within the Armed Services. In 1968 there were more than 53,000 desertions and 155,000 AWOLs. At the Presidio Army Base in San Francisco the stockade was bursting with double the number of prisoners it had been built to hold. Conditions were awful, including beatings, overcrowding, terrible food, and arbitrary harsh discipline. In October a sick prisoner began to jog away from a work detail and was shot and killed. Three days later, twenty-seven white prisoners staged a peaceful sit-down to protest the killing and awful conditions in the stockade. They were charged with the capital crime of mutiny.

Fourteen of the soldier/prisoners were defended by leftist lawyer Terence Hallinan. His defense was that the men suffered a collective psychological disturbance brought on by oppressive environmental conditions. The young men were a cross-section of working-class and poor white America: only five of them had graduated from high school; only one had even attempted college; their civilian jobs had been as a gas station attendant, fry cook, miner, millworker, seasonal fieldworkers, and as various unskilled laborers.

Hallinan's primary expert witness was Dr. Price Cobbs, coauthor of *Black Rage*. His testimony was an application of the black rage defense to white men:

I was struck by their similar background. They were all white. They have low self-esteem. Very few had ever felt themselves the object of concern and care. They have always fled when anxiety threatens. But on October fourteenth the killing of Richard Bunch, another AWOL with whom they identified very strongly, meant that this course of escape was no longer open to them. They defined themselves as oppressed and began to feel some identity with the black soldiers, with black people. . . . They became "niggerized." They responded as black people, and sang "We Shall Overcome," a song they hardly knew.

The other side of grief is rage, and they stopped one step short of rage. They weren't thinking about the consequences. It was unpremeditated, and they didn't have the ability to form an intent.

Reporters called Cobbs the most impressive witness they had ever seen in a courtroom.

In a powerful closing argument, Hallinan tied the stockade conditions to the psychological defense:

When Richard Bunch was shot and killed escaping from a shotgun work detail, the prisoners no longer had the alternative of running away. All of a sudden they had to look around them. What are they doing to us? What kind of a place are we living in? How can they treat us like this? We're human beings. We're nothing but AWOL GIs. Our only difficulty is we can't adjust to the military. We want to go home and see our families. We haven't committed any crime. How can they put us in places where we have to sleep so close together? Where we don't have enough food? Where our toilets are overflowing? Where we are mistreated; where we don't understand what's happening; where we are lost?

Suddenly they saw themselves as people who had something in common—not losers, but people who were being mistreated, who were being abused. And suddenly they became gripped with this idea of "We must get the word out. We must tell somebody else. This is not fair. Human beings cannot be treated this way. Americans cannot be treated this way. We are American citizens. They can't kill us, that's not right."

And somewhere in the middle of their terror, of their confusion, of the anxiety, somebody grabbed on the idea, "We have to petition our grievances." . . . They had no choice. They *had* to do that. They had lost entirely the ability to distinguish right from wrong. They were convinced that what they were doing was right, *even in military terms.*

The "Presidio 27" were convicted but given extremely light sentences. Their case was an impetus for the growing GI dissent movement. It also showed the potential of a defense grounded in environmental conditions.

2. The name of the defendant has been changed to protect his privacy.

Notes to Chapter 13

1. Holly Maguigan, *Cultural Evidence and Male Violence: Are Feminist and Multiculturalist Reformers on a Collision Course in Criminal Courts?* 70 N.Y.U. L. REV. 36 (1995).

2. One legally *incorrect* appellate decision disallowing evidence of black culture is *People v. Rhines*, 182 Cal. Rptr. 478 (Cal. Ct. App. 1982). In that case the defendant, who represented himself, offered to produce testimony that black people

speak loudly to each other, and that therefore his rape victim was not intimidated into having sex by his loud and demanding tone of voice. The proposed testimony was totally irrelevant to the rape charge because the defendant had *physically* forced the victim to have sex. But the court was so offended by the defendant's proposed testimony and his demeaning statements about black women that instead of limiting their ruling to the legal issue of irrelevance, they went on a tirade against race-based evidence. For a fuller discussion and criticism of *Rhines* see Maguigan, *id.* at 89–90.

3. *People v. Wu,* 286 Cal. Rptr. 868 (Cal. Ct. App. 1991).
4. *Yreka, California, Community Economic Profile,* 1995, 6. Prepared by the Yreka Chamber of Commerce.
5. Norma Jean Croy's case is currently on appeal. She is now represented by Diana Samuelson, cocounsel in Patrick Hooty Croy's retrial, and Jim Thomson.
6. Tony Serra was assisted in court by cocounsels Diana Samuelson and Jasper Monti. Attorney Denise Anton wrote the brief, which was printed in full by the California Public Defenders' Association. See 5 CALIFORNIA DEFENDER No. 4 (1993).
7. *California Lawyer,* July 1995.

Notes to Chapter 14

1. RICHARD DELGADO, THE RODRIGO CHRONICLES 164–189 (1995).
2. Crime has not been visited on my entire family. Although I have worked and lived for many years in high-crime neighborhoods, I've never been a victim of a crime other than my car being broken into. My sister grew up in the heart of Chicago and lives in New York and has never been assaulted or robbed, nor (knock on wood) has my daughter.
3. See, e.g., the excellent discussion of prisons, law, and policy by Luke Hiken and Marti Hiken, *Imprisonment—America's Drug of Choice,* 52 NATIONAL LAWYERS GUILD PRACTITIONER, No. 3 (1995).
4. Enlightening articles by numerous contributors on the information economy and its consequences for all of us can be found in *cy. Rev: A Journal of Cybernetic Revolution, Sustainable Socialism and Radical Democracy,* 3411 W. Diversey, Suite 1, Chicago, Illinois 60647. World wide Web Home Page is http://www.eff.org/pub/Publications E-journals/CyRev/cyrev.html
5. Since the assassination of Martin Luther King in 1968, the African American middle class has become four times as large, but one-third of African Americans are worse off. Although American scholars and commentators are reluc-

tant to discuss "class" divisions, more and more recognize the increasing inequality of the distribution of wealth. Cynthia Tucker of the *Atlanta Constitution* has twice taken on the issue in editorials, in which she contrasts the
success of the "black upper-middle-class" with the failure of the "black un-
derclass" and rails against the lack of a governmental response to growing
poverty. One illuminating example of government action that is likely to increase rather than decrease crime is the 1995 Republican "recession" bill
signed into law by President Clinton, which eliminated a summer jobs program that had employed 615,000 low-income students.

According to a prominent group of sociologists, the United States is now
more unequal than at any point in the last seventy-five years. FISHER, HOUT,
JANKOWSKI, LUCAS, SWIDLER, and VOSS, INEQUALITY BY DESIGN:
CRACKING THE BELL CURVE MYTH (1996).

6. *Mak v. Blodgett,* 970 F.2d 614, 619 (9th Cir. 1962).

7. *Siripongs v. Calderon,* 35 F.3d 1308, 1315 (9th Cir. 1994).

8. One of the foremost experts in death penalty litigation is Bryan Stevenson at
   the Equal Justice Initiative, 114 N. Hull, Montgomery, Alabama. Stevenson
   cautions lawyers against trying to convert jurors to a single world view.
   Rather, it is necessary to explain how racism and poverty have shaped the
   individual defendant's history.

9. Letter to the author from Rick Wagner explaining the legal strategy in the
   Noble Drew Ali housing project case.

10. Mercedes Marquez and other attorneys such as Chris Brancart of Pescadero,
    California, have used various legal remedies such as suing under state war-
    ranty of habitability statutes and federal civil rights laws. Marquez, who has
    settled numerous cases on favorable terms, says that slumlords often target
    immigrants to be their tenants because immigrants are unaware of their rights
    and have less access to lawyers to enforce them. A black rage–type defense
    could be expanded to include immigrants, confronting head-on the stereo-
    types and prejudices other people hold against those who emigrate to
    America legally or illegally.

11. From 1981 to 1996 HUD has had to list more than three thousand projects as
    "distressed" housing. The overwhelming number of projects on this "dis-
    tressed" list are, in turn, overwhelmingly occupied by racial minorities. This
    is true despite the fact that there are hundreds of thousands of whites who
    also live in subsidized, albeit de facto segregated, housing.

    Wagner once asked a high-ranking HUD official in Washington, D.C., to
    identify a single privately owned, HUD-subsidized project on the "distressed
    list" that had a majority *white* occupancy. Her answer was, "I'm sure there

must be one or two, but I can't think of any." He told her to let him know if she ever did think of one. He did not hear from her.

A Noble Drew tenant told Wagner that "if 383 white families were subjected to these conditions in a government-subsidized project, the authorities would not have waited seven weeks, much less seven years, to fulfill their legal duty and stop it."

Index